Exuberant Praise for

Mr. S

from Around the Globe

"Set[s] your heart aflutter. . . . With its improbably witty prose, this exercise in deep dish never makes you feel like taking a shower. It's the one Sinatra tome that doesn't stint on rageaholism or sexual addiction or the affection this kind of split personality still engenders. A." —*Entertainment Weekly*

"I doubt you will find anything as memorable all year. . . . Almost every page contains some jaw-dropping vignette. . . . So wittily and stylishly written that it goes straight to the top of my showbiz memoir league." —*Daily Telegraph* (London)

"Graduates in Sinatra studies will appreciate the many intimate revelations that this memoir has to offer. . . . [A] remarkable story in an authentic voice." —*The Times* (London)

"A juicy tell-all book that entertains mightily. . . . The book runs with the kind of spicy details that make for the most captivating cocktail hour chatter. . . . While much has been written about Sinatra's life and times, Jacobs adds more with his intimate personal spin on the legendary man." —*Denver Rocky Mountain News*

"A complex portrait of two complex men at a crossroads in history . . . full of the expected tantalizing tidbits about Sinatra, his women, the mob, Joe and Jack Kennedy, Dino and Sammy. . . . The requisite sex and drink and dusk-to-dawn parties are in there." —*Los Angeles Times*

"A unique, gossipy perspective on Sinatra's relationships with some of the glossiest women and dodgiest men mid-century Hollywood has to offer."
—*The Observer* (London)

"Deliciously gossipy, yet Sinatra is recalled with affection rather than spite."
—*Kirkus Reviews*

"Promises to make the recent rash of tell-all books on Princess Diana look tame in comparison. It's bursting at the binding with great characters, if not people of great character."
—Michael Gross, New York *Daily News*

"The cascade of filth, gossip and chuckles never stops in Jacobs' book."
—*Vegas Magazine*

"A bombshell . . . blows the lid off the seedy side of Ol' Blue Eyes' long and colorful connection with the Kennedys."
—*New York Post*

"The Sinatra described in the book is even darker than I remembered him. . . . [Jacobs] has got some good stories to tell."
—Peter Bart, *Variety*

"Enough betrayal, seduction, and intrigue for a decade's worth of soap opera plots. . . . *Mr. S* offers a curious sort of double voyeurism, with Jacobs inviting readers to vicariously experience his own vicarious access to the life of one of pop-culture's preeminent icons. . . . Packs a powerful punch."
—*The Onion*

"A hip patois worthy of a cool-jazz film noir. . . . Sinatra, of course, had more facets than the Hope diamond—a neat-freak who was harder on hotel rooms than Keith Moon, a man who tried to bed every starlet in Hollywood yet made unrequited yearning the center of his art, a close friend who cut people out of his life forever."
—*New York Times Book Review*

"A vivid account of [Jacobs'] many years serving The Voice. . . . *Mr. S* is a curious and convincing portrait not only of Sinatra but of Mr. Jacobs himself, and of the kind of mentality that breeds such passionate attachment to a man so spectacularly unworthy of it."

—Robert Gottlieb, *New York Observer*

"One of the year's most applauded books. . . . High-octane show-business gossip is mixed with psychological insights in an authentically hip-sounding voice." —*Sunday Times* (London)

"I can't help myself. . . . I read one page and I'm hooked. . . . A wickedly entertaining, unashamedly low-down, raunchy, titillating, tell-all memoir in which the author gossips in salacious detail about the sex lives, foibles, and hijinks of Sinatra and his friends. . . . I love this kind of thing. If I had my way, that's all I'd read."

—*Washington Times*

"A memoir devoted to deep dish on the life and times of the Chairman of the Board and those who loved him. . . . [It] has gone from being one of this summer's guiltiest pleasures to this fall's."

—Alex Witchel, *New York Times Magazine*

"Many examples . . . give this yarn more vibrancy and candor than other Sinatra books. . . . Jacobs' open, honest style and his mix of adoration and abhorrence at his boss's behavior brings the Sinatra kingdom to life. . . . That Jacobs (with journalist collaborator William Stadiem) waited until after Sinatra's death to write this tell-all account of his period in the fast lane has perhaps as much to do with his ex-boss's tyrannical influence as it has with respect. Even so, this is not a bitter book. In fact in one sense it's a celebration of Sinatra's legend—one that is true—and how a poor boy from the back streets of New Orleans grew up to be a part of it."

—*The Weekend Australian*

Mr. S

Mr. S

My Life with Frank Sinatra

George Jacobs and William Stadiem

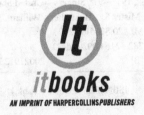

itbooks

AN IMPRINT OF HARPERCOLLINS*PUBLISHERS*

To my children who are still with me.
—*G.J.*

A hardcover edition of this book was published in 2003 by HarperEntertainment, an imprint of HarperCollins Publishers.

HarperCollins books may be purchased for educational, business, or sales promotional use. For information, please e-mail the Special Markets Department at SPsales @harpercollins.com.

First paperback edition published 2004.

Designed by Bernard Klein

The Library of Congress has cataloged the hardcover edition as follows:
Jacobs, George, 1927–
Mr. S : my life with Frank Sinatra / George Jacobs and William Stadiem.
p. cm.
ISBN 0-06-051516-3
1. Sinatra, Frank, 1915– 2. Singers—United States—Biography.
I. Title: Mister S. II. Stadiem, William. III. Title.
ML420.S565J33 2003
782.42164'092—dc21
[B] 2002191257

ISBN 0-06-059674-0 (pbk.)

RRDPrintCode

Contents

Last Tango
in Beverly Hills

SUMMER 1968. The only man in America who was less interested than me in sleeping with Mia Farrow was her husband and my
boss, Frank Sinatra. Theirs had to be one of the worst, most ill-
conceived celebrity marriages of all time, and after two years of one
disaster after another, it was all over except for the paperwork. Mr. S's
lawyer, Mickey Rudin, who was a combination bag man, hit man,
and Hollywood hustler, was planning to take Mia down to Juárez for
a Mexican divorce that would get her out of Mr. S's life once and forever, which, for everyone who knew them as a noncouple, couldn't
have been soon enough.

I may sound like Mr. S's friend and idol Humphrey Bogart in
Casablanca when I ask myself, of all the gin joints in the world, why
did Mia have to walk into the Candy Store that hot night? But she

did, and because I danced with her, and because the spying eyes of America, courtesy of an undercover scout for gossip queen Rona Barrett, were upon us, that frug, or watusi, or whatever it was, got blown up into a wild affair. And because I was Sinatra's valet, and because I was black, and because Mia was America's reigning Love Child, the rumors got particularly crazy, sort of *Upstairs, Downstairs* meets *Shaft*. Mr. S, who was the lowest he'd ever been in the fifteen years we'd been together, got even crazier. It cost me the job I loved, and it cost him a guy who loved him.

The summer of 1968 had been a particularly bad one for the generation gap. There had been the student seizure of Columbia University and the subsequent police riots and brutality. Then the same thing happened again in Paris. Soon there would be the Days of Rage at the Democratic Convention in Chicago, and before too long Mr. S, who had been King of the Democrats, was supporting Richard Nixon. Because he thought that the permissive youth culture was a threat to the American Way, or at least *His Way*, Mr. S wanted all the police brutality he could get. On the other side of the fence, Mia was getting all moony about student radicals like Mark Rudd and hippie radicals like Abbie Hoffman, with the end result that Frank and Mia wouldn't even speak to each other.

At first they would argue politics over our Italian dinners that Mia would barely touch. Mr. S thought she wasn't eating as a kind of hunger strike against his "capitalist pig," power elite, "get a haircut" attitudes, but it was more that Mia just wasn't much of an eater beyond yogurt and trail mix. Mia wasn't really a debater, either. She would just look at Mr. S with a betrayed look in those save-the-world big blue eyes of hers, as if to say "How can you possibly think like that? How cruel, how insensitive, how unloving!" And those big blue eyes that Old Blue Eyes himself had been such a goner for would just drive him up the wall, and certainly away from the table. Then she'd turn those guilt eyes on me, as if I were the voice of the ghetto. But I wasn't about to get into that trap. I stayed as neutral as Switzerland. "The only thing that'll save this world is my eggplant parmigiana," I'd say, carefully avoiding the mention of any animal protein. Then she'd give up and go read a script or call her agent. For an unmaterialistic hippie, Mia was wildly ambitious.

The Bel Air house we were renting, a big *Wuthering Heights* number just north of Sunset Boulevard, got to be like Berlin before they tore the Wall down. Separate rooms, separate meals, separate lives. The weirdest part about it was that there was no music. Mr. S didn't play his jazz, didn't play his Puccini, and Mia didn't play her Beatles or her Moody Blues. It was truly the sounds of silence, and it was loud as hell.

It's probably a good idea for me to point out that while I sometimes refer to the Chairman as Frank, or Sinatra, when we were together, I only addressed him as Mr. S. He generally called me George, but when he was being rambunctious, particularly with his so-called gangster friends, with whom he loved to act as "bad" as he could, he'd call me Spook. I know these were the days of Black Power, but somehow it didn't bother me. After all, one of the few times I ever saw the guy cry was earlier that year when Martin Luther King Jr. was killed. (He did *not* shed a tear for Bobby Kennedy, but that's another story.) He called his plane the *El Dago*. He called Dean Martin Wop, Gene Kelly Shanty, Cary Grant Sheenie, Jerry Lewis Jew, Laurence Harvey Ladyboy, Johnny Mathis the African Queen. Those were his terms of endearment. This was way before political correctness, and because he loved being the Bad Boy, he insisted on doing the opposite of whatever was political and whatever was correct, *except* around the kingpins of his youth like Sam Giancana with whom, ironically enough, he was always on perfect behavior, like a little altar boy.

But now Sam Giancana was long gone, in exile down in Mexico, in Cuernavaca. Johnny Rosselli would soon be going to prison. Because he grew up in a New Jersey subculture of godfathers, *padrones*, mob bosses, and such, Mr. S always seemed to need some power figures to look up to. His new kingpins became the Old Guard of Hollywood royalty, Claudette Colbert, Rosalind Russell, Leland Hayward, and, above all, Bill and Edie Goetz, he being the big-time producer of everything from *Ma and Pa Kettle* to *Sayonara,* she being the daughter of Louis B. Mayer and the Queen Bee of A-list Hollywood hostesses. I had gotten my start in showbiz nearly twenty years before as a liveried waiter, at their Holmby Hills estate, which was L.A.'s answer to Versailles. The Goetzes were the ones who actually pushed Mr. S into marrying Mia, because the Goetzes had embraced her as "one of them," so Frank thought he was marrying royalty himself. But he didn't account for the huge generation gap. Frank was then fifty-two, and Mia was twenty-three. Thirty years is a wide age gap at any time, but in 1968 it was as if they were a hundred years apart. What was worse, though, was that Mia's star was starting to shine more than Frank's.

Mia's film career was taking off, and Frank's was dying an ugly death. The fact that *Rosemary's Baby* had just come out and was the number one movie in America was killing Frank, especially since his new movie, *The Detective,* despite respectful reviews, lagged far behind it. But it was a lot more than box office. *Rosemary* was everything Mia embodied and embraced, occult, spiritual, freaky, out there. *Detective* was pure tough guy Frank. It was also, despite some attempts at kinky sex and gay murders and black cops, totally square and retro, as out of it as Frank had become. Moreover, Mia was supposed to be in it. The Chairman was going to "make her career" by creating what he considered a breakthrough part for her, but which was actually only the second romantic lead (romantic with Sinatra's character, of course). Mia turned him down to stay on in the title role in *Rosemary*, which was running way over schedule, and ended up making her *own* career.

Frank may have thought he was punishing Mia by having an affair with his *Detective* costar Lee Remick and flirting with Jackie Bissett, whom Frank "discovered" in England and cut her beautiful long hair short to replace Mia in the movie. It didn't make Jackie's career, though. It took the wet T-shirt in *The Deep* to do that. In addition to teaching Mia a lesson, these relationships were important for Frank to reassure him that he was still the Man. The problem was that Mia didn't seem to care. Without Mia's remorse the *machismo* factor didn't kick in to make Frank feel better about himself. So they retreated to their separate rooms and their separate ways, Mia with her crunchy granola, Frank with his olive-oil-fried-egg sandwiches. Because of their different schedules (she'd get up early to go to the set, he'd sleep late) Mia and Frank each had his/her own bedroom suite, both on the second floor. In their lovebird days, they'd start the evening together, usually retiring to Mr. S's chamber after dinner and rarely earlier than two A.M. After about an hour or so of whatever they were doing, Mr. S would doze off, and Mia would go into her room to sleep a few hours before going to the studio. Once the *Rosemary* conflict began, these slumber parties came to a crashing end.

On the rare occasions when Frank and Mia did interact, I always wished they hadn't tried. Mia had a big white cat named Malcolm that she adored. She always talked in sign language to the cat, who was deaf. Mia's obsession with Malcolm was bad enough, but the sign language really got on Frank's nerves. He didn't mind cats in general, but he came to despise Malcolm in particular. One day Mia was out by the pool, reading one of her Maharishi books and doing signs with Malcolm. Frank came out, didn't speak to her. He took out a cherry bomb, quietly lit it, and placed it next to the cat's food bowl. Kaboom! The poor thing ran off like a cat out of hell. Frank, who was obsessed with stupid practical jokes, and particularly ones with Three Stooges-type explosives, burst out laughing and couldn't stop. I honestly hadn't seen him so happy since he married Mia. "Deaf?" was all he said. Mia started bawling. "How can anybody be so cruel?" she cried. It got a lot worse when Malcolm never came back. He must have run all the way to Mulholland and gotten lost, maybe even eaten by the coyotes. Mia tried to find him, but couldn't.

I felt almost as bad as Mia did. This was the second pet Mia had lost on my watch. The year before Liz Taylor had given Mia a little Silky. Mr. S didn't mind dogs, so this pet didn't bother him. One day I had my three young kids up playing by the pool, and they threw the poor dog in. They didn't know he couldn't swim. I dove in and pulled the dog out, then tried to give him mouth-to-mouth resuscitation, but it was too late. The kids were crying, Mia was crying. Frank was nicer then, got her a new Silky, but it was the cat she really loved. When that one went and Frank didn't even apologize or try to replace it, I knew there was no healing this marriage.

Mia and I actually got along pretty well. Mr. S basically had me babysitting her all the time. We'd go shopping in the organic food stores, New Age bookstores, funky dress shops. I'd almost fall asleep listening to her spirituality rap. I actually preferred smoking pot with her and getting stoned, because then she'd zone out and shut up with the psychobabble. I obviously never told Mr. S about this. Like kids, we'd go off in the car to some secret park, usually up on Mulholland staring out at the psychedelic lights Mia loved. We would *never* do anything countercultural in the house. That would have been a death wish. Despite his own Jack Daniel's binges, Mr. S detested drugs, and everything that went with them. He detested hippies, detested long hair, even had his screenwriters write in jibes about them in his films that preceded *The Detective*, 1967's *Tony Rome* and *The Naked Runner*. The latter film turned out to be a major debacle, because Mr. S hated London, where the film was set, for being taken over by the Beatles and the Stones, and hated the swinging, Carnaby Street Mod atmosphere so much that he basically dumped the picture, went back to L.A., and let the producers worry about putting together what footage they had. It had to be one of his worst films.

Mr. S didn't care how good the new music was, whether British Invasion or San Francisco psychedelic rock. To him it was all one big excuse to take drugs. The Doors's "Light My Fire" drove him around the bend. DJs played it so often that he smashed one of the car radios with his heel when it showed up on three stations in a row. I guess that, for him, in time there was nowhere to hide from the all-consuming youthquake, except in the all-comforting, Republican, antidrug arms of Richard Nixon.

I remember Mr. S getting paranoid when I let my hair and sideburns grow a little bit that I had been "body-snatched" by some hippie cult. He was dumbfounded when I got a motorcycle. I blamed it all on Steve McQueen in *The Great Escape*, and since McQueen was one of the rare actors of the new generation whom Frank liked, probably because he kept his hair short, Frank let it go by. I was lucky it would be another year before *Easy Rider* would have made having that bike impossible. I guess I should have been flattered that Frank cared so much about me that he wanted to protect me from the rise of the drug culture. I was thirty-seven, he was fifty-two, and he liked playing Big Daddy to me, protecting me from all those evil influences he feared I would be unable to resist. To him, the hippies were the coming scourge of the earth, as savage and destructive as the barbarians who sacked ancient Rome.

Yet Frank had married the ultimate hippie. How could the sharpest, most hard-boiled guy on earth not see what he was getting? I guess it was because he liked what he saw. Ava Gardner, the greatest love of Frank's life, described Mia to me as "a fag with a pussy." (Forgive Ava's pungent language, but she didn't mince words.) She's also been quoted as saying Frank had always wanted to fuck a boy, but I don't believe it. If anyone knew how straight Frank was, it was Ava. No, Mia was very sexy. Even though she was compared to Twiggy, she was anything but a stick. She was much more like supermodel Kate Moss, and she would flaunt her body, using self-effacement as provocative bait. She always paraded around almost naked and would say, "It doesn't matter 'cause I don't have anything for anyone to get excited about," when she knew damn well that she did. In fact, she was totally confident that she was beautiful, and that confidence was the sexiest thing about her.

Mia, at nineteen, had snared Frank when she was on the TV show *Peyton Place* by showing up on the Fox set of *Von Ryan's Express* wearing a totally translucent veil dress with absolutely zero underneath. Plus she "accidentally" dropped her purse right in front of him. It was filled with tampons and condoms. Although Frank tended to go for more voluptuous women like Ava, or Kim Novak, or Marilyn Monroe, he definitely didn't have a single type. Mia actually brought back sweet memories of his affair with the teenage and similarly built Natalie Wood, whose own insanely ambitious Russian mother had pushed her on Frank, who needed no pushing himself. Also, Mia's naughty purity and blondness reminded him of Grace Kelly. The day he met her, he sent me out to buy copies of *Mademoiselle, Glamour,* and *Seventeen,* all the young fashion magazines, to admire the endless versions of Mia who filled their pages. It was as if he was testing himself to see if he could truly get excited by this new breed of creature. Then he got his dear friend, favorite composer, and whore wrangler

Jimmy Van Heusen to have their favorite madam send over a number of Mia "types," just to sample the future merchandise. Before they had had their first real date, he was already obsessed. Aided by her mother's friends, the Goetzes, hyping her fancy pedigree to Mr. S, Mia had expertly laid her tender trap. Pretty clever for a teenager. I suppose she wasn't on *Peyton Place* for nothing.

So if on the surface Mia seemed like one of the million hippie drug chicks you would see on the Sunset Strip in those days, she was anything but. She knew she had the right stuff, but part of her come-on was pretending she didn't. She was so confident that even though Mickey Rudin was preparing the divorce papers, and had even had her served with them on the set of *Rosemary,* Mia thought she could get Frank back if she wanted to. She also thought she could get him to give her a child, which is what she wanted more than anything else, and what Frank, who already had all the children he could barely handle, wanted least. Mr. S always had felt bad about his life as an absentee father, particularly after the nightmare of Frank Jr.'s 1963 kidnapping. He surely didn't want a new baby to feel bad about.

Mia didn't care what Frank thought. Motherhood was, only after stardom, the most powerful imperative for her. At times, she'd sit with me and go down her list of all the great and famous men she wanted to have children with after Frank. She knew the relationship would end sometime, but she assumed it would be at *her time,* and only after she had created one of what would be her master race of offspring. She was talking some major names, on her wish list: Leonard Bernstein, who was gay, Picasso, who was almost dead, J. D. Salinger, who had disappeared, and Bob Dylan, who was badly disabled from his motorcycle accident and underground. The girl thought big. She was that focused, and maybe if the Candy Store fiasco hadn't occurred, Mia might have even gotten her way with Frank and stopped the divorce at the eleventh hour.

But it did occur, and the rest is history and Woody Allen. Mr. S was down in Palm Springs. The tension in the Bel Air house had gotten so bad that even the big mansion was too small for him when Mia was there. Out in the 115-degree desert, he holed up watching television, which he never normally did, except for the old Friday night fights on the *Gillette Cavalcade of Sports*. Now he would watch *Mod Squad*, but without bothering to arrange to meet Peggy Lipton. He didn't even want to dial up Jimmy Van Heusen's endless parade of call girls. I knew the man was depressed, and I was worried about him.

I had to stay in L.A., though, because Mr. S wanted me to look after Ava Gardner, who was coming into town from London, her new home after living in Spain for over a decade. In addition to this major relocation from the land of sun to the land of rain ("What does it matter?" Ava said. "I sleep all day anyway." Like Frank.), Ava was coming off of a disastrous romance with George C. Scott, whom Frank hated, and an end of starring roles in her film career. She had just played second fiddle to Catherine Deneuve and Omar Sharif in the flop *Mayerling*. Getting older was a nightmare for a movie star, bad for Frank and far, far worse for someone like Ava who lived—and died—by her looks. Frank was worried about her and had always been protective. But he was in such a deep funk himself, he sent me in to sub for him.

Ava was staying in a bungalow in the Beverly Hills Hotel. Some friends were taking her to a Count Basie concert that night. I was going to meet her after the show at the hotel and hang out. Ava and I had developed a real bond, which was easy to do considering she was the earthiest, and most down-to-earth, movie star you could ever imagine. She always told me she was part black, that "poor white trash," the stock she came from in North Carolina, always had black blood in them. (Maybe that was why so many of them joined the Klan, going overboard to conceal their true roots.) Ava totally identified with her role as the mulatto in *Show Boat*, though she never forgave MGM for dubbing her songs. Like me, Ava was a frustrated singer. I knew that tonight I would go over to her bungalow, get plastered, and we would sing to each other until daylight.

But first I had an evening to kill. It was a pretty dead weekday in Beverly Hills, which was never what anyone would call a party town. The stars had to get up too early to be on the sets to support a real nightlife. It was usually dinner, at Romanoff's, Chasen's, the Bistro, then home to bed. Still, there were a few hangouts, which is a few more than there are now, which is nothing but fancy designer chain stores catering to rich Asian tourists. First I stopped in at the Luau, which was a Trader Vic's-style Polynesian fantasy right on Rodeo Drive, big banana trees and koi ponds and hurricane lamps and giant clam shell urinals that were the restaurant's chief conversation piece. The Luau was owned by Steve Crane, the ex of Lana Turner, who had been an ex of Frank in his early Hollywood years (who wasn't?). But it was dead, as was the Daisy, which was owned by Jack Hansen, whose across-Rodeo boutique JAX was where Marilyn Monroe, and every other star in town, outfitted herself in the California casual look. But the Daisy was dead, too, so I ended up at the Candy Store two blocks away from Rodeo, on Canon Drive.

The rise of Black Power notwithstanding, there weren't many brothers who could get into the Candy Store. Jim Brown, Wilt Chamberlain, Sidney Poitier, the Candy Man himself, Sammy Davis Jr., and me. I may have been riding on Mr. S's coattails, but who in this town wasn't riding on someone else's coattails? Everyone needed his or her Savior, his or her Messiah. Otherwise, they wouldn't get into Hollywood Heaven. Mr. S played Messiah to a lot of people. At his prime, in the JFK years, he was the most powerful man in the entertainment business. Now it was starting to slip away, but no one, absolutely no one in this town, was about to show the slightest hint of disrespect for Frank Sinatra. Hence I was one black man who would always get past the velvet rope, would always get a great table, would always get the run of the house. I also got a lot of beautiful girls in the process. Celebrity is a major aphrodisiac, but even celebrity adjacency can cast its own spell. It wasn't as if they wanted to use me to meet Frank. Except for Mia, hip young chicks had no interest in meeting Frank Sinatra in those days. He was off the radar of coolness. But the idea of my working for him, of my being that close to him, that was what was cool. It was like working at the White House. It made folks want to meet you. It gave you a mystique.

The Candy Store was the disco of the moment in Beverly Hills. Because it was new, it was the place to be. The owner, Gene Shacove, who was partnered with Tony Curtis, George Hamilton, and other stars who could draw a scene, was one of the two hairdressers to the stars in Beverly Hills. Gene, the inspiration for Warren Beatty in *Shampoo,* slept with a lot of his clients and rode a motorcycle, just as in the movie. But his biggest kick was making over these women into something they never dreamed they could be. One of his greatest makeovers was Jill St. John, who had been a rich, overweight Beverly Hills High School princess. Gene convinced her to change her last name from Oppenheimer, lose weight, get her nose done, and let him give her what became her trademark red hair. It worked like a charm. Frank was crazy about her, as were Sid Korshak, the Teamster lawyer who everyone feared as the Mafia *consigliere* in show business, Henry Kissinger, and Robert Wagner, with whom Jill finally settled down. The other celebrity hairdresser was Jay Sebring, who would come to the house to do Frank's hair, or what was left of it. Frank was supersensitive about his baldness and his wigs. It was one of the few things he couldn't control. He would never set foot in a barber shop, so Jay would do house calls, even driving down to Palm Springs when summoned. The next summer he would be a tragic victim of the Manson family.

There were a lot of pretty girls that night at the Candy Store. But because I was meeting Ava later, I wasn't planning any pickup attempts. I was just hanging out at the bar, when who should come in but Mia, with her dear friend John Phillips. If the world thought Mia was in seclusion mourning her upcoming divorce from the Chairman, they would have been surprised by the gay party mood she was in that night. And if anyone symbolized the drug-rock culture, or lack thereof, that Frank Sinatra detested and feared, it was the long, greasy-haired, always stoned John Phillips, Mr. California Dreaming himself. Despite the drugs, Frank did covet Phillips's gorgeous blond wife, Mama Michelle, which probably made him hate Phillips even more. "Georgie Porgie, pudding n' pie, kiss this girl and make her sigh," Mia greeted me in a playful singsong voice, as if she hadn't seen me for years, though I had just been with her at the Bel Air house that afternoon. I thought she was high, high as a kite. "Dance with me, Georgie Porgie," she insisted, dragging me out to the floor while John Phillips went into the men's room to smoke a joint, or do something stronger. "John won't dance," she complained.

We danced for what seemed an eternity. I kept looking back to the men's room to see when John was coming out, but he must have been having a wild time in there. Frank had never told me *not* to go out with Mia; on the contrary, he was grateful for what he called my "babysitting" her to keep her out of his orbit. And he never, ever spoke one bad word about her. But he never said anything good about her, either. At any rate, given the pending divorce, the scene at the Candy Store, innocent as it was, made me uncomfortable. Each dance felt as if it would never end. "Sunshine of Your Love." "This Guy's in Love with You." "Love Child." But when the DJ put on

"Somethin' Stupid," the previous year's number one duet by Frank and daughter Nancy, it was time to give up the floor. Mia didn't see the humor, or the horror, of the situation. I'm not sure she was even aware what the song was. Finally, John Phillips returned, stoned and smiling. I left Mia in his hands and went out into the night. The air of Beverly Hills never seemed more refreshing.

I went up to Sunset and the Beverly Hills Hotel. Ava had had a wonderful time at the Count Basie concert and was in great spirits, unusual given her loathing of Hollywood and its denizens. She was so up that she insisted we go for a nightcap in what was then Hollywood's lion's den, the Polo Lounge of the hotel. This was the place with the banana leaf wallpaper and the Philip Morris midget and the telephones at every banquette, where, if you were anybody in the business, you had to be paged. The polo players like Darryl Zanuck and Howard Hawks who inaugurated the place were gone, but everyone else would come there. I hadn't been in the Polo Lounge for nearly two years, since the big fight there where Frank's friend Jilly Rizzo broke a phone over the head of a powerful local businessman who had asked Frank, Dean, and a crew of their friends to hold down their noise. As Ava and I entered, the lounge was crawling with lizards like Paramount studio head Bob Evans, another guy Frank hated, not least because he was the executive in charge of *Rosemary's Baby.*

Evans had even more women running through his house than Frank did. Because he and his brother were big Seventh Avenue garment tycoons, they had endless model connections on both coasts, and Bob was using them strategically to do sexual favors for everyone and rise to the top in showbiz. That night Evans was so surrounded with starlets that he didn't even look up to notice Ava as we made our way to a back booth. He had been a bit player in Ava's 1957 film *The Sun Also Rises,* and she had thought he was so miscast as a matador that she, Hemingway, and Tyrone Power all signed a telegram to Darryl Zanuck demanding that Evans be fired. Zanuck refused, issuing his famous command, "the kid stays in the picture." Evans could deliver pussy, and pussy always trumped talent in Hollywood. Ava figured Evans still resented her and was ignoring her, gloating that now he was on top, and she wasn't. She couldn't have cared less. At forty-five, she was, for a Hollywood goddess, way over the hill, yet she was somehow relieved to be there, to be earning her living doing character parts rather than star turns. To her, acting was a job, not a passion. Now the heat to be fabulous was off. The paparazzi cameras had stopped clicking. The Bob Evanses of the world had stopped looking up.

London was a fresh start. Ava liked the city as much as Mr. S hated it. She had a townhouse in Knightsbridge, she had her Corgi, she had culture everywhere, and she had rain. She said she had been in Spain for more than a decade, so long, she had forgotten what rain was. Her best friend at the time was the singer Bobby Short, who often flew over from New York to visit her, and she said she was hanging out with some other black jazzmen in England. She felt she was out of the fast lane forever.

We talked about Frank and Mia, which Ava knew was a ridiculous match from the outset. Everything she predicted had come true. However, she wasn't the slightest bit pleased with the accuracy of her predictions. She felt as bad for Frank as I did. I urged her, as always, to try to get back together with him. It seemed to me that the entire fifteen years that I had been with Frank were a kind of crazy odyssey on his part to do everything in the world, and I mean the entire world, to get over losing her. I often wondered how much different my own life would have been if they had only stayed together. Ava laughed it off. She always laughed it off. She would always love Frank, but it was more as a friend, or actually a wayward son, than as the grand passion he once had been for her, and, alas, she remained for him.

One of Frank's favorite songs was "I Can't Get Started with You," and he always had Ava in mind when he sang it. "I've been around the world in a plane, I've started revolutions in Spain, I'm down and brokenhearted, 'cause I can't get started with you." What he meant was that he couldn't get started *again,* and that was the story of his life. Every love song he sang was for Ava, and every woman he had was an attempt to make him forget her. Nothing worked. Ava wasn't at all melancholy about it. She was a no-bullshit woman, totally realistic. She called it the way it was, and the way it was with Frank was not meant to be. Poor Mr. S.

We gorged ourselves on margaritas and the Polo Lounge's famous guacamole and Fritos. Ava said she didn't care if she gained weight. Eating well was the best revenge. We went back to her bungalow and listened to her new jazz albums. We drank, sang, laughed, like old times. Then I went home at dawn to the haunted house in Bel Air. Mia never came back that night. The next day I took Ava to the airport, to see her off to San Francisco to visit some friends. Then I drove east to Palm Springs. The three-hour drive through the rapidly dwindling orange groves that were being replaced with a suburban wasteland of shopping malls, car lots, and junk food emporia was especially miserable in the blast-furnace heat of summer. It was a true descent into American Hell. And to think that all my friends around the country had this fantasy about how wonderful California was. California Dreamin', all right. That John Phillips had the last laugh, he and the Beach Boys. They had sold a major load to the public. I wasn't hearing any songs about West Covina, or Loma Linda, or Redlands. This was the real California, and it was nothing to write about.

Neither was Palm Springs, which was at its ghost-town worst in the summer. The place was in the process of being trashed with cheap motels and bad restaurants. When Frank Sinatra had first come out, in the early fifties, Palm Springs was a secret Hollywood hideaway. I used to come down to the Racquet Club, which was super clubby then, with my old boss Swifty Lazar, and meet people like Cole Porter and Moss Hart, and the real Polo Lounge social crowd that actually played polo at the Zanuck estate, Ric-Su-Dar, named after the mogul's kids. Frank Sinatra, even with Ava Gardner, was considered a second-class citizen, a *nouveau* New Jersey outsider, by this entertainment royalty. Maybe he never got over it and that was why he was toadying up to the Goetzes the way he was. But he didn't have to. At that point, as far as Palm Springs was concerned, no one was bigger royalty than Frank Sinatra. He was the emperor of the desert. Even though President Eisenhower was still alive here, Frank Sinatra owned this town, and the world knew it.

But Palm Springs was on the downhill slope. Even Mike Romanoff, Frank's dear friend and the ultimate restaurateur to the stars, couldn't make his magic work. He had tried to open a branch here called Romanoff's on the Rocks, a black-tie supper club in this wild concrete bunker on the side of a mountain, and, despite Frank's help, he had to go out of business, which broke his heart. There were still stars around, but the spirit was drained. I would see Elvis Presley driving around aimlessly in his pink Cadillac convertible, looking for action that he was never going to find.

Palm Springs had lost its glamour, just as Mr. S was beginning to be losing his. His movies were duds, his last hit, "Somethin' Stupid," was more than a year before and vastly further from Cole Porter, and his child bride was making him look silly. Still, I believed Mr. S would come back. He was too fierce a survivor. This was no quitter. He had resurrected himself from show business purgatory in 1953, just when I went to work for him, and I knew he would do it again now. The times had indeed changed, but wasn't Mr. S timeless? I was devout in my belief that I had the greatest job a man could have. At thirty-seven

I was earning $1,500 a week, plus endless fringe benefits. Wall Street lawyers and bankers my age weren't making anything like that. Nor were most movie executives. I wasn't a rich man, but I *might* be, and I sure was living like a prince, the fresh prince of Bel Air, long before Will Smith.

So it was the greatest shock I'd ever experienced when I found that my key to the Sinatra compound didn't fit the lock. It had been changed. I rang and rang the bell. What was wrong? Finally one of the Filipino houseboys came to the gate, but refused to open it. "Mr. Sinatra very crazy," he warned me. "No good to come in. You must go. Before it be too late." Too late for *what?* I pressed him, but he wouldn't elaborate. And what about all my stuff? "Movers pack up." And he disappeared into the house. I stood in a daze in the baking desert sun. In one split second, my life had been turned upside down, inside out, and I didn't have a clue why. Then one of the black maids came out. She had been there for a year, and I knew her well, but she was clearly too terrified to show me any sympathy. Instead, she handed me a letter, cut her eyes downward, and scurried away. It was from Mickey Rudin's law office. I read it. It was short and anything but sweet. I had been dismissed, as of this instant, from Mr. Sinatra's service. I was not to reenter the premises, nor telephone, nor in any way approach or try to contact Mr. Sinatra. My belongings would be delivered to me in three days. There was no explanation, no apology, no severance pay. Do not pass go, do not collect $200, do not darken this door as long as you live.

Frank had done it to Peter Lawford, to his original manager Hank Sanicola, and to Jack Entratter, the Copa and Sands boss, who stood up for Frank when few others would. No one could bear a grudge like Frank Sinatra. He did it to these great friends, and he did it to others, but for all the tantrums I witnessed, all the fury, all the venom, I never imagined he would do it to me. It turned out that nothing traveled faster than gossip, and as much as Frank scorned and attacked the press, he believed the gossip before he would his best friend. He was a one-man Spanish Inquisition, and, at his worst, just as cruel.

And so it went, the job of a lifetime destroyed by a spin on the dance floor. I was devastated. I had lost my best friend, my idol, my boss. I loved the guy, and I assumed he loved me, too. I had no idea what to do. I had the greatest life in the world. But now I realized that it was *his* life, and now I had to figure out how to get one of my own. It was amazing how things changed, literally overnight. From being the toast of the town, or two towns, Beverly Hills and Palm Springs, I became the *ghost* of those towns. It was as if I didn't exist. Even Mia, whom I saw on Beverly Drive a few days later, crossed to the other side of the street to avoid me. She never spoke to me again, not to say she was sorry, not to share old times, not to offer to set the record straight. Not that Mr. S would have listened to her. Unlike Yogi Berra, who said it ain't over till it's over, when Mr. S said something was over, it *was* over.

Word had gotten out that Frank Sinatra had fired me, and people, even people I thought were friends, didn't dare even to speak to me for fear of incurring the wrath of the Chairman. The folks in show business feared Sinatra the same way the folks in Communist Russia had feared Stalin. There a party leader who had fallen from grace was known as a "nonperson." Now that's what I was, frozen out Moscow-style right here in sunny California. In those first cruel weeks of alienation and isolation, my only solace was in my memories. For nearly two decades I, too, had been a party leader, at one of the greatest parties the world had ever known. I had partied with the kings and queens of the planet, movie stars, record stars, sports stars, princes, presidents, gangsters, goddesses. It was an amazing trip, and even more amazing that a poor black kid from Louisiana like me got to take it. Although Mr. S had turned my world upside down, he couldn't destroy what he had helped me become. The incredible experiences we shared had made me one interesting man. That was the armor I would wear out into the world, and the shield of confidence I had to deal with whatever came up, good or bad. I could honestly say, without an ounce of boast, that I had seen it all. As I pulled myself together and tried to figure out the next chapter of my life, I looked back at the past twenty years and couldn't help but smile. If I could pull all *that* off, I could handle anything. As Mr. S loved to sing, ". . . the memory of all that, oh, no, they can't take that away from me."

2

Swifty

$\mathcal{T}$ HE only thing the superphobic superagent Swifty Lazar feared more than germs was failure. "It smells worse than shit," he would say, "and you can smell it from even farther away." By that token, Swifty was very uncomfortable with Frank Sinatra, his apartment house next-door neighbor. "He's a dead man," Swifty would say of the fabled crooner whose career had taken a southerly turn. "Once you lose it in Hollywood, you don't come back. Even Jesus couldn't get resurrected in this town." Although Swifty was always smiling and polite to Mr. S, he never invited him into the apartment and almost had to take one of his multiple showers whenever he ran into him. "I wished he'd get so broke that he'd have to move out," Swifty often said, because Swifty felt that having a loser in the complex somehow made him look less like a winner to his famous friends and clients.

"He makes them uncomfortable," he'd say, but the one who was most uncomfortable was Swifty, who judged everything and everyone by appearances and how they ranked in *Variety*. To Swifty, Frank was one more Hollywood has-been who was particularly inconvenient because the shadow of his decline happened to be darkening Swifty's door. So here I was, George Jacobs, Swifty Lazar's Man Friday, pitying Frank Sinatra, feeling awful for the biggest star in the world. What a totally weird state of affairs that *I* could be feeling sorry for *him*. I guess for a black man in his early twenties, I was riding pretty high at the time.

I was born in New Orleans in 1927 with show business in my blood. Actually, the blood was on the show business. My father had a nightclub called the Joy Tavern, near the old red-light district of Story-ville. He and my mother were divorced when I was three. She became a cook and housekeeper for a rich white family in the Garden District. I had a split-personality childhood, living with these plantation aristocrats by day, visiting my daddy and his hepcat jazzmen at night. My uncle was a cornet player. He introduced me to Louis Armstrong. I loved the life I saw these guys leading, with the music, the booze, the girls. It was bad, and it looked good. But my mother warned me that bad was bad and to stay away from it and anything to do with my father. Because my mother was half Jewish and half Creole, and my father also had a Jewish grandfather, hence our last name (New Orleans, being a port city, was one big gumbo pot), ethnically I wasn't quite sure what I was. These were the days of *Plessy* v. *Ferguson,* the "separate but equal" Supreme Court case that kept blacks in the back of streetcars. Even if you were an octaroon (one-eighth black) and had blond hair and blue eyes, in the eyes of the law, you were as black as tar. I didn't have blond hair, and while a lot of people thought I was Italian, I never tried to "pass." I was what I was. Whatever that was.

One thing I was for certain was patriotic. In 1945, as soon as I was old enough to enlist, I joined the Navy, and sure enough, I saw the world. I enrolled in the Cooks and Bakers School in Bayonne, New Jersey, where I was the valedictorian of my class. If you learn anything in New Orleans, it's how to eat and drink, and my mother's Creole recipes put me in good stead. From Bayonne I went to Portland, Maine, where I saw snow for the first time, and then to Naples, where I became aide to Adm. Charles Beatty of the Mediterranean Fleet. I traveled throughout Italy, Greece, Spain and France and learned how to cook the entire range of the Mediterranean Diet, even though few of us realized how healthy it was at the time. I also had no idea that my acquired skills with Italian food were going to be my passport into the stomach, and hence the heart, of a skinny *paesano* from Hoboken whose music I wrote off as white-boy stuff for silly screaming white girls. My favorites at the time were Herb Jeffries and Billy Eckstine. Everyone said I resembled the latter, which I took as the ultimate compliment, so much so that I developed delusions of becoming a singer just like Billy once I got home. By 1947, I was one sophisticated gentleman. I had seen the Colosseum, the Parthenon, the Eiffel Tower. I could say courtly things in three foreign languages. I thought I was some kind of *boulevardier,* a black Maurice Chevalier. It took coming home to New Orleans after learning that my father had been shot to death to bring me back to earth.

I was on a tour of duty on an aircraft carrier in Korea when I found out. My commanding officer called me in, offered me a cigarette, and told me to sit down. What did I do wrong, I asked. Your father's been murdered, he told me, and I fell apart. It got worse when I arrived in New Orleans. I went to police headquarters, where I was told that Dad had been putting out Coke bottles one morning after closing time at his Joy Tavern when two robbers riddled him with bullets. "Why?" I asked. "Your father acted like a white man," one officer said. "My father *is* a white man!" I shot back, as if Dad were still alive. I was lucky they didn't book me. I did some sleuthing and found out Dad had been killed, not in a robbery as the police had put down, but for not having paid protection money to a racket of which the police were a key part. Dad had been ambushed in a back alley by two contract killers the cops had sprung from Angola Prison. He ran away down an alley, trying to get to safety inside a neighbor's house, but the neighbor refused to open his back door. My father was executed, gangland style. I was so furious at the police, the neighbors, the whole rotten system that I decided never to set foot in New Orleans again. I was too upset, too angry, even to visit Dad's grave.

I married my high school sweetheart Dorothy Pasley, who had lived across the railroad tracks from us in our mixed black and Italian neighborhood called Girt Town, on the edge of the French Quarter. Dad had liked Dorothy, and that had meant a lot to me. Luckily, given the way I had come to hate New Orleans, Dorothy had a father in Los Angeles, which was where my mother and stepfather, a Pullman porter who was one of the most elegant men I had ever met, were just moving. After the war, the West was seen as the Promised Land, with the prospect of good jobs and fresh starts. There was a big Louisiana contingent in Watts, which was supposed to be the Los Angeles ghetto. But it was a ghetto with palm trees and night-blooming jasmine and perfect weather; it wasn't Harlem by any means.

Dorothy had only seen her father once every few years and had never visited him in California before we arrived there. We were both surprised by what we encountered. Chick Pasley had left Dorothy's mother and come to L.A. in the midthirties. He had prospered there. Like my stepfather, he was an elegant guy, with gorgeous clothes and diamond stickpins. He was also a big-time pimp, sending his beautiful mulatto girls to see white movie stars at the Beverly Hills Hotel and the Beverly Wilshire. Chick lived in high style in a huge house at the corner of Western and Jefferson. He had three Cadillacs. For all the luxury around us, Chick's mansion didn't seem to be the best place to start a family. I quickly found us a little apartment in Watts. Chick was delighted that I was getting Dorothy out of the house, and he never suggested I join him and his brothers in the "family business." In fairly short order we had three kids, two boys, George Jr. and Rene, and a girl, Brenda, whom I had to figure out how to support, by legal means, which proved not to be so easy in the Promised Land.

For all my naval spit and polish, the best first job I could get was as a gardener in Beverly Hills, which made the Garden District back home look like Harlem. I had never seen mansions like these. Beverly Hills was a small town then, the nicest small town in the world, where people rode their horses down Rodeo Drive, your neighbors were people like Clark Gable and Gary Cooper, and the pink palace that was the Beverly Hills Hotel was the town clubhouse. Still, I was a lowly servant. None of whatever skills I had were being utilized, nor did I have a particularly green thumb. Luckily, the garden belonged to a powerful lawyer named David Tannenbaum, who quickly upgraded me to a process server in his firm, Pacht, Tannenbaum, and Ross, at the corner of Roxbury and Wilshire. I was the only black guy in the office, or in the entire office building, for that matter.

The patriarch of the firm, Judge Isaac Pacht, was a true pillar of the Jewish community, and he represented a large number of the stars of the day. One of my first assignments was to serve some papers on Ingrid Bergman, who was scandalizing the world by leaving her Swedish husband for the Italian director Roberto Rossellini. I caught her at the airport just before she was to get on a plane. I never saw so much icy venom in anyone's eyes. That was my first lesson that stars were real people and not perfect, happy gods and goddesses, though Ingrid Bergman resembled one until you got up close. I also met Aly

Khan and Rita Hayworth, who were renting one of the several houses the Tannenbaums owned in the hills. Khan was not only Hollywood royalty, but world royalty, my first genuine prince. His father, the Aga Khan, was the ruler of a vast Muslim sect, though his son, who was a world-famous playboy, didn't seem spiritual at all. There were champagne bottles all over the house, and he and Rita Hayworth were constantly screaming at each other and smashing furniture, which Mr. Tanenbaum would send me up to replace.

My wife Dorothy was much less impressed by, or even interested in, this world of fame and fortune than I was. She had a job at a Brother Sewing Machine store on Crenshaw Boulevard and couldn't understand why I didn't get a "normal" job in Watts, too. Aside from our childhoods in Louisiana, we didn't have much in common, and our interests grew further apart the longer we stayed in L.A., a place I loved, because of how different it was from where we came from, and she didn't, because, to her, there was no place like home. And that's exactly where she went in 1953, taking our kids with her and remarrying with disastrous results for her and our children. But that came later.

Meanwhile I began taking singing lessons, courtesy of the GI Bill, at the Westlake College of Music above a shady place called the Bimini Bathhouse on Vermont Avenue in Hollywood. My teacher had taught Scatman Crothers, so I figured the place must be all right. At nights I would hang out at the jazz clubs on Central Avenue, places like the Club Alabam, the Downbeat, the Jungle Room and the Bird in the Basket, where I'd hear people like Dexter Gordon, Dizzy Gillespie, Art Tatum, and Miles Davis, whose lady worked at a hamburger stand I went to near Beverly Hills that served blacks, mostly servants to the stars. The Central Avenue scene was a hot one, kind of seedy, with lots of pimps, whores, and dealers, but it reminded me of New Orleans. Stars would come slumming here with their Cadillacs parked outside. I saw Cesar Romero, and Alan Ladd, and one night at the Jungle Room there were Aly and Rita, drinking and fighting. I worried for a second about losing my job if I spoke to them, then I said, what the hell, and came up and said hello, and Aly bought me two rounds of drinks.

I was so starstruck from being in Los Angeles (who wasn't, except for my wife?) that I also began auditioning to be an extra in the movies. I did get a few parts; unfortunately, they were all nearly identical. I was cast as a restless African native in some cheesy MGM *Tarzan* knockoffs. We all had the same one line: "Ungawa!" Whatever, I couldn't have been more thrilled. Here I was, George Jacobs, a prince, if not the king, of the jungle. I was in pictures! I was on the MGM lot! I was going places! Thus bitten by the Hollywood bug, I looked for other ways to get inside the business. One way I found was to work for a caterer who did the Hollywood party circuit. As it turned out, I was just the man for the job. I'm not sure whether it was inspired by *Gone With the Wind* or by Eddie "Rochester" Anderson on *The Jack Benny Show*, but Southern black manservants were highly in vogue in Beverly Hills. They had far more cachet than an English butler or a French maid. The bottom line was that I immediately got a lot of work as a waiter at all the best parties.

The best of the best were those of Bill and Edie Goetz, whom Frank Sinatra came to idolize. In the early 1950s, the Goetzes would have been unlikely to have Frank Sinatra in their house, even as entertainment. Even when they were young (they were barely around forty then), they were that grand. "Whatever Edie wants, Edie Goetz," was the line on her. Propelled by his father-in-law, Bill Goetz had run 20th Century-Fox during the war and now was the kingpin at Universal. Their mansion in Holmby Hills was filled with more French Impressionist paintings, Renoirs, Monets, Cézannes, than the Louvre. The décor was all original furniture by Billy Haines, the preeminent decorator to the stars. There was a staircase grander than the one in Tara. A Toulouse-Lautrec covered the projector in the living room; a Gauguin covered what became the screen, on which would be shown movies months before they were released. The food was by a French chef they were said to have hired away from Maxim's in Paris, and every menu at every place setting was written by hand. Edie, followed by Doris Warner, had been the most eligible girl in Hollywood (Frank Sinatra would hold on to an awful crush on her for years), and I wondered how Bill Goetz, who was a sweet guy who cracked awful vaudeville jokes that he learned from his idol Al Jolson, had beaten out every other ambitious Jewish suitor in the business for the hand of the ultimate princess. The answer, I observed, is that he paid an inhuman amount of attention to her, and she ate up every iota of it. In contrast to Aly and Rita, Bill and Edie were always hugging, kissing, stroking each other's hands and back. For the two decades I knew them, they stayed like lovestruck kids. The staff called them "the Snoogies," because "Snoogie" was each one's pet name for the other. "I love you, Snoogie. I love you even more, Snoogie. Oh, no, Snoogie, you can't love me more than I love you." And on and on. Anyone who says that Hollywood romance is a big fake obviously never saw the Goetzes in action. Theirs was the genuine article.

I saw every big star at the Goetzes, Fred Astaire, James Stewart, Cary Grant, Bette Davis, Lana Turner, Joan Crawford, old legends like Marion Davies and Gloria Swanson, directors such as Alfred Hitchcock and Howard Hawks, Broadway icons Cole Porter and Ira Gershwin, and a weird dwarfish man with huge eyeglasses and very dapper English-cut clothes who kept staring at me as if I looked equally as weird as he did. I was kind of self-conscious about the livery I was forced to wear, and I tried to get out of the dwarf's line of vision, but he kept stalking me around the Goetz palace, out into the formal gardens, wherever I was serving drinks. And then he disappeared. I thought nothing more of it until, a few weeks later, I was browsing at a record store in Beverly Hills at the corner of Charleville and Beverly Drive, when the dwarf reappeared, looking at me through the window. This time he came into the shop, and without asking my name, he introduced himself as Irving Paul Lazar and said, without the slightest possibility that I might have an opinion in the matter, "You're coming to work for me." The time was late 1950.

Lazar had already had me completely checked out. He knew precisely what I was making at the Pacht firm and offered me a 15 percent raise, to the princely sum of $100 a week. His office was just down the block on Beverly Drive, but he had much more in mind for me than office work. Lazar was a curious mix of totally confident and totally insecure. He had to make me acknowledge to him how cool it was that he found out all about me, from my naval record to my father's murder. Wasn't he a genius? He had to hear the answer. Then he gave me a list of all his famous clients, starting with Moss Hart, and going through George S. Kaufman, Howard Lindsay and Russel Crouse, Garson Kanin and Ruth Gordon, Alan Jay Lerner and Frederick Loewe, Cole Porter, all the giants of the New York stage whom he was now selling for top-prestige dollar to the class-starved studios. But then he had to list all of their credits, as if to prove how great they were. Either that, or how ignorant he thought I was. Yet if the latter were the case, why was he hiring me, except maybe to do some Pygmalion number? Whatever the reason, I looked at the whole thing as a wild adventure, Man Friday to the world's leading writers' agent. From Call Me Bwana to Call Me Shakespeare. Suddenly I was a man of letters, or at least next to one. In Hollywood your fate could change in the blink of an eye. That's what made it so exciting.

I soon learned that Irving Paul Lazar was not much more literary than I was. He rarely read his clients' works, he merely sold them. What a massive bluffer, what a masterful bullshit artist he was! And what a nutcase. Lazar lived in a two-bedroom duplex garden apartment on Wilshire and Beverly Glen that he rented from Loretta Young's mother. Frank would take an apartment here in 1952, when it became increasingly clear that he and Ava could not coexist under one roof without killing each other. Lazar's friend, director Billy Wilder, had lived here before Lazar and had put him on to it. Audrey Hepburn had lived here, too. Everything that wasn't part of the furnished flat had Lazar's initials, IPL, on it, the towels, the sheets, the napkins, the salt shakers, his English underwear. Lazar was a total Anglophile, which was about as far from his roots in Brooklyn as he could go. He had all his clothes made in England, and he sent all his shirts back there to be laundered in some ridiculous cleaner in Mayfair that charged him more than new shirts would have cost. But he was terrified a local cleaner might crease the collars. He had more towels than the Beverly Wilshire. I soon understood why. Lazar refused to walk barefoot on Loretta Young's mother's carpet. He was convinced it was infested with deadly germs, so he laid towels on the carpet to protect himself, and he insisted on changing these towels at least twice a day, and more often, whenever he had company.

"Company" often consisted of sultry large-breasted hookers, who were the type little Lazar preferred. How anyone so phobic about cleanliness and illness could consort with prostitutes was bizarre to me, but bizarre was Irving Lazar's real middle name. "I need them to help me relax," he would explain. "I have to be content. I can't deal from anxiety." For a man who was afraid to take pills or even aspirin for fear of rare side effects, sex was the drug he was willing to mainline. He never had a girlfriend, though his occasional dates, starlets like Barbara Rush, whose big break was *It Came from Outer Space*, tended to be dark and voluptuous just like the hookers. Regardless of her identity, he always made me throw the sheets away whenever a woman would lie on them, which was rarely longer than fifteen minutes. No one was allowed to spend the night, including me.

I would arrive around eleven, when Lazar would wake up, lay out the towels so he could pace the apartment and talk on the phone, then drive him in his Rolls-Royce to Romanoff's for lunch at one, after which he would walk down to his office and work the phones for the rest of the day until it was time for another meal at Romanoff's, or maybe Chasen's, or one of his many parties. Other times I would cook Italian food for Lazar, deliver scripts to producers and studios, and do all sorts of errands, delivering gifts to everyone he wanted to cultivate. He would often send me to Nate 'n Al's, the celebrity New York delicatessen on Beverly Drive, to buy huge supplies of caviar. "Be careful with that stuff," he would warn me. "Blacks can't digest caviar. It gives them gout." The idea was that blacks lacked a special enzyme to digest the sturgeon roe, and the caviar could make us deathly sick. How nice Lazar pretended to be on that point, how concerned about my health. That enzyme was called cheapness. For such a big spender, Lazar could be like Uncle Scrooge. He was only a big sport if the object of his generosity could do something for him or was his social superior.

Most of my job was standing around waiting, usually in the Rolls outside restaurants and parties. But sometimes the waiting could get interesting. I got to know George Raft, who lived in a fancy European-style apartment building across from Romanoff's restaurant where Jill St. John would later live. Raft used to stand in the street flipping silver dollars as if they were worry beads. He'd come over and talk to me. He had the very best clothes in Hollywood, spats, waistcoats, like Legs Diamond. He knew I admired his outfits, and one night he came out with a pair of amazing patent leather shoes that were just my size. "Learn to dance the rhumba in these," he said as he gave them to me.

My first falling out with Lazar was when he insisted I wear a livery uniform to chauffeur him in his Rolls, which he had acquired in lieu of a commission in a deal as a way to avoid income taxes. He was always on the prowl for the clever scam. I had hated looking like a lawn jockey at the catering events, but they were only part-time. To wear a monkey suit full-time was flat-out unacceptable. I refused to wear these "Nazi costumes" with the leather jackboots that went with them, I told Lazar. I would rather go back and serve process. But every other driver wears them, he pouted. Why can't you? Because I'm not like every other guy, I told him, and I didn't think you were, either. That shut him up. So he let me keep dressing in the collegiate, Brooks Brothers-style blazers and tweeds that I liked to wear. And he helped me buy a sporty used MG-TD convertible to drive from my new apartment in Hollywood to work for him. He wanted me to seem as English as possible, even in my off hours, during which I got too lazy to keep up with my singing lessons. I think, deep down, Lazar might have gotten to me a little bit. The singing business was rough. Maybe I would become an agent myself.

The work seemed amazingly glamorous, especially when Lazar began taking me on trips with him, to drive him, carry his many bags, prepare his outfits, and do all the little errands, the real-life stuff, that he was clueless about doing himself, like going to the drug-store or the post office. Again, things here began on a rocky note. On our first road trip, to Palm Springs, Lazar was going to the Racquet Club to work on some deal with the producer Charlie Feldman, who had previously been one of the biggest agents in town and helped Lazar fill his shoes. Lazar worshipped Feldman, as the model of what an agent could become. Feldman, another obsessive Jewish Anglophile, had a Goetz-like mansion in Coldwater Canyon and a wife who had been a showgirl in the *Ziegfeld Follies*. He later divorced her to be with the French beauty Capucine, who dumped him for William Holden, and was one of the few women who wouldn't give Frank Sinatra the time of day. Such is the game of Hollywood musical beds.

When we got to the desert, Lazar announced to me that I couldn't stay at the Racquet Club, that there were no servants' quarters. I wasn't expecting the presidential suite, but when I saw where blacks were allowed to stay, a kind of outhouse/stable near the Indian reservation, with fleas and bugs that looked as if they came from outer space, I got disgusted and said I would drive back to L.A. and pick up Lazar whenever he was ready. But he couldn't live without me. The Racquet Club was totally restrictive, but there was a nice place called the Bon-Aire down the street where Lazar made a reservation for me. When I drove up in the Rolls-Royce, they thought I was Ralph Bunche. The red carpet treatment I got was amazing. Whenever Lazar ordered me around too much, I would begin talking right back to him. "Abraham Lincoln fixed it so we wouldn't have to live like this," I protested to him one night. He sat back in the back seat of the Rolls and started whistling "Dixie." It wasn't your typical master-servant relationship. It was actually more like a sitcom. The trick to getting along with Lazar was never to take him very seriously and to know that he liked to be abused.

Our next trip together was to London, for Lazar to do some deals for Noël Coward, but mostly it was an excuse to go to Savile Row to get suits made, to John Lobb for custom shoes, and to Turnbull & Asser on Jermyn Street for his precious shirts. We were to stay at Claridges. The English were a lot more civilized than America was at that time about race relations. I was supposed to stay in a maid's room on the top floor of the snooty hotel. But when we got there, they put Lazar in the maid's room and gave me a huge suite. They thought I was some kind of African prince, and they treated me like royalty. There were a lot of other African princes staying there, and they all bowed and greeted me like I was one of them. I bowed back.

I only knew one word from my extra days: "Ungawa." I used it and it seemed to work. Lazar was fit to be tied, but it wasn't the style of the English gent he aspired to be (he'd even start talking with an accent the minute we got off the plane, and call everyone "lovey" and "cheerio, old chap") to throw a temper tantrum, so he let me keep my suite and keep up the charade that he was traveling with royalty for the whole week.

We went to Europe a lot, to see Lazar's client writer Peter Viertel, who later married Deborah Kerr. We skied with him in Switzerland, ate with him at Tour d'Argent in Paris, went to a bullfight with him and Ernest Hemingway in Málaga. Hemingway drank more than anybody I had ever seen. Even Dean Martin couldn't have matched him. He was also more bloodthirsty than Attila the Hun. He just loved it when the matador stabbed the bull, and the blood went flying all over the place. Hemingway had a big Sinatra-style entourage of beautiful girls, who doted on his every word, though Hemingway paid much more attention to the bottle, the bull, and the blood than to the broads. He left the girls to Lazar, who'd put on his biggest fake English accent and try to impress them with how much he knew about bullfighting, which was all bullshit. Hemingway was polite to me but drunkenly distant. After the bullfights, Hemingway would throw these all-night dinners, which I skipped and went off to the fancy brothels Lazar had showed me. In Spain you could be thrown in jail for being caught in bed with a woman who wasn't your wife, but the whorehouses, which were like elegant men's clubs, were totally protected.

Wherever I went with Lazar, I was rarely left out. In London, Noël Coward took me to the theatre when Lazar was too restless to sit through the plays. He hated stage drama as much as he did reading novels. Musicals were okay. The thing that surprised me most about this very fast world was how gay it all was. "Gay" wasn't the word then. It was "queer," but you never said it. You never said anything, and you weren't supposed to say no, for fear of offending these great creative geniuses. Both Coward and Cole Porter made passes at me. Coward brazenly held my hand at the theatre, while Porter kept giving me this funny handshake where he'd tickle my palm, which was supposed to be a code or something. Here was the man who wrote all our greatest romantic songs, "Night and Day," "I've Got You Under My Skin," and he was completely gay. Lazar told me he wrote "I Get a Kick Out of You" after being beaten up by some truck driver he'd picked up. My illusions were shattered, but that came with the territory of going backstage in show business, and this was merely the beginning. I had so many surprises that my life in entertainment was a two-decade shock treatment. But, for the moment, I played for time by telling people like Coward and Porter that I was almost engaged to some wonderful girl that I was making up. "How quaint," Coward sniffed.

For the first two years I was with Lazar, I never laid eyes on Frank Sinatra. They were in two different orbits, winners and losers. Lazar was packaging such movies as *An American in Paris*, which won every Oscar, while Frank was in bombs like *Double Dynamite*, with Groucho Marx, another has-been by now. There were no more hit records, no more screaming bobbysoxers. The only time you heard of Frank Sinatra was if you opened *Confidential*, the top scandal magazine. Then you could read what a shit he was to leave his loyal wife Nancy for that Jezebel Ava Gardner, and how he was getting payback by being dumped by MGM, by Columbia Records, even by Ava, who was reputed to be having affairs with every costar and every Spanish matador who crossed her path. Every few months there seemed to be a story about another Sinatra suicide attempt. I'm not sure if any of this was true. It sold magazines. But Irving Lazar certainly seemed to believe it. "He should go back to New Jersey," Lazar would say, as if

Hollywood could only be inhabited by the currently successful, which, sad to say, is pretty much the case.

The first time I met Frank Sinatra while working for Lazar was at a party where I was keeping the Rolls warm for a quick getaway. Lazar would sometimes go to five events a night. This obviously wasn't an "A" party; if it were, Lazar would have been staying. I was keeping to myself. The other drivers, all in their Nazi uniforms, were giving me a wide berth. I didn't dress like them. And I was black, which they weren't. So there wasn't much common ground. I did, however, feel like a cigarette, which was forbidden in the presence of the phobic Lazar, and I didn't want to give the other drivers the satisfaction of saying no to me. So I decided to ask the first guest who came up the street. And that guest was Frank Sinatra, who had just parked his own car. I asked him for a smoke. He said, sorry, but he didn't have one. I thanked him, and I assumed that was that, and waited for the next partygoer to ask. But ten minutes later out comes Sinatra with an entire gold bowl of cigarettes. I was shocked. I took one cigarette, but he said to keep the whole bowl. He patted me on the arm and went back into the party. From that moment on, I knew I liked the guy.

A year or so later, when he moved into the apartment complex, I knew Lazar wanted me to give him the swerve, to avoid him, but how could I? Here was a man in pain. Sometimes I would see him wandering on Beverly Glen, down to Mapleton Park, head down, all alone. Where were all those screaming teenagers now that he needed them, I'd think to myself. Where was *anybody*? If I ever made eye contact, I'd smile at him, and no matter how down he looked, he'd always pull it together and smile back. I'm not sure he remembered the cigarette incident. He was just a naturally nice guy. "Everybody's nice when they're down and desperate," was Lazar's take on the situation. "Losers have the *time* to be nice."

Lazar may have been the worst cynic in the world. Actually most of his friends were nicer than he would give them credit for being. My favorite was Humphrey Bogart. The world-famous tough guy was the softest touch in the world. The first time I met him was one night outside of Romanoff's. Lazar was down the block having drinks and would be coming to Romanoff's for dinner. I, of course, was there to wait. Then Bogart came up. He had seen me with Lazar, knew the Rolls. "Come on, kid, we're gonna get you something decent to eat," he said out of the blue. And he took me into Romanoff's, sat down with me and ordered me a fabulous dinner, which we were in the middle of eating when Lazar finally came in. You should have seen the look on his face! And it got even worse when Bogart stuck him with the check. Bogart loved playing jokes like that on Lazar, he loved giving him the needle. And nothing needled Lazar more than the nickname "Swifty," which Bogart gave to him. He wanted to be perceived as an English aristocrat, and Bogart rechristened him as who he really was, a sharpie hustler. Yet just because Bogart had Lazar's number didn't mean he didn't like the guy. Bogart was the best friend Swifty had.

Humphrey Bogart and Betty Bacall (Lauren's real name was Betty Perske) were Lazar's favorite couple, the most glamorous star marriage in the business. They lived a few blocks away from his apartment in Holmby Hills, near the Goetzes, which thus stamped the area as *the* place to live in Lotusland. Also nearby was another Lazar intimate, the great director Billy Wilder, who was extremely nasty and unforgiving and never once said hello to me or thanked me when I'd bring him a drink or a cigarette. He always made me feel like hired help, but Lazar told me that he acted that way to everyone. Another member of this group was a depressed screenplay-rewrite guy, one of the original script doctors, named Harry Kurnitz, a Lazar client, who everyone said was a comedic genius but always seemed to be whining about not having a girl. And there was the debonair

David Niven and his Scandinavian wife. Niven was so smooth, so slick, he never seemed real to me, but because he was Central Casting British, Lazar had to be around him. Niven was exactly what Lazar wanted to be.

Lazar and these people seemed to be the "youth group" at the frequent parties held at Ira and Lenore Gershwin's house, where there was, as might be expected, fabulous Broadway music being played or sung by people like Judy Garland or Oscar Levant or Kitty Carlisle, many of whom were, or would become, Lazar clients. This crew, who never liked to go to sleep, would continue the evening at the Bogart house, where they would drink until two or three in the morning. They would be joined by Mike Romanoff after he closed his restaurant for the night. Romanoff was a phony prince, an ex-jailbird and the biggest bullshit artist in the world, and because his lies were so outrageous, he somehow got away with it. Lazar thought he was the greatest man on earth. He admitted that his own lies were nothing compared to Romanoff's, hence his deep respect for him. I could see why an agent would admire the con man, though I never saw why Bogart embraced him as well, maybe because Romanoff would always bring great wines, and salmon and foie gras that he hadn't sold at the restaurant. I guess he did tell great stories, even if none of them were true. Other late nighters at the Bogarts were the genuinely clever writers (and actress) Ruth Gordon and Garson Kanin, as well as the incredibly nice Spencer Tracy, who came most of the time without Katharine Hepburn, so she wouldn't get on his case about his heavy boozing. This became the core of what got to be known as the Holmby Hills Rat Pack, which, five years later after Bogart died, was taken over by Frank Sinatra and his own crew.

It was only when Frank started being considered for the Maggio role in *From Here to Eternity* in the fall of 1952 that he simultaneously began being invited to the Gershwin parties, and, later, those of the Goetzes. When your stock starts going up in the business, your social stock will rise as well. Even though they were apparently at war with each other most of their brief marriage, which had taken place in late 1951, Ava wanted to have children with Frank, but only if he had a career that could support them. Consequently, she began her own campaign with her friend Joan Cohn, the beautiful, long-suffering wife of the ogre who ran Columbia Pictures, Harry Cohn, the guy who invented sexual harassment, to get Frank the supposedly classy, serious role that might restart his dead career. The casting process seemed to go on for months, and whether or not Sinatra got the part became everybody's favorite cocktail party bet. Lazar bet against Frank, though to his face, he'd tell him that he would get this big shot or that to put a word in with Harry. He didn't do a thing. I'd hear him talking about how ridiculous it was for Sinatra, whom he called a nonactor, to try to compete for the part with the front-runner for it, the "real" Broadway actor Eli Wallach. The only thing Sinatra had, Lazar would say, was that he was Italian, as was the character, and he was a loser, as was the character.

Nevertheless, Ava, and good sense, prevailed. Frank got the part. Of course Lazar began low-rating this as well, saying it was only a *supporting* role, and it was no big deal, and, besides, he doubted that the movie would be a hit. Yet Lazar hedged his bets. He sent Frank congratulatory champagne and flowers, and began inviting him to join his parties and those at the Bogarts'. "Maybe we can get him to sing," he'd justify his neighbor's presence. The minute he got cast, Frank Sinatra was a changed man. The gloom lifted. He was all smiles. He walked differently. Even though shooting wouldn't start in Hawaii for six months, all of a sudden he had a future again. He could hold his head up.

Frank Sinatra loved hanging out at the Bogarts'. That may have been the best perk of all of being back in the film game. A lot of times

I'd play late-night bartender, so I could see the pack in action. Sinatra was like a starstruck kid, in awe of Bogart, and watching his every move. With all the people around, it was hard to be alone with Bogart, but Sinatra tended to shadow him, following him into the kitchen or out into the garden, hanging on everything he said. Sinatra saw Bogart as his mentor, though I doubt that he ever told Bogart that. Bogart would have laughed at him. Be your *own* mentor, kid, or you'll never get anywhere, he'd probably have said. This time Bogart was wrong. Sinatra learned his lessons with straight A's. The two men had a lot of natural attributes in common. They were about the same size, short and skinny, and both men were losing their hair, though Bogart's was in much deeper retreat than his younger fan's. Bogart had fabulous clothes, cashmere jackets, Italian shirts, and velvet slippers, and a certain cool and grace in the way he'd smoke, in the way he'd put away the Jack Daniel's, eventually a trademark taste Sinatra acquired from Bogart. Bogart had an effortless physical grace, which Sinatra only had when he sang. Otherwise, Sinatra was tense and jumpy, and remarkably insecure for someone used to playing to screaming fans. That they had stopped screaming was probably what made him this way. The Jack Daniel's definitely helped loosen him up. I noticed that he was much more "on" around Bogart than he was when I saw him at other gatherings.

Even though he played the tough guy in films, and had a tough-guy growl in his voice, Bogart was really an East Coast aristocrat-type with a top background and a polish he got at prep school at the Phillips Academy in Andover, Massachusetts. His father was one of the leading surgeons in Manhattan; his mother was a well-known illustrator. They were accomplished, as well as pillars of society. It was an unusual background for a movie star, most of whom came out of nowhere, or from Hoboken. But that pedigree was just one part of the whole Bogart mystique. Another was his enormous talent and success (he had won the Oscar that year for *The African Queen*), and the third part of what made Bogart Bogart was his fabulous wife, Betty. Even though she was a head taller than him and looked like a sleek, tawny lioness, and had this deep sophisticated voice, Betty was just a young girl from the Bronx, as in awe of the whole scene as Frank was. Bogart was in his fifties, Betty was in her early twenties, and when he called her "kid," he meant it. Frank was about thirty-seven at this time, but around his idol he seemed like a kid, too.

Sinatra never showed up with Ava, or with any other woman. Everyone knew that Ava was his woman, and that she was hurting him terribly by not loving him the same way he loved her. No one would even mention her, or say, "Frank, how's Ava?" She was off limits. Once, somebody put on a new Sinatra record, "I'm a Fool to Want You," without realizing it was his own personal torch song to Ava. There was an interminable silence until the song was over. No one even dared to compliment Frank on it. I think it was Ruth Gordon who broke the ice by suggesting they all play charades.

By and large, this first Rat Pack was a pretty tame lot. It would be hard to imagine Frank, Dean, and Sammy, in their latter incarnation of the Rat Pack, playing charades. The Bogart pack was like a civilized, witty New York cocktail party, an Algonquin Round Table kind of experience. There was a lot of drinking, not just Jack Daniel's, but martinis, mixed drinks, champagne, and no one ever got really drunk, except for Judy Garland on a few occasions. When Judy got plastered, the worst she would do was get up and start belting show tunes like "You Can't Get a Man with a Gun," and everyone would join in. I never had to drive guests home who couldn't make it on their own. The discussions at these parties would usually revolve around the movies, how bad they were, who was screwing whom, both at the studios and offscreen. Everyone was great friends, but they were all very concerned with who was making the most money and who was getting the best parts. They were united in their hatred of the studio moguls like the Warners, the Cohns, the Goldwyns. There was a great divide between these artists and the money that they seemed to covet even more than their art. All in all, the Bogart evenings were models of decorum, dialogue, and taste. It would get a whole lot raunchier in the years to come when Frank would take control.

The taking of that control was beginning to happen bit by bit before my eyes, especially after Frank returned from Hawaii from shooting *Eternity*. He seemed to know, six months before the movie was released, that this was a winner. He also recorded what would become his first hit record in years, "Young at Heart," on his new contract with Capitol. It was a nice way to say "Fuck you!" to Columbia Records, which had dropped him the year before. He even had a nice way to say "Fuck you!" to Swifty Lazar, who was sucking up to him more and more with each bit of proof that Frank was going to be that rare person to beat the Hollywood curse, and, like Jesus and the South, rise again. Once when Lazar and I were in New York, Frank, the great practical jokester, enlisted Harry Kurnitz to get the landlady to give them the key to Lazar's apartment. They came in during the middle of the night with a contractor and bricked up the wall to the closet that contained all of Lazar's beloved English clothes, and then painted the whole thing to make it look like one big wall. Lazar went crazy when he came back. If there had been *Candid Camera* back then, this would have been the perfect stunt, just to see the look on Lazar's face. On other occasions when Lazar was getting ready to go to some fancy party, Frank would sneak in and steal some vital element of his outfit, like a cummerbund, or one of his cuff links, or the shoes he had me set out for him to wear. The crazier he would drive Lazar, the better I knew he was doing in his life.

In the winter of 1953, Lazar sent me over to the Goldwyn Studio to drop a script off for Billy Wilder, who was working there at the time. Wilder took the script from me as if I weren't there, and, as usual, did not say thanks. It was a treat, then, to run into Frank Sinatra on the lot. Instead of waving hello, he charged right over to me with something important to say. "George," he greeted me with a big handshake and a bear hug. "I want you to go see my secretary. She's got an important message for you. Go there right now. Right now." He shook my hand again and he was off. I had no idea what that message could be, but I sure was curious. So I found my way to this little office on the lot, and I met Gloria Lovell, a plain schoolteachery woman in her thirties who was in the middle of signing Sinatra's name to a pile of glossy photographs that were being sent to fans. "Oh, hello, George," she trilled, as if she had known me all my life. Then she handed me a thick envelope. "Open it," she insisted. It was a set of keys. "Welcome aboard," she said. Aboard what, I asked her, totally confused. "You're starting today," she said. Starting where? "At Mr. Sinatra's. He wants you to go there now. It may be a bit of a mess. He really needs you." But what about Mr. Lazar? I sputtered. "He'll manage," she replied with a slight grin. What can I say to him, I continued in a near panic. I didn't want to be blackballed, to see my brilliant career ended before it began. I was terrified of incurring the wrath of Swifty Lazar, who had grown to depend on me. It's been three years, I tried to explain. I can't just pick up and . . . "Mr. Sinatra will take care of Mr. Lazar," Gloria Lovell stated with schoolmarmish authority. "You just worry about Mr. S. You're working for him now." It took a bit longer for it to settle in, but soon I understood that I had absolutely no choice in this stunning turn of events. Frank Sinatra had stuck the ultimate needle into the little man he loved to needle. It was almost as if Sinatra somehow knew how little faith Lazar had had in him and wanted to show him once and for all who was the real boss. Whatever it was, my life was about to be turned upside down, and I was about to embark upon the wild ride of the century. Frank Sinatra had just made me an offer I could not refuse.

3

From Eternity to Here

ONE of the nicest things about Swifty Lazar was that he didn't hold a grudge, at least not if the person who had done him wrong was more powerful than he was. I thought I'd never be able to face Lazar at the apartment house, but the next time I saw him he was all smiles. He took Frank's "stealing" me with the same good humor he took Frank's walling up his closet. Not one snide remark, like "I hope you're satisfied." Or "I hope you're enjoying these Jersey *goombahs* as much as you did Noël Coward." Or "I'm leaving for Switzerland tomorrow and Irwin Shaw is so disappointed you won't be making it to the slopes with us." He could have, but he didn't. He put on a great face, though he did seem a little lost for a long time, going through a lot of new help. The main reason he didn't complain was that Frank Sinatra, with the huge success of *Eternity*, was quickly getting just as hot as he had been cold, and I'm sure Lazar wanted to work this for-mer "loser" into one of his big deals.

My first day working for Frank was very exciting. When I opened his apartment door, I was surprised he needed a valet at all, the place was so immaculately neat. I knew he had tried a Filipino houseboy a few months before, but the fellow hadn't lasted a week. Sinatra wanted someone who spoke his language. The five-room, two-bedroom unit was a shrine to Ava Gardner. There were pictures of her everywhere, in the bathrooms, in the closet, on the refrigerator. There were a couple of framed photographs of his children and of his parents but none of his ex-wife Nancy. Aside from one bookcase, almost all biographies (Washington, Lincoln, both Roosevelts, Booker T. Washington, and a lot of Italians—Columbus, da Vinci, Machi-avelli, Garibaldi, Mussolini), most of his possessions were records and clothes. There was a whole wall of sound, though it wasn't all jazz as I would have guessed, but albums and albums of classical music.

The closets were in perfect order, with all the clothes organized by color, fabric, and style. Most of the colors were orange (his favorite) or black. I figured the guy wanted to come off like a tiger. There were more sweaters than I'd ever seen, cashmere, mohair, lamb's wool, alpaca, you name it. And as for shoes, Imelda Marcos had nothing on Frank Sinatra. He had a whole closet just for shoes, dozens of wingtips predominating, with a good number of elevators. No won-der he seemed taller than his given five seven. There were also a lot of hats, which seemed odd for casual Los Angeles, but because of a receding hairline, hats had become his thing, just as they were Humphrey Bogart's. It was clear from his wardrobe that he had been keeping his eye on Bogart, because a lot of Sinatra's clothes were identical to Bogart's. The biggest surprise in the apartment was the industrial supply of Wrigley's Spearmint Gum. I had no idea the man was a gum chewer, like his original teenage fans, but he was.

What I did, waiting for my new boss to arrive, was to go shopping and prepare him a great dinner. I figured, with him being Italian, I should cook Italian, so I made baked clams, spaghetti marinara, veal marsala, zabaglione, the works that I had learned in my travels. After working for hours, I had everything ready at seven o'clock. Everything, that is, except Frank Sinatra. Eight o'clock, nine o'clock, ten, the hours went by without an appearance, without a call. I thought about calling Gloria Lovell and asking her where he was, but I didn't want to be a pest, not on my first day. By one in the morning I gave up. I cleared off the table, wrapped up everything that was wrappable, put it in the empty refrigerator and went home at two in the morning. I was really depressed. I felt like I had been stood up on the date of a lifetime.

I reported to work the next day at one P.M. Gloria Lovell told me that Mr. Sinatra never woke up before two except when he was shooting a movie, and that coming in any earlier would disturb him. Imagine my surprise when I found him fully dressed, drinking coffee, smoking a Lucky Strike, and listening to what I learned was his favorite composer, Puccini. I was embarrassed that I was late. One more strike and I would be out. But he was as nice as could be. He apologized, without further explanation, for being "tied up" the night before.

There with him was a motherly black woman named Hazel Washington, who had been his regular maid for the year or so he had lived in the apartment and came twice a week. Hazel's husband was a Los Angeles police department officer who would rise to be a commander on the force, while Hazel herself would go on to work for Marilyn Monroe. Hazel showed me the ropes concerning the apartment, where everything was, which sheets and towels to use, all the housekeeping stuff. She told me which markets to use, where to get the right kind of Italian bread, the right coffee, the right milk, and where to stock up on Campbell's Franks and Beans, which was Mr. S's favorite snack, one that he ate cold right out of the can. That was so disgusting, I thought, no wonder the guy was going downhill. I made him a beautiful steak for lunch, which he asked me to cook some more until it was medium, not rare. He thanked me for how delicious it was, though he only ate a few bites. Hazel told me not to take it personally. Mr. S was not a big eater. How did I think he stayed so skinny?

That night he took me over to Carolwood Drive near Sunset to meet his family. He drove us in his Cadillac Brougham Coupe, black body, silver top. He also had a Chevy station wagon, a woody like the surfers all drove. It was odd, after driving Swifty Lazar for years, to be driven by Mr. S. He insisted on driving, loved to drive. It was also odd being introduced to his ex-wife Nancy, who didn't seem ex at all. The house was a typical Beverly Hills five-bedroom sprawling fifties ranch-style affair, though a lot of the furnishings were of the more rococo New Jersey style. In fact, the house looked as if Mr. S still lived there. There was a predominant bright orange and black color scheme, and countless family pictures everywhere, with Mr. S in all of them. A big meal had been laid out for us, and Mr. S was like a little boy who had just gotten out of camp coming home for a home-cooked dinner.

Nancy, Big Nancy as she was called, as opposed to Little Nancy, who was just turning thirteen, wasn't Hollywood at all. I couldn't imagine her in the same room as Swifty Lazar, or even the same town. She was warm and down home, and took an hour in the kitchen after dinner while Frank played with the kids telling me exactly how he liked everything. The correct way to prepare the paper-thin steaks and pork chops, the scrambled-egg sandwiches, the bread to be sautéed in Italian, never Spanish, olive oil, the soft, never crisp, bacon he wanted for breakfast. She emphasized his disinterest in most vegetables, except for eggplant parmigiana and roasted peppers, and precisely which brands of pasta were acceptable, how many minutes to cook each, and how much salt to put in the water. Finally, of course, that marinara sauce, with the Italian plum tomatoes, crushed just so, and the prescribed balance of garlic, parsley, and oil. It was food chemistry a la Nancy.

Big Nancy was so maternal to Frank, she seemed like his mother rather than his wife, and I could see how the bull-in-a-china-shop boy in him could get tempted by the sirens of the movie business. There was nothing "bad" about Big Nancy, and, alas, that wasn't good. Something about her even made *me* feel guilty about being with her husband, as if I were at work destroying their happy home. And I had not even begun to party with the guy. It was what the Catholics call a Madonna/whore thing. Big Nancy was like the Virgin Mary, and the whores, well, I had no idea at the time. I sensed absolutely no resentment on Big Nancy's part over having lost her husband to the sleazy lure of showbiz, only resignation to the reality of the situation.

The whole scene was sad, because it was such an adorable family. There was a fat old black woman who had been with the family for years as a nanny to the kids, though Nancy rarely left them alone. She was an old-fashioned, lovingly hands-on mom. Little Nancy, Frank Jr., who was ten and the spitting image of his dad but so, so shy, and Tina, a doll at five, all seemed thrilled to see their father, who usually came by once a week. Yet there was something "special event" about these occasions, like papal visits. Mr. S was very touchy and huggy with the kids. He truly loved them, and always arrived with either toys, gifts, or, as they got older, money. But at the same time the situation was awkward, especially the goodbye part. The kids never begged him to stay, but their longing expressions conveyed the powerful message, and it hurt. Driving back to the apartment, Mr. S looked down. I told him how much I liked his family, and all he could say was, "I know, I know." He would call them every single day, wherever he might be, at six o'clock just before their dinner, and be the best telephone father there ever was.

I often went over to the Carolwood house on my own, to do errands, deliver presents, drive the kids somewhere. They seemed so excited to see me, as if I were a surrogate dad, bombarding me with questions about what their real dad was up to. The kids rarely came over to the apartment, which was Mr. S's "bachelor pad" and which he didn't want them to see. When they came down to Palm Springs, he made me get rid of all evidence of whatever women visitors had been around. Dates were off-limits whenever the kids were there. Mr. S was very prudish and old-fashioned in thinking he could shield his children from his reputation and reality as the world's biggest playboy.

I also got to know and like Big Nancy, who was in reality more prudish than her ex-husband pretended to be. There was no way she would ever get remarried, or even go on a date. The closest was Cesar Romero, who looked like the handsomest Latin lover in the movies, but in reality was totally gay. In what *Confidential* magazine might have tried to sensationalize as a *ménage à trois*, Cesar would take Big Nancy and her best friend Barbara Stanwyck out to Chasen's once a week, though the reality was about as naughty as a bridge club. The friendship with Stanwyck was pretty ironic. The main thing the women had in common was that each had lost her husband to Ava Gardner. Stanwyck had been married to Robert Taylor when he succumbed to Ava's charms in 1948. The Taylor-Gardner affair, which was consummated at the house of Taylor's mother, never approached the mad passion of the union with Sinatra, but for the ex-wives, the result was the same. Still, I never heard Nancy utter one unkind word about Ava. She was a very classy lady, some might say a saint, and her sacrificial goodness instilled in Mr. S a nagging guilt he was deeply uncomfortable talking about. One thing, however, he would never say was that he regretted having married Nancy.

I realized that Frank and I had a lot in common, a divorce and three kids, though my Dorothy wasn't anything like the sweetheart that Big Nancy was. With any other boss, I might have felt it was presumptuous to compare my situation with his. But something about Mr. S was so vulnerable, so real, at least at that stage of his life, that it wasn't long before I let him know how much my own situation allowed me to relate to his. He could have easily said, George, don't you go dumping your real world onto mine, but he didn't. I struck a chord in him that made him open up about the deep frustrations he was feeling, loving his family, loving Ava Gardner, and loving his career all at the same time—none of them were giving him an easy time of it.

But at the beginning of my job with him, the thing he would most talk about with me was work. That was almost always in the forefront of his mind. In what would become a continual aspect of my working for Sinatra, we'd sit and play cards late into the night, and he'd drink "Jack" (Daniel's) and obsess about his career. He was on the comeback trail, though he didn't feel he was home free again by any means. As far as he was concerned, his career was still up in the air. Although *Eternity* was doing big box office, Oscar nominations had not been tallied, and Mr. S still did not have his next film job. He thought he had, but he had been screwed, which had made him as insecure as ever, teetering on the brink of celluloid oblivion.

The first (of many) people I would see Frank Sinatra hate was the man who went on to be considered one of the grandest of all Hollywood producers, Sam Spiegel. One day I arrived to see the living room half destroyed. Two lamps had been knocked over, broken glass was covering the floor. At first I thought there had been a burglary, until I began cleaning up and found the remnants of several drafts of a script entitled *On the Waterfront* by Budd Schulberg, who I knew had written the nastiest novel about Hollywood sleazebags, *What Makes Sammy Run?* I found Mr. S in bed nursing several bad paper cuts on his hands, which he got ripping up the script. He apologized for flipping out and told me he had just lost the role of a lifetime and that he had been fucked over by the worst real Sammy Glick in the business, Sammy Spiegel. I said, hey, you just had the role of a lifetime in *From Here to Eternity,* and he said, very dejectedly, this one's a role for *two* lifetimes. Then he went into a tirade against Sam Spiegel that lasted for the next couple of weeks.

Sam Spiegel was the Mike Romanoff of producers, a European con man and ex-jailbird who went on to fool all of the people all of the time. He was the total caricature of the fat cat movie mogul, gold chains, big cigar, pinky rings, "Frankie baby" this and "Frankie baby" that. He was always surrouded with beautiful women, whom he graciously dispatched to his friends, or whomever he wanted to sell something to. He seemed like a joke. Yet he was the real deal. He had made, and would continue to make, some of the greatest classic movies, *The Bridge on the River Kwai, Lawrence of Arabia.*

One of the many people Spiegel fooled was Mr. Doubting Thomas himself, Frank Sinatra. Spiegel had promised Sinatra the part of the tormented, poetic hoodlum Terry Malloy in his upcoming production of *On the Waterfront.* Spiegel had hyped Sinatra to kingdom come, promising that Maggio might get him a Best Supporting Actor Oscar, but that Malloy was guaranteed to garner him the Best Actor statuette, ensuring Sinatra's career literally from here to eternity. Spiegel had brought home the Oscar bacon for Sinatra's idol Bogart in *The African Queen.* Now Sinatra was trusting Spiegel to do it for him. Sinatra naturally wanted to believe Spiegel, who assured him time and again what a great, natural, earthy, and real thespian he was, how he was the symbol of the working man, the voice of the people, and that there was no other actor in the world who could do justice to this part of parts. The film was going to be shot in Hoboken. "For Chrissakes," Spiegel said, "you *are* Hoboken!"

But, as it turned out, there were too many people in Hollywood who, like Swifty Lazar, lacked confidence in the resurgence and staying power of Frank Sinatra. The bottom line, and producers believe in nothing except the bottom line, was that Sam Spiegel could not get his dark tale of labor unrest in the New York docks financed with Sinatra carrying the film. So, for all his declarations of Sinatra's uniqueness, he found another actor who could do even better justice to Terry Malloy, the ultimate justice of getting him to the screen. That actor, who would become Sinatra's continuing nemesis, was Marlon Brando. Brando had originally refused to work with the *Waterfront* director Elia Kazan, because he hated Kazan for being a stool pigeon, a name namer in the Communist witch-hunt of the House Committee on Un-American Activities. That's why Spiegel came to Sinatra, telling him "you're better than Brando." Spiegel totally snowed Frank, put him under his ether. And then, when he was finally able to put Brando under that same ether, getting him to forgive Kazan, he stabbed Frank in the back.

I had never seen Frank Sinatra pissed off before; he had seemed so sweet and downtrodden the whole time I had known him I didn't know he had this venom in him. (Man, did I underestimate that one.) Sam Spiegel had spoiled Sinatra's Oscar party before the party had begun. He was ruining his comeback. Worst of all, he had lied to Frank. He had made a promise and he had broken it, and, as Frank told me, fighting back the tears, where he had come from that was the worst thing a man could do. Frank really beat up on himself for getting suckered by Spiegel. He'd talk about how Spiegel had done prison time for writing bad checks and other frauds in England and had been deported for his crimes. He should have known, and he felt stupid. I was about the only one he could complain to at that point. Bogart loved Spiegel, because he had helped him win the Oscar. Lazar loved Spiegel, because he wanted to sell him things. Romanoff loved Spiegel, because he was pretty much the same guy himself, and Spiegel was one of his best customers. So there was nowhere Frank could go with his rage. All Frank could do was rant to me and look for the next best part that the buzz from *Eternity* could help him get.

Mr. S and I spent our first month or so getting to know each other. I was pretty awkward at first. I'd shine every pair of shoes twice, and press his pants and coats three times, just to be sure they were 100 percent right. I was much more compulsive than I had had to be in the Navy. I wanted so much to please him, I know I overdid it. Once I was hovering so close to him over dinner that he said to me, "Who do you think you are, Ted Lewis?" He was referring to the guy who sang "Me and My Shadow," and it gave both of us a big laugh and was helpful in breaking the ice. So was a time when he had some people coming over for drinks and hors d'oeuvres and I spilled something on my shirt so he gave me one of his. We were just about the same exact size, so his stuff all fit me. The only problem was the initials on the shirts. One of the guests, a Broadway music type, began giving me a hard time about the shirt. "What's your name?" George. "Then what are those FS initials for?" the wise guy kept sticking it to me. "Fast service," I improvised, and Sinatra broke out laughing. "He's a bullet, George is," he said. "Don't mess with him." That got his respect.

We bonded still further on his first sleepover conquest during my watch. She was a pretty starlet from the studios whom neither he nor anyone else ever saw again, but he had me put on a candlelit spread as if he were entertaining a princess. I had to go to Parisian Florist in Hollywood, the best in town, to get roses, to Jurgensen's fancy grocery shop in Beverly Hills for the best champagne and chocolate, to Monaco's Italian deli for prosciutto, plus a long trip downtown to Bullock's Wilshire, the top department store in L.A., for a gift of an engraved notebook because she had said something about wanting to become a writer. When it came to women, and to his friends, Mr. S was the most thoughtful man I ever met. He didn't miss a thing. The girl barely touched her meal, but, when Mr. S told me I could leave for the evening and she was still there, I knew all our military operations for this romantic D-day had not been in vain. The morning, or rather afternoon after, I accidentally ran into Mr. S as he was coming out of the shower. Stark naked. It was the first time I had seen him *au naturel*, and it looked so unnatural, I couldn't stop myself from blurting out, "My God, that thing's so big you must rub olive oil on it!" He turned beet red, then broke out laughing. "I bet somebody had a good time last night," I went on. He grinned that big conquest grin and said, "About time I got lucky."

Whenever Mr. S would be impressed or amazed or shocked by something, he would exclaim to me, "Holy mackerel, Kingfish!" quoting his favorite radio and TV show, *Amos 'n' Andy*. He got off imitating a black dialect. He wasn't doing it because I was black, though he liked the fact that I understood the genuine article. He'd do Amos and Andy imitations with all his friends, so it made me feel like one of the guys. And he liked telling black jokes. "What's long and hard on a black man?" "The third grade." Or "Why are blacks sexually obsessed?" "If you had pubic hair on your head, you'd be sexually obsessed, too." Or one of the corny ones he inexplicably fixated on, "What's black in a tree?" "A branch manager." If he told any of this shit today, he would be sued for racial harassment. But not then. He'd tell these stupid jokes to Sammy Davis Jr. the same way he'd tell them to Humphrey Bogart, and pretty much the same way he'd tell them to me. Being black was never discussed, nor did it seem to be considered. He never used the "n" word, except to complain that someone like Sam Spiegel was "treating him like a nigger." He would use it as an adjective of oppression, but never as an oppressive label. He wouldn't stand for that. He saw himself as a member of an oppressed minority and had total empathy for anyone who was similarly situated. Where race was concerned, the man was color blind, even if today he'd be viewed as criminally insensitive. Whatever he was doing came from the heart. A year or two later, when he'd sometimes call me "Spook," I took it as a brotherly nickname, not a racial epithet. Everybody in the Rat Pack had a "ratty" nickname, and now so did I. I thought I had "arrived."

Mr. S didn't keep many secrets from me. I had to deal with all his inadequacies. The biggest one was his hair. Every morning after he shampooed, I'd have to spray hair coloring on the ever-expanding bald spot on the back of his scalp. Like Humphrey Bogart, who had the same hair problem, Sinatra would never go out without this cover-up, and without one of his trademark hats, though he'd only wear one of the many custom hairpieces made for him by Max Factor when he was shooting a film or performing at a show. His other main point of self-consciousness was the entire left side of his face, from his ear down to his neck. When he was born, it was a difficult delivery. The doctor had to use forceps, which scarred and deformed Sinatra's face and punctured his eardrum. The latter injury had kept him out of the service in World War II, while the former deformation forced him to personally apply makeup over the rough, cratered scars every day of his life. It was funny watching Mr. Tough Guy pat his face with this little powder puff, but I didn't dare tease him. Mr. S wasn't vain about his appearance; he was embarrassed.

The thing that bothered Mr. S the very most may have been his lack of education. He felt bad that he had never gone to college and was a flop in high school. He wasn't a big talker, mainly because he wasn't sure what to say. He was constantly in fear of putting his foot in his mouth, of using the wrong word, of exposing his lack of learning. So whenever he'd have a quiet hour, whether at home, at the studio, on a plane, he would always have a leather-bound hardcover dictionary with him, and he would sit there reading all the words he didn't know, from A to Z. New words, which he'd mark and circle, were like new toys, which he loved playing with. What's more, each new word he learned made him feel more secure. He would have actually enjoyed going back to school. "Growing up, I was told reading made people go blind," Mr. S often joked. He wasn't a big talker, but his love affair with the dictionary gave him unique patterns of speech. For example, instead of saying "I need this like a hole in the head," he'd go on entire medical riffs. One day he'd say "I need this like hemophilia." Then the next he'd say, "I need this like Parkinson's." And then "I need this like peptic esophagitis." He sounded like a doctor, all from poring over that Webster's. Apparently, Cole Porter got many of his rhymes the same way.

For all his playboy antics, Frank Sinatra was dead serious about his career, which he placed before everything else. By career, I mean singing. Movies, he was coming to realize, were a crapshoot out of his control. In that game, there were slicker players than he, guys like Sam Spiegel. He wanted to be a top actor, wanted to be a star, wanted to *succeed* as in everything else he did, but he understood he couldn't be the Best There Was. Music was another matter. He had been at the very pinnacle of pop music. He knew what it was like at the top there; it wasn't a fantasy like films. It was a reality he had savored, and he wanted to savor it again. "Fuck movies!" he declared defiantly when "Young at Heart" topped the Hit Parade, at the depths of his despair over Sam Spiegel. He had the same reaction when his rendition of the theme song from "Three Coins in the Fountain" also topped the charts. Knowing what his trump card was, he was totally disciplined about his singing. He'd religiously spend an hour every day before he went to the recording studio listening to classical music and to opera. His favorite singers were Richard Tucker and Lawrence Tibbett.

Mr. S approached his first big Capitol album recording session in the spring of 1954 with the rigor of one of his seductions. Retreating to his Palm Springs home to avoid any distractions, he would rest as hard as he normally played. He would only drink hot tea with lemon and honey, no Jack Daniel's, and no cigarettes. If you saw him at the studio with a drink or a smoke, they were merely props. His voice was his moneymaker, and he treated it with the utmost respect, which is what he had for his new arranger, Nelson Riddle, who helped channel the rage and pain of Sinatra's turbulent thirties, midlife in those pre-youth-culture days, into turning the man from the ultimate crooner to something much deeper and stronger, the ultimate stylist. Those spring sessions, for the album called *Swing Easy!*, turned out such classics as "Just One of those Things," and "All of Me."

That same spring he finally won his Academy Award. He had never pretended it didn't matter. In fact, although Mr. S was one of the least religious men I had ever met, the entire month before the Oscars he'd go down to the Good Shepherd Church in Beverly Hills and pray. He didn't even see any girls that much, he wanted God's help so bad. I remember the day of the Oscar show, I helped him dress in his tuxedo and a "good luck" toupee he would wear on opening nights. He also had special underpants made, a cross between a panty girdle and a jock strap. The idea was to hold down that big thing of his, so it wouldn't show through his tuxedo pants. He wasn't quite John Dillinger, but he was hung enough to have to take special precautions. This was the Eisenhower era, and "family values" prevailed. Speaking of which, Mr. S brought Little Nancy and Frank Jr. as his dates to the ceremony at the Pantages Theatre in Hollywood. Big Nancy had given him their own ceremony earlier in the day, where the family presented him with their own Oscar, a medallion with the statue engraved on one side and a saint on the other. Later that night he beat Brandon de Wilde, the blond kid in *Shane*, Jack Palance, the villain in *Shane*, Eddie Albert, the sidekick in *Roman Holiday*, and Robert Strauss, the comic captive in *Stalag 17*. There was no wild celebration afterward. He took the kids back to Nancy, then returned to the apartment and called his mother in Hoboken and put me on the phone as "your new son, Giorgio." He seemed shell-shocked, more relieved than happy. So many things had gone wrong, especially the *Waterfront* fiasco, that he couldn't believe he would get the Oscar until he held it in his hands.

Although there was no orgy that night, the games were about to begin. First Sinatra had to finish his *Swing Easy!* album, and then his new film *Suddenly*, a B picture in which he played a psycho who wants to assassinate the president. This choice of subject matter reflected how down and depressed Mr. S was when he agreed to make it. Yet it reflected a theme, that of political assassinations and how easy it was to pull them off, in which he was deeply interested and would come back to again in both *The Manchurian Candidate* and *The Naked Runner*. Mr. S thought such movies would get Americans talking as well as buying tickets to see what he considered one of the ultimate "what ifs." Mr. S's explorations into this deadly heart of political darkness got him into big trouble in 1963, when the rumors arose that his Mafia chieftain friends may have been behind the assassination of John F. Kennedy, who was seen as having betrayed both them and Sinatra.

Once the recording and filming work was over, it was time to party. The revels were led by Jimmy Van Heusen, who was Sinatra's best friend and the role model for the swingin' music man that Frank would now become. Unshackled by the constraints of family and of failure, as well as of Ava, who had left him for a famous bullfighter and for good, the joker could now go wild. Jimmy Van Heusen was a decadent womanizer, an Olympian boozer, a war hero, a daredevil pilot, and one of America's best songwriters. Bogart may have been Sinatra's role model for style, but for lifestyle, it was Van Heusen "All the Way," the Oscar-winning song Van Heusen wrote with his lyricist Sammy Cahn. Sinatra called Van Heusen "Chester," after his real name, Chester Babcock. Van Heusen, who had won his first Oscar composing "Swinging on a Star" for Bing Crosby, was the ultimate swinger. Balding and WASPy, Van Heusen had the reassuring presence of the military test pilot he had been. (His Sinatra song "Come Fly with Me" was completely autobiographical.) He was also a wild man.

As a young guy, Van Heusen had spent some time in an upstate New York seminary before going on to Syracuse University, where he earned tuition by playing piano in a brothel. His whole life seemed to be a debauched backlash from that early religious schooling. Van Heusen had his own place in the hills above Palm Springs called the Rattlesnake Ranch, which was all sex, all the time. He would have entire plane crews of stewardesses, when stewardesses were the big sex symbols, crashing there at once.

He also loved hookers. His own "whore wrangler," the guy who rounded up the ladies, was a fat song plugger named Murray Wolfe, who looked like hell but was a brilliant salesman, especially with the name Frank Sinatra to drop. Wolfe was a precursor of the payola people who would bribe disc jockeys to play songs on the radio. Wolfe would bribe anyone to do anything, and he got results. Wolfe worked closely with a madam in the Valley named Joyce, who was tight with all the casting people at the studios, keeping long lists of which starlets were new, which ones were hot, and which ones needed extra money—basically all of them. She also knew lots of non-Hollywood California beauties who wanted to earn extra pin money, girls like

Judy Campbell, who would later pull a sexual trifecta with Sinatra, Jack Kennedy, and Sam Giancana.

Some people would call Jimmy Van Heusen, who, bored with his original name, chose his new one from a shirt ad, a bad influence. His own songwriting partner, the nervous, milquetoasty, pun-spouting Sammy Cahn, was horrified by Van Heusen's nonstop debauchery. But these excesses were just what Frank Sinatra needed, or thought he needed, to make it through the long Ava-less nights. Van Heusen, while not corrupting, had written "Nancy with the Laughing Face," about Little Nancy, to show his respect for Frank's family-man side. At his lowest depths, Sinatra was said to have slashed his wrists in Van Heusen's New York apartment in 1953, before I started with him. It didn't seem like his style, but the despair was there. If it was true, then Van Heusen's mission was to never let his friend get so low again, and, to that end, he kept the booze and the broads flowing nonstop. Van Heusen, with his military training, had the stamina for this sexual boot camp. I was actually surprised that Mr. S, who was frail and fragile, could keep up with him, but he did. It was an occasion he spurred himself to rise to.

Because I had never met Ava Gardner, I found it hard to believe that any woman could have such a devastating effect on a guy like Mr. S, who was no stranger to beautiful ladies. Then I did, and I was blown away. If I were going to slit my wrists over a woman, this would be the one. As for the whores, the starlets, the stewardesses, Sinatra would have dumped them all in a split second if Ava would have come back to him. She wouldn't, and she had made it quite clear to him time and again. But he still hung on to the hope and the dream. The winter I started with him, when Spiegel had knocked him low, he did a very masochistic thing and added insult to his own injury by flying to Spain to try to win her back one last time. He was up against some heavy competition. Ava's man was Luis Dominguin, the most famous, most fearless, most dashing matador in the bull-ring. Hemingway put the guy on a pedestal, and Dominguin put Ava on one. Even if Ava had been going with a bullshit sweeper, she wasn't going back to Frank. He was too possessive of her, she was too jealous of him. Neither trusted the other. I guess it was a case of loving each other too much, so much that they would have killed themselves. Love and death. Sinatra came home empty-handed, yet he still wanted Ava in his life, whatever the circumstances. Thus when she came to L.A. to discuss her next movie projects, he insisted she relax for a weekend in Palm Springs. She accepted, but demanded that if she was going to relax, that Frank couldn't be there. Fine, he said, and dispatched me to take care of her.

Ava Gardner was the most beautiful woman I ever saw, much less met. I picked her up at the airport, and she could stop planes, not just traffic. There was no movie star nonsense with her, no entourage, no fawning press agents in tow. She was pushing her own bags on a cart, trying to lie low in dark glasses and a tatty raincoat. But once I had her in the Cadillac and she took off the coat and the shades, I could barely steer straight. The first thing to hit me were those cats' eyes of hers, green with flecks of gold and hypnotic as hell. She wasn't wearing an ounce of makeup, and her skin was creamy and flawless. Her hair was thick and lustrous. Then there was her body. She was five seven, sleek, but with amazing curves. She wasn't wearing a bra, which was totally risqué in those days. Defying gravity, she had no need of one. She had the ideal body, the kind that stars these days pay fortunes to plastic surgeons for. The best thing about her, though, was that she didn't give a shit. She wasn't trying to be hot, and she wasn't trying to be grand. She was just trying to get away from it all. She made me stop for a Coke and some peanuts, which she pored into the bottle and ate and guzzled at the same time. It was a "Southern thing," she said, apologizing that MGM had made her lose her syrupy Southern drawl. When I told her I was Southern, too, that was the beginning of a beautiful friendship.

If you're a Southerner, the distance between North Carolina and Louisiana isn't all that far. Southerners somehow naturally relate to each other, even black and white, and especially black and poor white, which is where Ava was coming from. Her family were tobacco tenant farmers in a backwater called Boon Hill, outside the little town of Smithfield in eastern North Carolina. We were both Depression kids whose biggest treat was going to the "picture shows." We both sang in Baptist church choirs, both loved fried chicken and collard greens, both hated the swamp humidity we had grown up with. However, the fact that my father was a nightclub owner in New Orleans made me seem like a super sophisticate compared to Ava. Compared to Boon Hill, New Orleans was Paris, and compared to the boys she knew, George Jacobs was Jean Gabin. At least that's what she told me on the drive down to Palm Springs, and it made me feel pretty cool. She could have said anything, and I would have felt pretty cool hearing it from her.

Ava also told me that her dead father was such an awful racist that she was certain the gentleman did protest too much, that he had black blood in him, and hence in her, a touch of the tarbrush. Her idea of youthful rebellion was to sneak off with the kids of the black sharecroppers and go to church with them. She knew all the great spirituals, and got us singing along by the time we hit San Bernardino. "Rock of Ages." "Just a Closer Walk with Thee." "It makes you almost believe in God," she said. I told her what a good voice she had, and that was the biggest compliment I could have paid her. She despised movies, she said. She was only in it for the money. Singing was another matter. She'd do anything to sing, but the pigs who ran the studios wouldn't let her. Even though she was a true superstar at this point and her film career was much, much bigger than Frank's, she was as insecure as he was about how long it might last. She had just taken Clark Gable away from Grace Kelly, on the screen anyway, in *Mogambo,* and she was about to light things up with Humphrey Bogart in *The Barefoot Contessa,* yet she didn't act like the celluloid goddess that she was. She made me stop for cigarettes, for a bottle of cheap wine, and for Ritz crackers before we got to Sinatra's house, by which time she was dead drunk. I had to carry her from the car and put her in Mr. S's bed, where she slept until the next morning.

We were living in the original Sinatra house on Alejo at the time, which, like the Beverly Glen apartment, was filled with images of Ava. This was before the massive compound on Wonder Palms Drive where the Kennedys, and all the other celebrities on earth, were to stay. The Alejo house was pretty, in the postwar desert-deco style, but rather small. Then again, in 1954 Frank Sinatra was anything but rich. He was paying off a crushing six-figure debt to the Internal Revenue Service, which he owed for back taxes that his weak cash flow in the dark years of the early fifties had forced him to defer. In his divorce from Big Nancy, he had basically given everything he had to her, except this Palm Springs house, to buy his freedom to marry Ava. His bankability as a movie star based on *Eternity* was just kicking in, his records were just beginning to sell again, and he was negotiating for a piece of the rock or, as it were, the Sands in Las Vegas, which would prove to be a major cash cow. At that moment, he was a struggling thirty-nine-year-old entertainer with a famous soon-to-be ex-wife. Proof of this was that I was getting the same $150 a week that I had under Swifty Lazar. But I had faith things would be getting better. In the meanwhile I liked my boss and I liked his world.

Ava and I had a great weekend. We cooked Southern feasts—the glory that was grease, we called them—fried everything, vegetables obliterated in pork fat, rich cakes made in Crisco, pecan pie. She was one of those rare women who could gorge on everything she wanted and never gain a pound, though somehow I sensed she wished she could get fat and bail from the business altogether. She was a terrible drunk, and would drink anything, cheap sangria, bad beer, expensive champagne, it didn't matter. We played a lot of Mr. S's record collection, mostly Duke Ellington and Billie Holiday, but Sinatra's albums as well. Ava loved his voice, but the songs didn't make her sentimental over "them," even at her booziest. The one she was a little misty about was her ex before Frank, bandleader Artie Shaw, on whom she had developed a teenage crush after seeing him and his big band in Raleigh. Music was only one of Shaw's aphrodisiacs. A bigger one, she told me, was his brain. He was the first man to treat her as an intelligent person, rather than a sex symbol, which had so turned her off about Howard Hughes, who was still stalking her. Shaw taught her how to play chess and had sent her to UCLA to take classes, which, she sighed, was something Frank would have never done. She did the crossword puzzle every day, which she said annoyed Frank. Mr. S basically detested anyone who had had anything to do with Ava, Shaw, Hughes, or Peter Lawford, whom he excommunicated for five years for taking Ava to dinner during one of their estrangements. The only "Ava man" he tolerated was her first husband, Mickey Rooney, whom Ava wrote off as a studio-arranged marriage. She told me the PR man came along with them on their honeymoon. We'd swim in the pool in the desert night, and being alone with a tipsy, half-naked randy-talking Ava was a temptation that made me very uncomfortable. I didn't feel like a valet, I felt like a friend, and I also felt awfully aroused, which was one Molotov cocktail of conflicting emotions.

I could now see exactly why Mr. S was so obsessed with her. Super-gorgeous women weren't like this one. The other movie goddesses were narcissistic, neurotic, concerned about no one except themselves and their stardom. Ava was only concerned about others. Moreover, she had that magic that made those others feel that, with her in their corner, anything on earth was possible. She was a cross between Miss Universe, a kick-ass girl-next-door, and a fairy godmother who could give you your dearest wish. The only problem was, once you met her, your dearest wish was *her*. "She's a gas, ain't she?" Mr. S asked me when I returned to L.A., wanting to know what we did every second of the stay. Thank God I didn't have to lie to him.

I don't want to give the impression that Mr. S was a Hollywood narcissist who only talked about himself, his career, his romances. As he got comfortable around me, he wanted to hear more about me than I did about him. Our card games would often go on until dawn, with his begging me to tell him stories of my Louisiana boyhood. To him my life in New Orleans was as exotic as life on Mars, and he was fascinated by it. So we would talk and talk about it all, things like my father growing up the one half-breed among eight white stepbrothers, about his nightclub partnership with the Cuban boxer Kid Coco, about my Creole grandmother with her 104 grandchildren, about my wife's pimp father, with his diamond stickpins and his Cadillacs and his starry clientele that included Lionel Hampton, Count Basie, Pegleg Bates.

He'd love my tales of how I would run away from home and show up on the doorsteps of the great moss-draped plantations of the River Road along the Mississippi. I was a cute curly-haired little boy, and I'd use that cuteness to get myself taken in by these white aristocrats. I'd tell them my parents had died, that I was all alone, so they'd feel sorry for me and ask me to live in their mansions and get waited on by their servants. I'd only stay one night, have one great dinner and live like a prince for a day, then vanish and go back home before my mother sent the law out to look for me. Every few weeks I'd do an Oliver Twist number like this. I had a huge fantasy life. I would read the *National Geographic* magazines at school and dream about the places I'd go. Now all those dreams were coming true, and Mr. S seemed very happy to be sharing his fantastic life with me. When I'd tell him a story about how I'd chase after the Italian girls in Girt Town who looked down on me, he'd match me with one about how he'd chase after the Irish girls in Hoboken who looked down on him. It was nice being buddies with your boss, something that would have never happened with Swifty Lazar.

It's amazing what winning an Oscar can do for you. I believe that if Frank Sinatra had been able to show the statuette on his mantel when they were trying to finance *Waterfront*, even Sam Spiegel would have been forced, by simple greed, to do the right thing and would have given him the Terry Malloy part. I say this because, after that March at the Pantages, no one, in Hollywood or anywhere else, dared say no, or even maybe, to Frank Sinatra. Even though at one low point Mr. S had declared "Fuck movies," he would never repeat that pronouncement now that he was hot again. Although movies indeed were a crapshoot compared to music, where Mr. S was undisputedly Numero Uno, cinema was the Everest Frank Sinatra felt compelled to conquer. Yes, he liked being a shrewd businessman, but he liked being a dreamer and a conqueror too much to be *totally* practical. Some dreams, like movie stardom, were beyond the bottom line.

In the next five years, Mr. S would make sixteen or so major Hollywood movies and nearly a dozen huge albums, not to mention television, Las Vegas, world, and national tours. And that was all before he got involved in politics as the ambassador from the State of Show Biz to Washington and the world. Forget James Brown. The hardest-working man in Hollywood was, and will forever be, Frank Sinatra, no contest. He was also the hardest-playing man in the game as well. And his love life, if that's what you would call it, went off the charts. He became the Casanova of Modern Times.

For every new movie, there was a new affair, and not merely for the benefit of the studio publicity apparatus. No man has ever slept with so many famous women. Pre-Oscar, the only celebrity I knew to have slept over was Dinah Shore, who was a long-running affair of Sinatra's. He knew the fine and difficult art of casual sex, keeping his girlfriends as friends, through lots and lots of attention. Yes, gifts and lingerie, but more valuable was the telephone and face time he would put in listening to their endless problems. "Get me a goddamn hooker," he'd often say, rolling his eyes at the end of a marathon phone session. "George, Romans, countrymen, somebody, lend me your ears." I got to know all of Mr. S's ladies, stars and nonstars. I'd pick them up, drive them home, pay them if they were pros, make the candlelit seduction dinner and buy the flowers and chocolates for them if they weren't, then listen to their laments when Mr. S let them down, which was inevitable. Sinatra never staged a conquest at the woman's place. He understood the home court advantage, plus he preferred sleeping in his own bed, usually by himself once the fireworks were over and I'd escort Miss Right for the Night back to her place.

Post-Oscar, Sinatra was always swinging with some star. The first big one was Kim Novak in *The Man with the Golden Arm,* and their on-and-off fling continued through *Pal Joey.* He complained to me that her legs were too heavy for him, but her face more than made up for it. Mr. S ultimately lost Kim to Sammy Davis Jr., who almost lost his career to the evil Columbia kingpin Harry Cohn, who did not want his platinum goddess tarred, as it were, with Sammy's brush. Frank did not begrudge Kim to Sammy; however, he did almost "Lawfordize" him for encouraging *Confidential* magazine to do a spread on him and Ava Gardner that created the illusion that they were a number, after Ava showed up at one of Sammy's shows at the Apollo Theatre in Harlem and then appeared with him in an *Ebony* photo shoot. Sammy begged forgiveness on career grounds, that it was merely an innocent publicity stunt. Ava backed him up, and that saved his ass. For Frank, that woman was sacred ground. If you messed with her, it would be scorched earth. Also, Sammy was a special case. Sinatra had just nursed him back to health and to performing again after the 1954 automobile wreck on the desert highway between Palm Springs and L.A. that cost him his eye.

I have never seen anyone more caring and generous than Mr. S in this crisis. He was the ultimate stand-up guy. Despite his hatred for hospitals, he visited Sammy constantly in the San Bernardino Community Hospital and made sure he had the finest specialists brought in from L.A. to treat him. On a psychic level, he used his own comeback as the example that gave Sammy the strength to return to performing, bucking him up every day and making one-eye jokes that somehow took the curse off Sammy's disability. Mr. S also used all his power to arrange Sammy's famous comeback engagement at Ciro's on the Sunset Strip, and making sure that every big name in Hollywood was there on opening night to cheer Sammy on.

Meanwhile he had installed Sammy in the Palm Springs house to recuperate and prepare for this fateful return engagement. Mr. S had me stay at the house to be at Sammy's service for the three weeks he was there, cooking whatever he dreamed of, rounding up the broads he dreamed of. I'd help him light his endless cigarettes until he could practice enough with his one eye to get his field of vision straight. Sometimes when he'd end up lighting the tip of his nose instead of the cigarette, he'd break down crying in frustration that he'd never get it all back again. "Shit, Sam," I'd console him. "You get to see more out of one eye than a thousand guys see outta two. You're gonna make it. Don't waste that good eye on fucking tears." And he'd stop, and try again, and soon he was striking up matches like old times.

Whatever Sammy wanted, Mr. S was going to be his fairy godfather, and all his caring worked wonders for Sammy, who ended up a greater entertainer than ever. Thus in the *Ebony* incident Mr. S had a lot of himself invested in Sammy and found it hard to hold a grudge, even a Sinatra grudge, against someone he treated as a son. Lawford, on the other hand was never "family," just an "English sharpie," as Frank called him, who just happened to have the best connections in the world.

One affair that, unlike the others, was conducted in top secret was with Natalie Wood, because she was a minor at the time, either fifteen or sixteen, though she didn't act like it. She wore skintight dresses, pushup bras, all the makeup that Saks could sell. She smoked and spoke like a world-weary New York sophisticate in a *Thin Man* movie. Then again, she was an actress, just a precocious one. Sinatra adored this tiny beauty, but he didn't want to go the way of Charlie Chaplin or Errol Flynn or, later, Roman Polanski. He had been taken with Natalie ever since she became a child star in *Miracle on 34th Street*. Somehow he met her mother, Maria Gurdin, a Russian woman who was the pushiest stage mom in history. She made Brooke Shields's mother look laid back. Mrs. Gurdin brought the teen Natalie over to the apartment for cocktails soon after Mr. S won his Oscar. She had her kid all dolled up, total jailbait, in a form-fitting black party dress, and Mr. S went for it in a big way. Nothing dirty-old-mannish, he was never like that. He played them cuts from his upcoming album, provided career suggestions, refused to let me serve Natalie an alcoholic drink until her mother allowed it. I made her a martini, which seemed to go with her outfit. She drank two and would have had a third had Mr. S not jokingly called a limit. I've never seen anyone so supportive as he was of Natalie's and her mother's ambitions. In the next week, after those cocktails, Natalie began coming over after her studio school, without her mom, for "singing lessons." Mr. S would send me away when she was there. "I don't want you to testify," he joked. He wanted to be "In like Flynn," but he didn't want to be ruined for it.

Natalie was much more than a fling. Their secret affair went on for several years, off and on, until she reached the age of consent, and even beyond that until she took up with Robert Wagner. Mr. S truly cherished her, and whatever went on in private, he was also a father to her more than her own father, very protective, advising her about all the many men who would come after her. In Frank's world casting was the sincerest form of flattery. He liked Natalie so much he put her, at age nineteen, in his 1957 movie about racism, *Kings Go Forth,* in which she plays a *mulata* living in WWII France in a love triangle with two GIs played by Sinatra and Tony Curtis, whom Frank always called by his real name "Bernie." Because of my own background from New Orleans, where half the city was of mixed race, I was Mr. S's informal technical advisor on that film. For all her many charms, I hate to say that Natalie was the least convincing black girl I ever met. We'd joke about it, calling her the "Black Russian."

Mr. S was also instrumental in encouraging Natalie's marriage to Robert Wagner, one of the handsomest young actors in Hollywood. If anyone *looked* like the town's dream couple, they were it. It was surprising that Mr. S liked Bob Wagner so much, he was such a pretty boy. I had met him as a young caddy at the Brentwood Country Club, carrying the clubs for Clifton Webb, the elegant British star of *Laura,* who was one of the reigning queens of Hollywood's gay world. Webb got Bob the powerful gay agent Henry Willson, who had made stars out of Rock Hudson, Tab Hunter, and Sal Mineo. Eventually, Willson also represented Natalie, who was one of his rare female clients.

Mr. S would bait even his straightest friends for the slightest "fag" mannerism, like the way they'd hold a cigarette or use a French word, or affectation, like ordering wine instead of hard liquor with dinner, real-men-don't-eat-quiche stuff. Anything that smacked of worldliness, culture, or sophistication was a "fag thing." Despite Bob's association with Webb and Willson, and despite his urbane manner, Mr. S gave him a pass on all that, and years later even gave him his blessing to get engaged to his daughter Tina, and when that didn't work, he forgave him, and gave him another blessing to wed surrogate daughter Jill St. John.

"What do you think of Bob, George?" Mr. S asked me one day.

"He's a nice guy," I replied.

Mr. S shook his head. "George," he said. " 'He's a nice guy' is not a valid answer to my question."

I didn't like being put on the spot like that. I didn't want to insult anybody. Yet I knew Mr. S counted on me to be honest with him. Mr. S did most of his "serious" talking to his girlfriends. With the guys it mostly drunken insults and awful jokes and puns. Was he being serious with me? "Bob could be too pretty for his own good," I blurted out. "What would people say if you looked like that?" I realized I had jammed my foot in my mouth.

There was a long, scary silence. I thought this was the end of a short and wonderful career. Then Mr. S broke out laughing. "George, I *do* look like that. I think we have to get you glasses." As time went by, the more I got to know him, the more candid I would be. But one rule was: never, ever, make a negative comment about his appearance. Some jokes just didn't play in Sinatraland.

Mr. S had a brief on-location flirtation with Sophia Loren on *The Pride and the Passion* in 1956. However, it went nowhere because his continuing passion for Ava Gardner was a fatal blow to Sophia's pride. The main reason Sinatra took the part in the costume epic, aside from getting to work with another of his idols, Cary Grant, was that being in Spain gave him an extended opportunity to pursue Ava in Madrid. The pursuit didn't work, nor did the film. He and the director Stanley Kramer went to war over Sinatra's refusal to do more than one take of a scene, and Mr. S eventually stormed off the picture and out of the country.

More revealing than the costars and starlets who shared Sinatra's bed were the ones who got away. On *Pal Joey* Rita Hayworth ignored him completely. She was close to forty at the time and still a knockout. Mr. S never cared about age anyhow, old or young. Somehow he was terribly impressed with her because of her romantic pedigree with Aly Khan and Orson Welles. Because I used to know her in my law firm days, he tried to use me as an opening wedge to try and get something going. It didn't work. She didn't remember me, or even Mr. Tannenbaum, from whom she rented her house. She often forgot her lines, and her general blankness and disinterest even in Frank Sinatra at the top of his game, singing "The Lady Is a Tramp" to her, may have been due to early symptoms of the terrible Alzheimer's disease that would destroy her.

Another pedigree that got away, though not totally away, was Grace Kelly in *High Society*. Sinatra got a kick out of "Gracie," as he called her, but he had felt humiliated pining around the set of *Mogambo* over Ava in front of Grace. He was certain she saw him as a major loser and he could not bring himself to make a play for her. But he had another problem on the set. He was deeply intimidated by his costar Bing Crosby, one of his childhood icons and one of the lords of the manor in Palm Springs. Crosby and Bob Hope were part of the Eisenhower elite, a WASPy Republican golfing aristocracy that would have nothing to do with Frank. I think this was why he worked so hard for John F. Kennedy, to gain acceptance and legitimacy. Crosby was particularly important to Mr. S because Crosby's brilliant career was the precise blueprint for his own. Crosby had begun as a crooner, became a singing idol, then got into acting and won an Oscar for *Going My Way*, and then became a multimillionaire businessman to boot. Plus he was a wonderful sportsman. It was a scary act to follow, yet Mr. S desperately wanted to follow it, to a T. He would have also loved to be buddies with Bing, yet Bing, though invariably friendly, kept his cool distance. Their relationship remained strictly professional, and it killed Mr. S to think that Bing considered him neither in his class nor in his league.

Everything about Mr. S had to do with paying debts and settling scores, all about the balance sheets of life. He would have treasured a Grace Kelly sexual credit, but he didn't want to try and fail in front of the august Bing. There had been lots of rumors about Grace, for all her outward virginal blond purity being a real vixen, having affairs with all her leading men, Gary Cooper, Clark Gable, Ray Milland, and even Crosby himself on *The Country Girl,* for which Grace won her Oscar. So for all his fascination with Grace, Frank, as they would say today, didn't want to go there.

Debbie Reynolds in *The Tender Trap* was off-limits because of her marriage to Sinatra buddy Eddie Fisher, though even if she were unattached, Sinatra found her too impossibly perky to be sexy. He thought Olivia de Havilland in *Not as a Stranger* was sheer class, but she was involved with director John Huston, who was Bogart's dear friend, which made Olivia untouchable. Nevertheless, Sinatra's frustrated attraction to her led him to perform some adolescent pranks to attract her attention. Robert Mitchum, their costar, was legendary for his imperturbability. Every day at lunch, he would engross himself in the newspaper and not speak to anyone. One day, when I was with Mr. S at the studio, in front of Olivia, Sinatra sneaked up on Mitchum and set the paper he was reading on fire. Mitchum barely noticed until his fingers were singed. Then he jumped halfway across the table. Mr. S thought this stunt was much more impressive than his role, and bragged to everyone how he had "gotten" Mitchum. He never "got" Olivia, though, who was amazed at how childish Sinatra could be.

Maybe for Mr. S, life did begin at forty, for this was about the time he started sending me down to Tijuana on cherry bomb runs. I would go south of the border and bring back entire trunkloads of explosives and fireworks, which he would set off in his friends' shoes, in their toilets, under their beds, whenever and wherever they would least expect it. "The Hoboken Bomber strikes again!" he would exult with as much glee as if he had connected with one of the many girls of his fevered dreams.

Mr. S's problem, if you could call it a problem, was that he was like a hyperkinetic kid. Today they'd give him Ritalin. He couldn't sit still, and he couldn't be alone. Thus he always needed a girl, and she didn't have to be famous. First he'd go for his leading lady. If she wasn't free, he'd try some famous ex, like Lana Turner, whom he'd dated in the forties, for old times. Then he'd work his way down the food chain, starting with the starlets, then the hookers, and, if all else failed, he'd call Peggy Lee, who lived down the block. The name of the game was Dialing for Pussy, and Mr. S played it every night, except when he was "in training" for an album. Then he was a monk. Movies didn't count. He'd astonish his costars by showing up on the set at seven A.M. straight from some all-nighter, dressed in his tux, his tie undone, and his whisker stubble starting to show, duck into makeup, and come out an hour later fresh as a daisy and in perfect control of his part. Just don't ask him to do a second take.

Mr. S got his one-take philosophy of acting from Boris Karloff. Boris Karloff? Frankenstein? Yes. Sinatra had been a huge Karloff fan as a kid in Hoboken and was deeply honored to have "the Mummy" as his friend. In the thespian department, Mr. S put Karloff up there with the Barrymores. The only stars in Hollywood he may have admired as much were Bogart and Fred Astaire. He had met the horror icon on a studio lot in the late forties and had been bowled over by what an English gentleman he was. Karloff's real name was William Henry Pratt and his two great passions in life were cricket and gardening, not torture and murder. Whenever Karloff came over to visit Sinatra and to mentor him on roles he was considering by having Mr. S read lines for him to see how they sounded, he'd bring the most beautiful bouquets of freshly picked flowers. Mr. S never suggested this act of hospitality was a "fag thing," as he would have if any other male had made the same gesture. Karloff's acting philosophy, in a nutshell, was simple: "Say your lines. Hit your mark. Get out." But Sinatra embraced this as the oracle of a legend and took it to heart. No multiple takes for him. In time, he became considered an efficient, naturalistic, often excellent actor. Whenever he was praised and asked how he learned to act, he didn't say Lee Strasberg or Stella Adler or Stanislavsky, but gave all the credit to Old Frankenstein.

I was never in the bedroom with Frank and his ladies, but I heard from a lot of them afterwards, though rarely from him. He was a true gent and didn't kiss and tell, unless it was really bad—or really good. One actress, Jeannie Carmen, got so annoyed on a would-be romantic weekend in Palm Springs that she insisted that she go back to L.A. a day early. A disappointed Mr. S dispatched me to drive her, and, man, did I get an earful. Jeannie Carmen was a classic blond starlet and pinup girl with one of the most perfect figures in Hollywood. Ava Gardner once described her as "a pale [as in blond] imitation of myself," which Jeannie took as an enormous compliment. She also had an unusual skill, as a trick-shot golfer. She would travel around the country and appear on television, this gorgeous girl doing these impossible shots. Hole-in-one-Jeannie, we'd call her. With a skill like hers, she was naturally in hot demand in golf-crazy Palm Springs. Sinatra only played at playing golf, but he really liked Jeannie, whom he dated both when he was down, and after he was up again. He appreciated her loyalty so much he bought her a Chrysler convertible, which wasn't that unusual a gift for him to give once he was rich again. He was the master of the grand gesture.

Jeannie both loved Frank and hated him. "All he does is whine about Ava," she whined, echoing a complaint by many other lovers that, once the deed was done, the postcoital pillow talk was a never-ending obsession about the one who got away. Otherwise, she enjoyed going to bed with Mr. S, whom she rated as one of the lords of foreplay, a great kisser and an even better cuddler and hand-holder, sentiments that many other of Sinatra's conquests repeated to me over the years. Jeannie Carmen worshipped Mr. S's hands, which were always perfectly manicured and baby soft. He wasn't exactly doing heavy lifting, other than skirts, with them. His "equipment" was, with her and others, a conversation piece. "I thought he was bending down to scratch his *knee,*" she marveled. He had no fetishes in particular. "The only place he liked lingerie was on the floor," Jeannie told me. He did enjoy being woken up, at any hour, with a surprise blow job, but woe betide any woman who disturbed his precious sleep for any other reason. I can't tell you how many calls I got from him in the middle of the night, screaming, "Come and get this bitch outta here." Among his other cardinal sins were wearing too much perfume, of almost any brand. His own cologne, Coty's "Jungle Gardenia," he wore in the tiniest amounts. Jeannie and others would tell me how Mr. S liked to talk gangster slang in bed, "smack this one, smack that one," "put the arm on," "get it in the neck," "ass is grass," "cement shoes," Godfather stuff, narrating the grisly tortures he had in mind for all his enemies. I would have liked to hear what he had dreamed up for Sam Spiegel.

This particular weekend, Mr. S had gotten very drunk. When that happened, he could get both nasty and self-pitying, and Jeannie couldn't take it. But she would come back, and he would take her back, and they stayed sexually friendly for many years. When he would train those hypnotic blue eyes on her, or anyone else, there was that magic moment when a woman was *the* woman, the only woman, and that was irresistible. In the early sixties, Jeannie, Marilyn Monroe, and I all ended up in the same apartment complex on Doheny Drive and had a different set of adventures.

By far the most exciting thing that happened in the Alejo house during my early tenure, the thing that made me realize I truly was not in Kansas anymore, occurred when Mr. S wasn't even there. As with Ava, my boss was ultragenerous with his possessions. He would readily lend his house to anyone, even if he barely knew the object of his largesse. The case in point here was Minna Wallis, the fiftyish homely sister of mega producer Hal Wallis, who as production chief at Warners had been responsible for such masterpieces as *Casablanca* and *The Maltese Falcon,* and as an independent had produced the Martin and Lewis comedies and would produce all the Elvis Presley films. Because of her brother's success, Minna Wallis was A-list, part of the Goetz charmed circle and someone Mr. S, who was admittedly a social climber, wanted to cultivate. Mi casa, su casa. And my valet, your valet. He sent me down to Palm Springs to prepare the house for her and whomever she happened to bring. Boy, was I unprepared when Marlene Dietrich and Greta Garbo showed up. Both women were in their fifties, and neither had made a film for years. As far as celebrity sightings could be rated, Garbo, who had "wanted to be alone" for over a decade, was by far number one, and Dietrich wasn't far off.

The two European superstars couldn't have been more natural, no makeup, no airs, no frills. Garbo had some weird dietary requests, no dairy, no animal protein, just exotic organic grains and stuff (now the regimen is known as "vegan" and very popular among star and model types). These edibles she had learned about through her friend, Beverly Hills's first celebrity nutritionist, Gaylord Hauser, but at that time no grocery store in Palm Springs had ever heard of them. I had to make a mad run back to L.A. and Jurgensen's, which had everything, to keep the ladies happy. When I returned that evening, they couldn't have been happier. Greta and Marlene were in the pool, completely naked, and Minna Wallis was lying on a chaise in a Moroccan caftan, drinking champagne and watching them like a hawk. They were oblivious to her, and to me. I slipped into the house and into my room so as not to spoil their party, though I couldn't resist peeping through the blinds. What mortal could? I rarely heard Garbo talk, but I did hear Garbo laugh. She was having a wonderful time, giggling, splashing Minna, dunking Marlene under water. Then fun turned to heat. Marlene pulled Greta into what seemed like a playful embrace, which ended up in a kiss. They got out of the pool, but didn't dress. They savored the privacy, the freedom, the night-time desert warmth.

Marlene lit up a cigarette, which she passed to Greta. They each took long drags, intercut with long, pregnant looks at each other. Then Greta sprawled out on a chaise, and Marlene lay down beside her, looking up at the constellations in the crystal-clear desert sky. Minna wouldn't leave them alone, but they didn't seem to care. If she liked to watch, let her watch. Marlene was the aggressor. She kissed Greta's lips, she stroked her, she began to slither down Greta's long slender frame. And then a coyote began to howl. The ladies jumped in fright and retreated into the house, and the best I could do was to serve them yogurt, steel-cut oatmeal, and organic honey for breakfast the morning after. But at this point, even before Mr. S made the cover of *Time* a few months hence, I had no doubt that I had the coolest job in the world.

4

Gangland

*I*F I thought that winning the Oscar was the ultimate for Mr. S, I was wrong. Getting on the cover of *Time* was an even higher pinnacle of accomplishment. That *Time* cover, combined with his being featured on the prestigious Edward R. Murrow television show *Person to Person,* was the *Good Housekeeping* seal of approval in American life in 1956. The Oscar, *Time,* and Murrow formed a magical anti-vampire crucifix that would do more than protect Mr. S from the bloodsuckers of Hollywood; this figurative talisman would also convert the naysayers into idolators. In the highest echelon of American life, Frank Sinatra was now a made man, in the best sense of the term. Yet, strangely enough, just when he had a free pass to the halls of power and prestige, he sought the company of a different sort of "made men," the folk heroes of his youth and, to be fair, the only people who had not forsaken him when he was so recently down and nearly out. Now he was high and mighty. He could consort with anyone he wanted. Like any conquering hero whose most triumphant journey is back to his roots, to "show 'em" what he had accomplished against all odds, in the mid-1950s Frank Sinatra's favorite journey was not around the world whose imagination he had captivated but back to Hoboken.

To go with his new life, Mr. S had bought a new home up on Bowmont Drive, off Coldwater Canyon in Beverly Hills. The early 1956 Murrow interview was a sort of public housewarming at this sprawling Japanese-style estate, which Hollywood people called "the Teahouse," after the hit Broadway play *The Teahouse of the August Moon*, and those who really knew what was going on called it the Whorehouse of the August Moon. But that wasn't Ed Murrow stuff. And neither was I. I was all excited about getting my fifteen minutes, or more likely fifteen seconds, of fame as valet to the Biggest Star in the World. I got a special white jacket, got my hair cut, was looking quite sharp, if I might say so myself.

But when all the television cameras began to arrive that day to do the live shoot (Murrow stayed in the studio in New York, smoking his cigarette; this was all high-tech for the period.), I saw two Asian guys, also in white butler coats, arrive at the house. They looked as though they had come from Central Casting, and I was close to right. Gloria Lovell had hired them from some domestic agency for the day. One was Filipino, the other from Japan. I assumed they were there to serve drinks and food to the *Person to Person* crew. Then Mr. S took me aside and broke the bad news. I wasn't going to be on the show. What? I was crushed. I felt as bad as Sinatra did when he lost the Terry Malloy part. "Are you ashamed of me, boss?" I couldn't stop my hurt self from blurting out.

"Just the opposite, George," he said. He chuckled at how badly I had misread the situation. "If you're on that show tonight, you'll be working for Jules Stein tomorrow. I can't risk losing you." Valet snatching was a crime that was rife in Beverly Hills. If I was on national TV, I would instantly achieve major status as blue-chip help, and Mr. S didn't want to lose me to some blue-chip mogul like Stein, the head of MCA and a social lion on the same level as the Goetzes. To salve my wounds, he doubled my salary, to $300 a week. He also gave me an envelope containing ten brand-new $100 bills. It was a small fortune in 1956, though I still would have preferred saying hello on the air to the great Ed Murrow.

Even if the show were live, it somehow seemed as fake and staged as the Asian houseboys. There was the signed photograph from Franklin D. Roosevelt and the award from the Al Jolson chapter of B'nai B'rith and the comment from Mr. S that, in terms of stage fright, the toughest number he ever had to do was singing "The Star-Spangled Banner" at the Polo Grounds. Then again, I shouldn't have expected Ed Murrow zooming in on Mr. S pouring Jack Daniel's for Sam Giancana with Judy Campbell draped over the couch. In plain and simple terms: Frank Sinatra *loved* gangsters, or at least the world they lived in, just as most Americans have had a fascination with this world from *Little Caesar* to *The Godfather* to *The Sopranos*. The big difference was that Mr. S could get a lot closer to the flame than the rest of us. In fact, aside from the so-called gangsters that were Sinatra's friends and at least honorary Godfathers, many of his close pals in show business were also somehow gang-related.

Humphrey Bogart *looked* and *sounded* like a hoodlum even if he wasn't one. George Raft, a dear Sinatra ally, the guy who gave me his dancing shoes, went way back with the mob, as far back as Al Capone. Dean Martin and Sammy Davis Jr. had been working in mob joints for years. Where *else*, as Sinatra would wonder, was a guy supposed to sing? If anything, Dean embraced the mob even more strongly than Mr. S, and Sammy embraced anything Mr. S embraced, maybe even harder. For all his genius and all his courage, when around Mr. S, Sammy would act like the Stepin Fetchit of the footlights. That's not really fair, because the one thing Sammy never played to was any kind of black stereotype. In fact, he was just the opposite. If he were performing in London Sammy would develop an aristocratic British accent that was more perfect than the Duke of Edinburgh's. He sounded like Noël Coward. But that was what bothered me. Sammy was always *trying* so hard to please everyone, he was like a court jester, even more of a servant than I was. He may have been the most exciting, entertaining servant in the world, but still a servant. By playing the jester, Sammy made Mr. S feel even more the king than he already did, and maybe this was all part of a Machiavellian plan to someday usurp the throne. Yet while Sammy played this "yes, master" game, until I got to know him better and saw that it may have been an aspect of his brilliant act, he was the only person in Mr. S's world who made me aware of being black, and made me feel second-class for it. Actually, Joseph Kennedy, JFK's father, made me feel black, too—like a Black Panther, who wanted to kill that racist bastard. But later about him.

Sammy was even more insecure than Mr. S about his lack of education. He basically begged people to teach him what they knew, whether singing from Sinatra, jokes from Rickles, boozing from Dean, acting from Eddie Robinson. He was a little hangdog acolyte. His personality cried out, "Help me!" Nobody who met him could resist. And nobody who ever taught him anything ever had a smarter student. He was the quickest study I'd ever seen. He could do dead-on imitations of anyone, from Cary Grant to Jimmy Cagney to Marilyn Monroe to Judy Garland. He actually would have made a great female impersonator. The only person Sammy was more solicitous of than Mr. S was Sam Giancana. Sammy would literally kiss the ring of this top *capo*, though it may have been more out of genuine respect and gratitude for the gigs Giancana had gotten him than the fear he seemed to feel for Mr. S. I say fear, but I must also say love, for Mr. S had helped save both Sammy's life and his career after his accident, and Sammy would have eternal gratitude for that. But Sammy was no saint. He could be a naughty boy, as we saw in his self-promotional episode with Ava Gardner in *Ebony*. Sammy may even have had designs on Ava, for he was the horniest of guys and Ava was crazy about him. I think Sammy felt secretly guilty that he fantasized about replacing Mr. S as the King of Entertainment, and his obsequious behavior was compensation for his massive ambition.

You might have thought Sammy and I would have bonded as brothers, but we didn't. He was always polite, but distant, as if there was a certain pressure for him to get down with me. I think I made him uncomfortable. One black in the Clan was enough. I was much closer to Sammy's valet, a black guy from Watts we all called Murphy. I'm not sure whether that was his first name or his last. He was just Murphy, like Liberace or Fabian or Valentino. His job made mine look laid-back. Even if Sammy were just doing a weekend in Vegas, he'd carry seventeen or eighteen big suitcases of clothes. Mr. S, on the other hand, liked to travel light, one suitcase, one hanging bag, one briefcase. That was it.

Sammy was the most fabulous dresser. He was always totally turned out. He didn't know the meaning of "casual." Even his lounge wear was theatrical, the silk robes, the Chinese pajamas, the ascots. Whenever Sammy would sit down and talk to me, I felt as if I was with the pope, or rather the chief rabbi of Jerusalem. Sammy took his Judaism very seriously. He observed every holiday, every ritual. He said it gave him the grounding, the moral center that he needed. It was Sammy who eventually got me interested in my long-lost Jewish roots. Whatever Sammy talked about, whether religion or golf, he could turn you on to it. He was a real pied piper. He was so on, so brilliant, even alone with me. If he had you in his presence for ten minutes, he'd have you for life.

As for Dean, he knew what he owed the mob guys, if that's what they were, but he was cool about it, just as he was cool about everything else. Dean simply Didn't Give a Shit about anything, except maybe golf. He was completely relaxed, which may have had something to do with his massive consumption of alcohol, far, far greater than that of Mr. S, who was a teetotaler by comparison. But Dean never got nasty; he got sleepy. He had a mobster's coolness, the laid-back nonobliviousness of a seasoned hit man. One thing that did make Dean a little nervous was race jokes. His natural inclination was to be about as subtle as Governor George Wallace, but he knew that was wrong and didn't want to hurt the "little guy's" feelings, be he a "Nig" or a "Hebe." Jerry Lewis had put Dean off Jews for two lifetimes, and he was naturally suspicious of anyone with anything vaguely Jewish about him, a name, a nose, a career, like agent or jeweler.

As for blacks, Dean used me as a sounding board for jokes, almost always written by someone else. Dean's forte was his delivery, not his originality. "Nothing could be bigger. Than to play it with a nigger. At the Copa." This was to "Carolina in the Morning." I think Sammy Cahn wrote this as Dean's intro to Sammy at the Copa Room of the Sands in Vegas. I thought it could piss some people off. Dean at first didn't get it. He saw it as a "tribute," and done with *amore*. And the "n" word? "Niggers don't go to the Sands," was his attitude. I eventually talked him out of it, though not out of a joke after Sammy's marriage to the Swedish actress May Britt: "What's black and white and has three eyes?" "Niggers won't care about this one, just blind people," was Dean's defense. If Dean would get upset with Sammy, the worst thing he could say was that Sammy was "Jerry turned inside out." Dean wasn't sensitive to any of this because he saw himself as an equally oppressed minority. Wops, nigs, hebes, what the fuck was the difference? We were all up against the wall and fucking well better stick together.

Because of the later Rat Pack, Mr. S is most usually identified in Hollywood with Sammy and Dean (Peter Lawford was strictly fair weather and was basically a bridge to the Kennedys, one that turned out to be a bridge too far). In actuality Frank Sinatra was, in the mid-fifties, closer to Eddie Fisher than to the others. If anyone could give Mr. S a run at bedding famous women, or any women, for that matter, it was Eddie. Once the money began rolling in for Mr. S, he took a penthouse apartment in New York in a cul-de-sac at Seventy-second Street and the East River. Good views, better privacy. Eddie Fisher had the penthouse next door, and even Mr. S was impressed by the sheer volume of Eddie's conquests. In truth some of the conquests were triumphs of the checkbook. In the high rise right next door to us lived dozens of fancy call girls. It was one of the highest concentrations in Manhattan. Because of the dead-end location of the block, limos could double park while celebs and politicians could pop in for quickies. Or the "girls next door," as we'd call them, could pop out. Eddie, like Mr. S, was so horny that it didn't matter if he had just had Liz Taylor. If there was a fuckable girl around, he had to have her, cost be damned.

Eddie proudly described himself as the Jewish son Sam Giancana never had. He'd also fill in for Mr. S at the Copacabana in New York or in Miami or Vegas if Mr. S would ever get sick or go chasing Ava or something crazy. Eddie wrote his own book on girl crazy, so he'd always understand. Luckily for their friendship, Mr. S claimed never to be attracted to Liz Taylor. He thought she was too high mainte-nance, higher than Ava. He also thought her legs were too short, and he was definitely a leg man, though I think it was his high regard for Eddie that stopped him far more than Liz's gams. Assuming you don't count Sammy Davis Jr., Eddie Fisher was one of the rare Jews in

Mr. S's entourage. Another was Jack Entratter, whom Mr. S knew from the forties, when Entratter was a bouncer at the Stork Club. The tall, handsome, dapper Entratter would rise through the club world to become manager of the Copa. In the early fifties, the mob dispatched Entratter to Vegas to run the Sands. The Sands would be Mr. S's Vegas headquarters for more than a decade and Jack his favorite "businessman" until they had a violent falling-out that saw Mr. S smash a golf cart into the Sands's glass doors. Then his best Jewish buddy became "that scumbag kike."

Not that Mr. S was antisemitic; he simply felt most comfortable with guys from his same background. As with Eddie and Jack, if the Jewish guy had ties to gangland, that somehow gave Mr. S that extra measure of trust. Trust was something that was in short supply for Mr. S where the Jews of Hollywood were concerned. No man could hold a grudge longer than Mr. S, and no grudge was bigger, not even his loathing for Sam Spiegel, than the one he held against Lew Wasserman and Jules Stein, his former agents at MCA who had dumped him in the early fifties. He blamed them for trying, and almost succeeding, to kill his career, and him. Murdering Jews, he called them, the real gangsters. He was complaining about them any chance he could get.

At his forty-second birthday roast at the Villa Capri in Hollywood in 1957, his friends were still making jokes about his hatred for these powerful Jews. Yet among these friends were other powerful Jews, Jack Benny, Eddie Fisher, Tony Curtis, Mike Romanoff, Sammy Cahn, who sang a ditty to "All the Way," making fun of Frank's Italian dining habits at the Villa: "Every meal's a bleeder. When you're eating with the leader. This life's not for Jewish stomachs. Pass the bicarb, I say . . ." Dean Martin, to "You're the Top," sang "He's a wop, Records sell like Nestlé's, He's a wop, But they don't top Presley's." Dean's jab about the hated Elvis showed how Mr. S needed all the business help he could get. Help from Jews. Hence Eddie Fisher serenaded the birthday boy with "Bert's His Papa," a tribute, to the strains of Fisher's trademark song, to Sinatra's William Morris agent Bert Allenberg. "All roads lead to Jerusalem," Mr. S conceded. When in Dean's number he tried listing rhyming Italian Hollywood names, Tommy Leonetti, Annie Alberghetti, Tony Franciosa, Pori Rubirosa, the drunken table pointed out that Rubirosa wasn't Hollywood, nor was he Italian. "Shows how hard up we are," Mr. S shouted.

There was one song-and-dance man, probably Mr. S's biggest idol, who probably didn't know who Sam Giancana was. That was Fred Astaire. Once we were on the Warner lot, and we saw Fred Astaire walking by. Mr. S was as excited as the schoolgirls used to get excited by him. He insisted we follow Astaire around the lot, hiding in the shadows to make sure he couldn't see us. They must have met at the Goetzes or somewhere, but Mr. S didn't think he was worthy to go up to him. "Look at how he moves. Just look at him," Sinatra would whisper to me. "I feel like a klutz." Sinatra may have had total self-confidence as a singer but very little as a hoofer. His nonmob friend Gene Kelly had taught him his steps in *Anchors Aweigh* and *On the Town*, but Mr. S claimed he forgot the moves as fast as he learned them. "It's not natural for me," he'd lament. That's why Astaire was a god to Sinatra, because for him it *was* natural, just as being cool was natural for Bogart. Astaire never spotted us that day at Warners, but if he had, I'll bet Mr. S would have asked him for an autograph. He was that starstruck.

I was pretty starstruck myself when I got to meet some of my own idols traveling with Sinatra on the concert circuit and to Las Vegas. I loved going on the road with Mr. S. I began our road trips in 1956, and he treated me royally on them. He was totally dependent on me, and I loved this kind of responsibility, like in the Navy. It feels great to be the right hand of a king. I'd make calls, book appointments, arrange dinners and parties, entertain waiting friends and dignitaries, coordinate everything. I was beside Mr. S twenty-four hours a day, always ready to jump to any occasion and please him. It was a pressure cooker, though he never blew up at me, probably because I never fucked up. He made me feel a key part of his life and work and introduced me to *everybody*. "This is George Jacobs," was all he had to say. He didn't need to explain what I did, because I did it all. Explaining would have taken way too long for Mr. S, who wasn't one to explain things, anyway.

Almost until the sixties, I was one of the only blacks allowed to stay in the Sands in Vegas and other hotels where Sinatra played. As Dean said, "Niggers don't go to the Sands." There was generally no room at the inn for blacks even if they were performing there. Even a star like Sammy Davis Jr. had to stay at the Moulin Rouge, which was the only black hotel, if you don't count the cabins on the outskirts of town, which were about as inviting as the Bates Motel in *Psycho*. And at one hotel, when Dorothy Dandridge went for a swim, guests demanded that they drain the pool so they wouldn't get some rare black infestation. Sounds like something Swifty Lazar would have come up with. Vegas was a Wild West, cowboy town back then, and these cowboys didn't cotton to colored dudes. Eventually Mr. S was the key man in getting these barriers dropped, so he could share stages, as well as floors, with the likes of Ella Fitzgerald and Sarah Vaughan, whom he called Sassy. My favorite was Billy Eckstine, who was so sharp that the second he saw me and saw how much we looked alike, he embraced me and cried, "My son!" On second thought, I bet Mr. S put him up to it, just to give me a thrill.

For all his Amos and Andy humor, his "yo mama" jokes, Mr. S genuinely loved his fellow black musicians and kept that humor to his largely Dago best buddies. He only saw talent, and I only saw stars. Both Frank and Sammy were very tight with these fellow performers, though their styles were different. Sammy liked to clown around, do impromptu numbers, show off. Frank was much more serious, though he would never talk about music with these great singers. He might talk about movies, or even politics, but never music. He figured they had enough of that on the job. Black or white, he rated Tony Bennett as his chief rival. He felt Tony's voice was every bit as good as his. He also admired the ease and charm of Tony's delivery. Then again, Tony was a much easier guy than Mr. S, and certainly no party animal. He was very quiet and loved to paint. In his down time, he'd go out by the lake at Cal-Neva or to the desert in Vegas and bring his sketch pad. Because Mr. S liked to paint as well, this was what he and Tony would talk about most. In New York, Tony would come drinking with us at Toots Shor's or, later, Jilly's, but he'd be long gone by the time we closed these places. In 1962, Mr. S decided to cut his own version of "I Left My Heart in San Francisco," but after making and releasing the single, he listened to it next to Tony's classic, then ordered it withdrawn from the market. Such was respect.

Back to the Sinatra circle, after Jimmy Van Heusen, Mr. S's closest music friend (and his music friends, like his music, were more essential to him than movie friends and movies) was Hank Sanicola, a physically big boxer-turned-roadhouse-pianist who became Sinatra's bodyguard in the Tommy Dorsey screaming-bobbysoxer 1940s and had graduated to being his Manager, with a capital M. The way to becoming a success in the Sinatra organization was often through your size, or brute force. Sinatra liked guys who could save his life, if necessary. Burly Hank was a protector, as were Jilly Rizzo and others like Brad Dexter, whose lifesaving skills elevated him from bit actor to big producer.

Rarely did any of these guys actually lift a fist for Frank. Jilly, who had an even crazier temper than Mr. S, did a few times, often with disastrous results. Once he did save Sinatra from a stalker who got into Mr. S's hotel bedroom in Melbourne, Australia. Jilly beat him over the head with a large standing ashtray and nearly killed him. Brad Dexter's bluff was far bigger than his bite. We used to call him "Superman" because he walked around with his chest all puffed up and out. Sanicola, on the other hand, was the real thing. He would break your legs if you even said anything bad about Sinatra. And if the adversary were bigger than Hank was, he had lots of friends whose specialty was "talking to people," which was Hank's euphemism for their distinctly nonverbal approach to handling problems. Sanicola had Sicilian roots, which Frank found *simpatico*. He called him "Dag," as in Dago. It was the same name he used for Dean and others of his Italian friends. (They called him "Sinat.") It was pronounced like "Day-Glo," not like Dag Hammarskjöld, the head of the United Nations, though Sinatra and company got the biggest kick mispronouncing his name, turning the distinguished Swedish diplomat into an Italian homeboy. Sometimes he'd even call me "Dag." I was thrilled to be included as a *paesano*.

Another beloved "Dag" had nothing to do with the entertainment business at all. Not if he could help it. Yet he couldn't help it, and it ruined a great deal of his life. He was married to the biggest movie star in America, and he was the biggest sports hero in America. It was a guaranteed recipe for disaster. The Dago in question was Joe DiMaggio, the Yankee Clipper, the Pride of the Yankees, Mr. New York, long before he was reduced to Mr. Coffee. He was the only Italian in the country bigger than Frank Sinatra. Mr. S was deeply honored to be his friend; it was a measure of how far the kid from Hoboken had come that he could hang with a hero, who was the Fred Astaire of America's pastime. One of the most Old World Italian characteristics of Mr. S was his deeply superstitious nature. Mr. S put great stock in the fact that DiMaggio's name and that of the character who had restored his career, saved his life, were the same. He saw it as an omen, a miracle.

I, too, was in awe of the guy, and I knew zip about baseball. At first he seemed arrogant, barely acknowledging my presence, but I came to see that he was painfully shy and private. Marrying Marilyn Monroe was suicide for a guy like that, but that's why she was Marilyn. The more Joe drank, which was a lot, the nicer he would get. He'd even try to turn me on to baseball by telling war stories about Babe and Lou and his own glory years, which was unusual for a guy who hated to brag. It wasn't so much boasting, but rather disbelief that I knew and cared so little about the national pastime, "What?! You don't know about my fifty-six-game streak?" And I was so out of it, I said something like "Was that really good?" And all the guys would roll their eyes, like what planet was I from. The answer was planet New Orleans, which was no baseball town. The people there were too busy eating and fucking, I'd defend my position. Once I mentioned Ted Williams, and Joe dismissed him with "He throws the ball like a girl." That surprised me, that Joe would put a fellow superstar down like that. I guess he liked being the Greatest and didn't want to hear about the competition. Joe was no jokester, but he thought he was being a real rib-splitter when he started calling me "the Commie," as in Communist. The idea was that only a Communist didn't dig baseball. Don't forget, these were still McCarthy times.

Mr. S and the Clipper had met at Toots Shor's restaurant, a famous booze, meat, and potatoes men's club of a joint thick with cigar smoke and filled with sports stars, gossip columnists like Walter Winchell and Earl Wilson, and musicians from the nearby jazz clubs of the West Fifties. Talk about mob ties. Toots, whom Mr. S also called "Dag," was a tough Philadelphian who had run speakeasies for Lucky Luciano and never met a mobster he didn't like. Toots never gave Sinatra a bill, not when he was down, and not when he was back up, either. Not that Mr. S was trying to get off cheap. At the end of an evening, Sinatra would hand out c-notes to every waiter, busboy, and bartender who had crossed his path. Beside that, the lure of having Frank Sinatra in the restaurant was worth a fortune in itself. Toots was no fool.

Toots Shor's was one of Mr. S's favorite New York hangouts, but he preferred being with all Dagos, all the time. There were too many tourists who might bug him in Little Italy, and Jilly's place was still in his future. So his hangout became a joint called Patsy's on West Fifty-sixth Street. It was a red-checked-tablecloth, red-clam-sauce kind of place with an upstairs dining room that Mr. S joked was "headquarters for Murder, Inc." He enjoyed being close to the action, particularly that kind of action. I had no idea who the clientele was, just a lot of heavy-set guys with big cigars, bigger pinky rings, and still-bigger-breasted companions, "floozies" was the word.

The first time I went to Patsy's, with Sinatra, Sanicola, Van Heusen, and some of their own floozies (Mr. S liked to travel in a pack), some big guy said "Who's the nigger?" I'd never seen Mr. S give a look that could kill like that before. By the time we reached our table, I looked up again and that guy was *gone*. His whole table was gone. And I never heard the "n" word in Patsy's again, though I never saw any other brothers, other than Sammy, in there until the sixties.

In Los Angeles, Mr. S's favorite hangout was another Patsy's (no relation). This was Patsy d'Amore's Villa Capri in Hollywood, one of the rare Southern California outposts for authentic New York / New Jersey red-sauced Italian food, the food Mr. S had grown up on in Hoboken. Patsy d'Amore (they mispronounced it "dee-amor," Hoboken-style) had a genuine New York wood-fired pizza oven. What's more, he delivered, and we used him all the time to cater parties. And the fancy, *real* dishes I had learned to make in Italy? Fugged-abboudit! Same with Romanoff's, which Mr. S might use for dates with movie stars and moguls, but which he felt was way too hoity-toity for normal wear and tear. He and Mike Romanoff, while cordial, would bond only after Humphrey Bogart died. The Villa Capri was the scene of the fiasco that ended Mr. S's friendship with Joltin' Joe DiMaggio. Perhaps the biggest thing the two men had in common, bigger than their Italian-ness, bigger than their stardom, bigger than their gargantuan cocks (Joe was supposedly the Milton Berle of swat), was their amorous travails at the hands of their goddess wives. Frank had been there first with Ava. He knew precisely the hell that the Clipper was going through with Marilyn. He also knew how insanely, murderously jealous these women could make their men, precisely because there were always *other* men, thousands, millions of other men waiting, drooling in the wings. Not that either guy would ever mention his amorous problems to the other. Each was way too macho to whine about love. Whenever I was around them, they'd only talk about sports, usually boxing and never baseball. That was a cornerstone of the Sinatra conversational philosophy: never talk to a pro about his *job* when he was off duty. So he wouldn't talk to Lionel Hampton about vibes and he wouldn't talk to Joe DiMaggio about Louisville Sluggers.

So here they were in 1954 at the Villa Capri, Frank still mooning over Ava, Joe in a state of shock over Marilyn just divorcing him on grounds of "cruel indifference" though neither actually referring to their tribulations. Yet Mr. S liked to talk about Joe's Marilyn problems with *me*. It seemed to make him feel better that he wasn't the only Dago superstar in the doghouse of love. The charge of "cruel indifference" was a laugh, Mr. S had told me. The Dago Slugger was anything but indifferent. He was blind with rage at the way his wife was being used as national cheesecake, what with that porno shot of the subway gust blowing her skirt over her head in Billy Wilder's *The Seven Year Itch*. Wilder had described the scene to Sinatra, said you could see Marilyn's pussy through her white panties. Mr. S arranged a prerelease screening at a friend's house, not the Goetzes, they were too square, looking for Marilyn's pussy. It sounded like the *Basic Instinct* of its day, but it was all quite innocent. No pussy made it to the screen, barely a flash of panties. But Joe was still bent out of shape. And for all their awful fights and all the whispers that Joltin' Joe was a wife batterer, the man was deeply in love. He wanted her back, and he believed she would come back if he fought hard enough. This man was the ultimate champion; he was not a quitter.

Mr. S knew and liked Marilyn, and he would come to love her, well, *almost* love her himself, but right now he was there for his hero. Mr. S indirectly pushed Joe to go and get her. He did this by hiring a private eye buddy (he had more than a few) to track Marilyn as a gift for Joe. That was the present for the star who had everything, his own private eye. That night at Villa Capri (I wasn't there, but I heard it all from Mr. S later) the dick called and said he had hit paydirt. Marilyn was shacking up with her drama coach. Acting lessons, my ass! Frank and Joe plus Hank Sanicola, who apparently were totally looped at this point, were going to stand up for Marilyn's honor, which was more than she ever did. These Old World Dago men of respect were going to throw this clown out, show Marilyn the error of her ways, show her how much the Clipper cared about her. However, when they joined up with the dick and his aides and the whole gang descended on the love nest and kicked down the door, all they found was an old lady in bed by herself. They got the wrong apartment. The right apartment was the one directly upstairs, the home of another member of Marilyn's drama class, who was letting Marilyn and her coach do a "cold reading" there. The old lady went on to sue Sinatra and DiMaggio.

It was deeply embarrassing. Mr. S didn't even talk about it at first, he was so humiliated. It seemed to me like a Keystone Kops comedy, but to Mr. S it was no laughing matter. The last thing he ever wanted was to be made a fool of like this. It was *his* detective, hence *his* fault, even if the detective was on the right track and had made an honest mistake. Mr. S would take a dishonest score over an honest mistake any day. He never used the detective again, and he blacklisted him with all his friends. It was tough for a Hollywood dick to survive under that cloud. The mistakenly raided woman got paid off, but Joe began to suspect Frank, like every other man, had his own designs on Marilyn and had set up the whole raid to destroy things with Joe, so Sinatra could have her himself. Mr. S thought Joe was preposterously paranoid, even more paranoid than he was about Ava. But as the years went by, and Mr. S got closer to Marilyn, and then introduced her to the Kennedys, treating her, in Joe's eyes, as power catnip, no better than the whore Judy Campbell, Joe cut Frank completely. He later would blame him for the death of the woman he loved and would never forgive him. So much for Dago solidarity. Joe was replaced by famed player and coach Leo Durocher as Mr. S's "base-ball friend."

Most of the time, however, as long as they weren't competing over some girl, which could make enemies out of brothers, the Italians did stick together. One of Mr. S's favorite "old neighborhood" guys was Skinny D'Amato, who was also a great friend of Joe DiMaggio. Skinny was the Toots Shor of New Jersey, the perfect host who never charged his famous guests. He was also a great impresario. Playing his 500 Club in Atlantic City was like playing the Colosseum in ancient Rome. It was the big ticket in the Garden State. It seemed like Valhalla to Mr. S when he was starting out, just as the Yankee Clipper seemed like Zeus. And now the boy could walk on Mount Olympus with his gods, and Skinny was the god of nightclubs. Normally among the Italian guys, Skinny would have been a fat slob. They liked to give each other reverse names. But Skinny, whose real name was Paul, was really skinny. He looked more like a senator, very distinguished, fine clothes and bearing. I guess he had come a long way from the Lewisburg Federal Penitentiary in Pennsylvania, where he had done time for white slavery. To Mr. S that sentence was hardly a blot on his record, but rather a red badge of courage. It proved why Skinny had a way with the ladies; he always treated Mr. S and his crew to amazing hookers. At Lewisburg Skinny had made great life contacts, especially with some Philadelphia crime lords who set him up after parole as their front man at the "Five." It was also at Lewisburg where Skinny made the connections that led 500 Club patron and Prohibition bootleg supplier Joseph Kennedy to turn to him when he needed to find out whom to bribe to ensure that his son would win the 1960 West Virginia primary. Skinny was Kennedy's "bag man" in the state, and, that, too, became a mark of honor.

In the same way that Skinny never charged Frank, Frank never charged Skinny. I'm sure Skinny paid Mr. S for his performances in the dark ages of the early fifties when few others would book him. But once the man was back on top, he would perform five shows a night for nothing but the honor of being there. On my first trip with Mr. S to Atlantic City, it was like a homecoming celebration. Here was Jersey's favorite son, and they all came out to cheer him. We took a whole floor at the Claridge Hotel on the Boardwalk, which was wall-to-wall beauties courtesy of Skinny. I would have thought that after five shows, at five in the morning Mr. S would have liked to get back to the Claridge and the ladies or at least to sleep. No way. He was home, and he was wired. We went down to the black belt of clubs on Kentucky Avenue, places with names like Timbuktu and Club Harlem, to a place called Grace's Little Belmont to visit Sammy Davis Jr.'s terrific mom, Baby Sanchez, who still ran the bar there. "Sammy's Mammy," Dean called her. Mr. S was passing out fresh hundred-dollar bills, like Rockefeller with his dimes, to everyone, waiters, patrons, winos on the street, guys in the band. I've never seen anyone so happy to be in one place. And he always gave credit where credit was due. "I wouldn't be here if it wasn't for Skinny."

That same trip to Atlantic City, Mr. S took me to Hoboken to meet his mother and father, Dolly and Marty. The first thing she says, right in front of me, is "You never told me he was a nigger! Who do you think you are, Ashley Wilkes?" Mr. S was embarrassed, like any kid would be with his mom. I had no idea what to do, to run for cover or what. Then she gives me this big hug and kiss and welcomes me into her home. That was the way Dolly was. She was a chubby, bubbly dynamo with a big mouth and an even bigger heart. She said whatever came to her mind, no censorship. She may have been something of a local politician, yet she was anything but diplomatic. Hoboken, when Mr. S was growing up, was one big race riot. The Germans and Irish, who ran the place, hated the Jews, who were up and coming, who hated the Italians, who were down and out, who hated the blacks, who were nowhere at all, and so on.

Everybody hated everybody. It was nothing personal. Because once you were a friend, that's what you were, not a black or a Jew or a Dago, but a friend. So if Frank liked me, Dolly liked me, and she quickly adopted me as her second son, her "Jigsilian," which was Dolly-ese for black Sicilian. She took me into the kitchen with her, taught me how to cook Jersey-style *braciole, scarpariello, cannoli,* though she lamented, like any loving mother, how little her boy would eat. She'd lament a lot, despite his vast success, all the basic stuff, his family, his home life, or lack thereof. She adored Ava, I think, maybe more than Nancy. Dolly had stayed close to Nancy on account of the kids. But Dolly understood her son's compulsive need for glamour and action. Because Dolly was, if anything, a realist, she knew Nancy wasn't going to work but hoped that, if her son got his act together and got over the Don Giovanni part, the Ava thing *could* work. She made me her emissary in trying to talk sense to him, not that that ever did any good.

I could see from meeting his mom exactly where Mr. S got his verve and his sass from. She should have been on stage. If she had, Marty, his father, would have been hiding in the wings, cringing. A boxer who became a fireman, Marty called his son "Mr. Big Shot," as if he still thought Frank was crazy to try to get into show business. Marty was a tough, quiet, little guy, the kind you see playing cards all day in those Italian social clubs in Little Italy. He was Old World, a little bit of Palermo in Victorian, run-down Hoboken. Marty had seen how his boy had almost lost it all once, and you could see he was afraid he could lose it all again. Take nothing for granted that comes too easy, that was his philosophy. That was why he had gone to the firehouse every day, even when his son would have gladly bought him ten firehouses. Dolly (whose heritage was Genoese) gave her only child unconditional love, but Marty, superstitious Sicilian that he was, would never give up his doubts. I could see the pain in Mr. S's face from his inability to get his father, of all people, to believe in him. In his own way, without meaning it, Marty Sinatra made him feel just as bad as Sam Spiegel had. As a result, Mr. S spent much more time talking to his mother, whom he'd call almost every day, like his kids, than his father.

Despite an awkwardness with Marty, Mr. S was great to his parents, whom he addressed as "Mom" and "Pop." He paid for everything for them, though Marty was much prouder than Dolly about taking money. Mr. S would secretly slip three or four hundred-dollar bills in his father's coat, so Marty could buy drinks for everyone down at the old bar he hung out in. He'd drag his parents to all his New York music openings and proudly show them off to his high and mighty friends. This was one man who wasn't embarrassed by where he came from, though Marty and Dolly may have been embarrassed by where he ended up. They *despised* everything about Hollywood and generally refused to let Frank fly them out to his gala film premieres or Vegas debuts. He begged his parents to let him set them up in high style in Beverly Hills, sort of an Italian Beverly Hillbillies, so they could be near their grandkids. But neither Dolly or Marty liked Los Angeles; they thought it was bogus and preferred New Jersey.

Marty especially hated the food in California. He thought Frank's beloved Villa Capri was a bad joke. Marty was actually an even better cook than Dolly. He made the greatest "pastafazool" and taught me how to do a perfect calamari salad, though he told me the squid in California was all frozen. "Fake" was his favorite word for everything Pacific Coast. I think he liked me because I was from New Orleans, which wasn't a fake place, because my dad had a bar, which to Marty was a noble calling, and because one of my dad's partners had been a big boxer, Kid Coco, and Marty considered boxing the true sport of kings. As a result of his parents' California antipathies, Mr. S would fly his three kids to his East River penthouse as often as their school schedules allowed, so they could keep in touch with their grandparents across the Hudson and with their bedrock immigrant values, which Mr. S deeply admired, even though he didn't necessarily live by them.

The tricks Mama Dolly taught me about making authentically inauthentic Italian food would soon come in handy. Mr. S was putting on a huge spread in Palm Springs for a special guest. He even hired a mariachi band to entertain. I had never seen him try so hard to have everything perfect, not even for Ava. He was extremely nervous about each little thing being just so, the linens, the soap, the caviar, which had to be the finest Beluga, from Iran and not Russia. "The guy hates Communists," Mr. S explained. Who was he, I asked,

Joe McCarthy? No, Mr. S laughed. He was as far from Senator Joe McCarthy as a guy could be. So who, I pressed my boss, was I going to all these pains for? "He owns Chicago," Mr. S said. Sam Giancana was one Italian Mr. S did not call Dag.

The thing that made the first big impression of this Mr. Big of American Gangland were his hands. He had the most perfectly manicured hands and nails I had ever seen. Yet these were the same hands that, according to the man's legend, in his youth had crushed tracheas and squeezed triggers. Mr. S never mentioned that side of Giancana. What impressed Sinatra about the capo was that he was a genius of a businessman. No matter that the legend labeled Giancana as a near idiot, with a double-digit IQ. To Frank Sinatra he was a genius when it came to money, and money was the only test that mattered in America, where anything was possible, even for an idiot to own Chicago. Where success was concerned, brawn could be better than brains, though "Mafia" was a word I never heard Mr. S use.

Sometimes they called Giancana Sam, sometimes Salvatore, sometimes Mooney, which was some kind of Italian usage for "crazy." He didn't seem crazy to me. He seemed very conservative. Sam Giancana, a small man, almost Sinatra's and my size, but a little heavier, was around sixty, balding, mousey. He was the kind of man you might have seen in Marty Sinatra's Italian social club, except his clothes were way too good. He had the fanciest clothes I ever saw, as fancy as his hands. He had silk suits, and silk shirts, and silk pocket squares, and alligator shoes even after alligator shoes became illegal. Everything was custom made. He wore a star sapphire ring that looked like the Hope Diamond, serious Breakfast at Tiffany's stuff. And he smoked Havana cigars that would have made Harry Cohn jealous. Yet at the same time, he had a high, almost girlish voice that mispronounced half of the few things he would say. He got everybody's name wrong, from President Eisenheimer to Clark Grable.

Sam Giancana looked dazed, lost, a scared rabbit. He carried huge rolls of dimes and quarters, to use in the pay phones he was constantly stopping at. He said all the regular phones he could use were being tapped. He seemed totally paranoid. Yet Mr. S insisted the man was a wizard, a business mastermind who understood big money better than anyone else in the world. Like Skinny D'Amato, Sam Giancana had kept Mr. S afloat when he was drowning, probably more so, because Skinny took orders from Sam. Sam had ordered Skinny and other gang-related club owners around the country to book Sinatra and to keep booking him, despite his voice problems, despite his dwindling allure. Sam Giancana's confidence that Sinatra would come back became a self-fulfilling prophesy.

Talk about the heat being on in the kitchen. I must have cut myself five times and burned myself ten, but that was nothing compared to what this mob kingpin would do to me if I fucked the meal up. And it wasn't just Sam Giancana. Throughout the day one mob boss after another showed up at the Alejo house. There was Johnny Rosselli, the original Dapper Don, with clothes and hands like Giancana but tall and handsome. Rosselli, who had done more time than a clock, was supposedly the Mafia's man in Hollywood. I used to see him at the best tables at Romanoff's and Perino's, with the prettiest starlets as well as with Harry Cohn, who had a huge gambling problem that Rosselli enabled. They were also frequently at Santa Anita racetrack together, and they wore identical "blood brother" ruby rings that Rosselli had given the mogul. After seeing Rosselli at his house, I asked Mr. S if Giancana had leaned on Rosselli to lean on Cohn to give him the part in *From Here to Eternity,* and he gave me a Cheshire-cat grin. "Hey, I got that part through my own fucking *talent,*" he said. And then he gave me a wink.

And there were more. There was a guy named Joe F. and another called Johnny F., and some others with Italian names no one could pronounce. Each guy came with at least one or two thick-necked bodyguards. Mr. S couldn't have been more thrilled. He'd say, "George, feed 'em all." Now I know how Wolfgang Puck must feel on a night at Spago when all the stars show up at once and want special dishes. One mobster wanted eggplant, another spinach, another wanted clams. There were no fresh clams in Palm Springs in those days, so I got canned ones and prayed to God the boys were drunk enough not to care about the difference. Luckily they were. I don't know what was going on out there that attracted so many heavy hitters. It was like the famous Apalachin Conference they had the next year, I think, 1957, when the capos from all over the country met in a little town in upstate New York. But there were no closed-door meetings, at least at Sinatra's house, and no whispers of dividing up Las Vegas, or Havana, or whacking some rival. No, the only talk I heard was about broads, boxing, and golf. Don't forget, Palm Springs was a place to relax, even for criminals.

That weekend I would drive Sam Giancana around Palm Springs to meet his visiting fellow mobsters, each of whom was staying in some gated mansion, not of celebrities but rather of the faceless fat cats from all over who owned manufacturing companies and heavy industry and came to the desert to golf. Those mobsters were certainly connected, although I'm not sure to whom. Giancana was a total gentleman, and I'm not saying this out of relief that he didn't strangle me to death. Once he got comfortable with me, he said a strange thing to me: "You know, I like niggers." Mob guys were not known for their racial tolerance, so this was a big confession. "Niggers made me what I am," whatever that was, he continued.

I wasn't sure how to pronounce his last name, so I called him Mr. Sam. "Tell me about it, Mr. Sam," I asked him, and between one golf course and another, he did. When he was in prison in Terre Haute, Indiana, in the forties, for what I didn't press him on, his fellow

inmate was a black guy who went on to become the king of the numbers racket in Chicago and a multimillionaire. It was one of the few
ways a black man could get rich in America at the time. Giancana
knew a good thing when he saw it, and, in a rare display of brotherhood, he became the black guy's partner. He eventually had to force
the black king out, because his own bosses "didn't want to be in business with no niggers," Mr. Sam said. When he said force, he meant
force. Sam didn't tell me the gory part, but I later heard that Giancana
and his henchmen had kidnapped the numbers king and brutalized
him until he turned over to Giancana his business and the details of
how to run it. Mr. Sam put a much nicer spin on this for me, boasting of how magnanimous he was in setting the black guy up for life
in a villa down in Mexico. "A lifetime of the shits is still a lifetime," he
said. The Big Boys wanted the black king whacked, and Sam saved his
life. He sounded as if he expected an award from the NAACP.

Mr. Sam also complimented me on my driving, which, I learned,
was a big deal from him. Giancana had begun his mob career as a
driver, or "wheel man," for the successors of Al Capone. "You oughta
come to Chicago," he said at the end of his stay. "I'll give you a *real*
job." "Hey, he's *mine*," Mr. S spoke up when he overheard him. It was
the only time all weekend that he had asserted himself to Sam in any
way. Otherwise, he had been as much of a valet as I was. He would
follow Mr. Sam around the golf course, hitting a few balls at first,
then giving up and just riding in the cart watching Giancana play.
That man loved golf as though he were Arnold Palmer. In between
holes, Mr. S would hang on every word Sam said. Sinatra wanted to
learn from Giancana in the same way Sammy Davis wanted to learn
from everybody else. Mr. S never acted that way, though, around anyone else. What he and Giancana talked about was business, the business of running casinos. The numbers I heard them throw around
made my head reel. They were never less than in the hundreds of

thousands. The word "skim" came up a lot, and I don't think they were referring to milk, as did the phrases "IRS," "balance sheets," "gross," "pension funds," and "Teamsters." I wasn't a *Wall Street Journal* kind of guy, and all of it went over my head, but I didn't think Mr. S was, either. I was surprised how slick he was at numbers talk, but I guess when you've got it, you like to talk about it. Sinatra owned a piece of the Sands, in return for his making it his exclusive venue in Vegas, and he loved the notion of being a capitalist, a proprietor. He wanted to own even more. Sam Giancana was his mentor in these ambitions that extended far beyond stage and screen.

There are endless conspiracy theories about Frank Sinatra being in the pocket of the Mafia, involving trying to kill Castro, killing Marilyn, killing the Kennedys. What about a theory that Sinatra and the Rat Pack were pawns of the Mafia, which controlled America's bar and liquor business? Wasn't the whole Rat Pack phenomenon nothing more than a three-year liquor advertising campaign? If it was about anything, it was about the joys of drinking. That might be far-fetched, but Mr. S was indeed strongarmed by Mr. Sam and friends to do car ads, not national campaigns for Ford or GM, but local radio spots for a small Pontiac dealership in Chicago that the "Chicago Boys" were involved with. The place was Peter Epsteen Pontiac in Skokie. Mr. S did his pitch to "Old McDonald Had a Farm," singing "Old McDonald had a farm, E-I-E-I-O. And on this farm he had a car, the swingin'est car I know. It was a new Pontiac with a dual wide track. What a kick to drive it, like ballin' the jack. Peter Epsteen Pontiac, he sold the car to Mac." Not only did Mr. S do an ad; Dean and Sammy also performed for Peter Epsteen, to "Come Fly with Me," and "High Hopes." If Mr. Sam could get these superstars to stoop to this, then *anything* was possible. That was "respect." Major respect. The Rat Pack song "My Kind of Town (Chicago Is)" was a declaration of loyalty to Mr. Sam.

The "mob circuit" of venues where I began traveling with Mr. S in the mid-1950s went from the Sands in Vegas, to the Villa Venice in Chicago, to the Copacabana in New York, to the 500 in Atlantic City, to the Fontainebleau in Miami. The drill was the same, endless nights, oceans of booze, gorgeous girls, and, of course, the greatest music on earth. Gangsters were everywhere. The faces were different; the muscle was the same. The only reason I was able to keep my bearings in this cavalcade of excess was because I had gotten married again. That gave me ballast, though I have to admit that the temptations were hard to resist. I had met my new wife Sally in music school while I was still working for Swifty Lazar. We had three boys, Gregory, born in 1955, Guy, in 1956, and Sean, in 1957.

Sally was Finnish, and very blond. Her family had emigrated to Oregon, where she had grown up on a farm. I had dated white girls before, and both my parents were part white, so Sally's whiteness wasn't exotic to me, but I was pretty exotic to Sally. However, blacks were considered totally cool and then some in Finland, where anything different was welcome. But then Sally's mother left her logger father for a local machinist, who was as much of a racist redneck as an Alabama Klansman. So we didn't go home to Oregon for Christmas. Sally hated her new stepfather, who went to jail a few times for robbery. Funny how I married into two criminal families. (The third time was to a preacher's daughter, just to even things out.)

In any event, we had a short, intense courtship. Sally had insisted on remaining a virgin until our wedding night, so I figured she was mine forever. Shows how much I knew! Sally's singing dreams got about as far as mine. She took a job at the telephone company, and later as a secretary at the Biltmore Hotel in downtown L.A. For my first three years with Mr. S, he never met my family. He barely saw his own, so it wasn't discussed. Home and work were separate but not necessarily equal. Mr. S was a jealous mistress. The kids were too young to take on the road, so Sally had to stay home and play mom while I gallivanted all over the world. It wasn't real gallivanting, but it seemed so glamorous no one would believe how hard the work and the round-the-clock pressure were. Even when I was in L.A., I'd never get home until two or three in the morning, if at all. Then I had to get up at six when the kids did. I drank a lot of coffee.

Sally wasn't crazy about my hours and my travels, but I was crazy about her and my kids, and love conquered all. At least for a while. At the beginning of our marriage, we didn't have a religious household at all. That was before I rediscovered my Judaism and before Sally discovered the faith of Jehovah's Witnesses, which I blame for destroying our marriage, even more than my dreadful hours. But later about that. In these early years with Sinatra, this new wife and family kept me grounded. If I hadn't embraced family values I would have embraced a lot of women who would have spelled a lot of trouble.

Even though I was true blue, sometimes my wife would get terribly jealous, just because my proximity to the goddesses of the world had such *potential* for incrimination. Take the time Mr. S sent me down to Acapulco to "take care of" three of the most beautiful women in Hollywood. In the "Come Fly with Me" days when Acapulco was the most glamorous of resorts, Mr. S had taken a villa on La Concha Beach. A big house party he had planned had somehow fallen apart. None of the men he invited could make it, including Mr. S, who had to stay at the studio for reshoots. So I was sent to take his place. The first of the women was Ava Gardner, who was in town and in a non-matador availability phase. The second was the lovely Jeannie Martin, Dean's wife, a former Orange Bowl Queen from Miami Beach. And the third was the equally lovely Bea Korshak, a former model and Ice Capades skater who was the wife of Sidney Korshak, the Chicago mob lawyer who had become the most feared Mr. Fixit-or-Be-Fixed in all show business.

I knew Ava liked to drink and listen to jazz, and Jeannie liked to drink and browse and laugh at soft-core pornography, when porn was much harder to come by than it is today. I used to drive around to these obscure bookstores in Hollywood and buy Jeannie under-the-counter sex comic books, with funny photos and silly stories. Whenever I'd go to Tijuana on fireworks runs for Mr. S, I'd bring Jeannie some really hard-core magazines. Remember that in those days Tijuana was one of the raunchiest places on earth, famous for the donkey show at the club the Blue Fox. Acapulco being Mexico, I was sure I could find some "literature" that would amuse Mrs. Martin.

I had no idea what Bea liked and was frankly afraid to find out. I didn't want to get too chummy with the wife of Mr. Big, who may have *seemed* like a typical I'll-sue-you-but-won't-kill-you Jewish lawyer but was someone for whom I didn't want to take the slightest risk of creating any impression of impropriety. Bea herself appeared to be the nicest lady, with no apparent kinks at all. Most of the time she and Jeannie sat on the beach making up guest lists for their charity SHARE, which was the ultimate do-good activity for A-list Hollywood wives. While they were out planning their good deeds, Ava would stay in the villa, napping, drinking, and listening to jazz. There was a great collection in the house, and, naturally, all of Mr. S's records, which got lots of play, in his absentee honor. All three women liked to swim, particularly on the balmy moonlit nights and, luckily for me, who liked keeping things simple, none was in a Dietrich-Garbo phase. Nor did any of them get a yen for one of the handsome cliff divers, or any of the local gigolos who were always lying in wait. I mostly hung with Ava, who gave me the nickname "El Matador de Moscas," or, the killer of flies, for swatting away the endless swarm of bugs. My wife was on my case about having a wild foursome, and the only action I was getting was playing exterminator. It wasn't always glamorous.

People remain confounded as to why Mr. S, now on top of the world, would continue to consort with, actually court, people like Sam Giancana, Johnny Rosselli, Sidney Korshak. Were these the folk heroes of his Jersey childhood? Did Mr. S have an outlaw streak? Were criminals simply more fun to be around than boring straight people? Was this the fantasy of the ninety-seven-pound weakling dreaming of becoming a strongman? Or was it gratitude, plain and simple? I have my own idea. It was all about business. Why did Harry Cohn hang with these same people? Why did Lew Wasserman? Why did Joe Kennedy? These guys had the capital, they had the labor, and they would take chances when conservative Wall Street wouldn't, chances in the entertainment business, which Wall Street viewed as unpredictable, unquantifiable, and "Jewish" to boot. Wall Street in the fifties preferred U.S. Steel. Look at U.S. Steel now, and look at entertainment. Sam Giancana wasn't a gangster; he was a *visionary*. He was the genius Mr. S said he was. If Wall Street disdained show-biz, as a crapshoot, Mr. Sam and his outfit were willing to roll the dice. Literally. That's how Las Vegas was born.

In truth, Mr. S had a little bit of Wall Street in him. Look how risk averse his father Marty was. Mr. S had rolled the dice and won, but he had rolled and almost lost as well. He had nearly crapped out. He saw how tenuous the whole game was, how it could vanish in a flash. Mr. S wanted to be part of the capital, not just the labor, fancy labor, that he was. He wanted to be an *owner*. Just as Marty treasured his tenure at the firehouse, Mr. S too wanted some major security of his own. His firehouse happened to be a Vegas casino. To achieve that end, he jumped into bed with Sam Giancana, who helped him acquire his own "piece of the rock." The first rock was the new Sands, which opened in Vegas in 1952, with its own Copa Girls, considered the cream of the Vegas crop, and its own Copa man, Jack Entratter, considered the host with the most. With his 9 percent share, the Sands was more than Mr. S's showcase. It was his *office,* the house that Sinatra built. He loved being an owner so much, he would go for a second round with Mr. Sam at the Cal-Neva Lodge at Lake Tahoe, this one with tragic results. Nevertheless, Mr. S had discovered the joys of capitalism. He preferred the odds on the croupier's side of the table. He liked talking business, going to his new offices in a bank building in Beverly Hills, reviewing balance sheets, nearly as much as he did getting on stage. It says something that his new "best friend" was Al Hart, the Jewish president of City National Bank in L.A. Maybe Mr. S's father did know best. Having a firehouse wasn't so bad after all.

Given Mr. S's quest for financial stability, I was surprised that he was showing zero interest in domestic stability, as I myself was pursuing. He turned forty in 1955, and he was still sowing wild oats like a teenage farmboy. He had way too many options to cash out of the sex game. In fact, he kept his own black book, not of past conquests, but of future ones. Aided by his chief pussy truffle hound, Jimmy Van Heusen, Mr. S kept a file on all the upcoming starlets in town. He'd read *Variety,* and *Photoplay,* and other movie magazines to see who was hot and fuckable, and he'd put them in the book of "people to do." I never read the list, so I don't know if it consisted only of new faces or others he had in mind, like Grace Kelly, Sophia Loren, Gina Lollobrigida. Whoever, the way he figured it, he couldn't get a better family than he already had, and he couldn't fall in love as deeply as he already had with Ava, so he might as well just go on a sex rampage.

He did, nevertheless, have a close call with Lauren Bacall. He called her Betty and she called him Francis, and they were virtually brother and sister. The Bogarts, almost alone in Hollywood, had taken Mr. S in when he was an orphan of the storm. Since they were the dream couple of the silver screen, their acceptance of Frank was not only rebellious, in the snotty, superficial Hollywood social scene; it also validated Mr. S, who, strange as it may seem, was desperate to be accepted by this snotty, superficial, largely Jewish world. He was the kid with his nose pressed against the glass of this candy store of fame. Once they let him in, he may have smashed all that glass, but he wanted in, nonetheless, in the worst way. Because he worshipped everything about Humphrey Bogart, Mr. S wasn't going to stop with his wife, but I think he worshipped Bogart enough to keep his impulsive lust in check. I say I *think,* because as Mr. S himself often said, "a hard dick has no conscience," and, whenever he and Betty would be alone together at the house for some innocent reason, like picking up a script or showing her a painting, he would usually send me away. But I'd bet he was loyal to Bogart, if no one else.

When Bogart got sick in 1956, Mr. S was devastated. It wasn't just sick, it was a death sentence. It started with a simple smoker's cough, and turned out to be esophageal cancer. That really hit Mr. S where he lived. Like Bogart, Mr. S smoked and drank as if there would be no tomorrow. Now for his idol, there wouldn't be. They hadn't established the connection between smoking, alcohol, and cancer back then. The health experts who sounded the alarm were regarded by lay people as crackpots, almost un-American. Smoking was as American as apple pie. Drinking was the dream of the leisure class. Mr. S thought Bogart was indestructible, and now that he saw his idol was mortal, it made him realize so was he, that maybe the health nuts were onto something. But instead of sobering up and stubbing out, Mr. S went on a multiyear binge that never stopped. I guess you call it denial.

Bogart suffered for over a year, slowly wasting away. It started as indigestion, heartburn, but what bon vivant didn't have that? Eventually, they did exploratory surgery and discovered the malignancy. Betty broke the news to Frank, who was shocked but confident the doctors would cure his friend. Bogie, the ultimate tough guy, was too tough for the Big C. The night before the first big operation to cut out the cancer, Mr. S gave a party for some of the old Rat Pack at the new Bowmont house, Swifty, Romanoff, the Nivens. Everybody drank and smoked like crazy, including Bogie, all laughing at death. Alas, death got the last laugh, though Mr. S's way of cheering Bogie up was to sit and smoke and drink with him until the bitter end.

Mr. S was badly shaken up watching Bogie waste away, despite the catered meals from Romanoff's and Chasen's, which the poor guy couldn't swallow, despite Bogie's "fuck it" courage. He dressed in his cashmere jackets and ascots until the end. It was so sad how shrunken he became. He was like a little marionette, whom they would roll out to say goodbye to his legion of pals. He was only fifty-eight when he died in early 1957. Like Swifty Lazar, Mr. S had a thing about germs and hospitals, though not so far as to put towels on the floor. He was obsessively clean, hated when people sneezed and coughed around him, avoided hospitals like, well, hospitals. Like Lazar, Sinatra also would shower at least four times a day, always after a girl, always before meeting someone, sometimes just for the cleanliness of it. But Swifty was much more neurotic than Mr. S. Swifty never went to the hospital when Bogie was dying, but Mr. S bravely showed up, just as he did with Sammy Davis Jr. after his car wreck. He loved the guys, and friendship came before any phobias. Nevertheless, Mr. S never concealed his problems with the institutional part of illness. "I much prefer visiting prisons," he said. "Not even close." One of the main reasons Betty kept Bogie at home until the bitter end was so that he could see his adored Swifty and Francis.

After Bogart died, it was only natural that Betty, who was thirty-three at the time, would spend a lot of time with Mr. S, who was forty-two, picking up the pieces. And it was only natural, knowing Mr. S and his libido, that he would try to sleep with her. It was like night following day, the most natural thing in the world, to make love to a beautiful woman. But because he loved Bogie so much, there was always that heavy guilt number, both for Mr. S and for Betty. "Here's looking at you, kid," took on ominous meaning. Bogie was up in heaven, or wherever, looking at his two "kids." He may not have been thrilled at what he saw. Talk about Catholic shame. Poor Mr. S was totally conflicted. I remember how nervous he was the first time he took Betty out in public, to a closed-circuit showing of a Sugar Ray Robinson championship fight. With his father being an ex-boxer, Mr. S loved the fights. I'm not sure about Betty, who was more a theatre girl. Afterward, the press was all over them, and he was sorry he had "gone public" with Betty. But he kept going, to the gala openings of his new movies *The Joker Is Wild,* and *Pal Joey,* to his concerts at the Sands.

Like Mia Farrow, Lauren Bacall was Hollywood "class," and Mr. S craved class like a junkie craves a needle. And Betty seemed to crave Mr. S's Life, after having to deal with death for such a long time. Still, Betty Bacall may have confused sex and love. Mr. S was confused, too. Maybe he *did* love her. Then again, maybe he didn't. Aside from the ghost of Bogie, she had baggage, two kids, her own career. Mr. S hated careers, if they conflicted with his happiness. Ava's was bad enough. Moreover, Betty was jealous of Ava and the continuing trance she had put Frank in. Even for Lauren Bacall, Ava Gardner was a tough act to follow. Who wouldn't be jealous, given Frank still called Ava every week, had his bedrooms festooned with her photos. But logic didn't matter. Betty was supposed to suppress these troublesome emotions. Mr. S wanted his women to be hassle-free, which, of course, would never be possible.

Betty came over to the Bowmont house far more often than Frank went over there. The idea of his sleeping in Bogie's bed was probably too much for either of them. He did stay over on occasion. He'd call me in the morning to bring him a new set of clothes. Mr. S didn't even want to make the ten-minute drive between the two houses in old clothes. He was that meticulous. Even though Betty had seen me around for years, and she knew that *I* knew what was going on, she never confided in me as did so many of Mr. S's other ladies. Maybe she was embarrassed to have to deal with me. In fact she rarely spent an entire night on Bowmont, always leaving before dawn. The whole affair didn't even seem like an affair, it was conducted so discreetly. "Just friends," was how both Frank and Betty described it to their friends.

Whatever it was, the Sinatra-Bacall romance was played out on a tightrope, without a net. It took Swifty Lazar to push them off. When Mr. S wasn't around, Swifty was Betty's other constant companion. He may have had his own lustful thoughts, but his own self-esteem, where females were concerned, was so low that he couldn't act on them. If he couldn't pay, he couldn't play. At one point, Mr. S had said, to hell with it, let's get married, to Betty over dinner at the Imperial Gardens on Sunset, a sliding-screen, very private Japanese restaurant that had replaced Preston Sturges's Players Club on the site. The first person she told was best friend Swifty, who was so jealous the first person *he* told was gossip queen Louella Parsons, who put it in her column and told the world. I'm not sure how seriously Mr. S even meant his proposal. He might have just said it in an off-hand way. He didn't give Betty the big ring, or anything like it. That would have been a characteristic grand Sinatra gesture on such a momentous occasion. But he didn't make it. He hadn't told anyone else, certainly not Big Nancy, who was deeply hurt, for both herself and the kids, when she read about it in the papers.

Whether it was a real proposal or not, Mr. S flipped out. He had enough guilt from Bogie up above. He couldn't take any more from Big Nancy down here. He took the firestorm as an omen that he was doing the Wrong Thing. When in doubt, get out, was his credo. He blamed Betty much more than he blamed Swifty, arguing that she was using Swifty to create publicity to shame him into going to the altar. If we're engaged, we have to go through with it, right? Wrong.

From *fait accompli* to party's over in one phone call. They had been dating nearly a year, and he dumped her over the phone. That was as ruthless as I had seen Frank Sinatra at that point in our relationship. I was taken aback at the cold way he cut Betty, whom he had truly cared about, completely dead. I had no idea that one day he would treat me the exact same way.

I felt awful for Betty, who had enjoyed such a classic romance with Bogie. Perhaps only one of these in a lifetime was all anyone could expect. By the same token, Mr. S could only have one grand passion in his life, and that was Ava. Betty, who had gotten spoiled by Bogie, simply wanted more than Frank could give her. Mr. S desperately tried to copy Bogart in every way, but when it came to loving Betty, the mold had been broken.

Not only did Mr. S now turn against Betty Bacall, he turned *on* her. He called her "the Jew bitch." He complained to his buddies how spoiled she was, how cold, how badly she kissed, and, worst of all among his friends, that she couldn't—or wouldn't, give a blow job. "All she does is whistle," Mr. S said, nastily referring to Bacall's famous suggestive line in her first film, *To Have and Have Not*. Cocksucking, in this group, was considered the highest feminine art. To fail here was to be less than a woman. Curiously, Mr. S did *not* turn on Swifty Lazar for dropping the marriage bomb to Louella. They had a "guy thing" going that transcended the slings and arrows of romance. Lazar remained Sinatra's friend, though Sinatra never ceased loving to play nasty practical jokes on him. *Nobody* in the Sinatra circle seemed to stand up for poor Betty. I guess if they had, they'd have been excommunicated from the group. The party line was that pushy Betty tried to pressure a harried Frank into a marriage he didn't want.

I had never seen the famously courtly Mr. S be so vicious about any woman, not even the whores he would pay off and ship out because they were wearing too much makeup or cheap perfume. He was turning on his dear friend, his idol's widow. Even if they weren't really engaged, she was his girlfriend. It wasn't as if she was some publicity hound, or some nutty fan trying to get knocked up. But for some reason, he treated her as one, and it was ugly. He must have fallen harder for her than he cared to admit, so he reacted violently in the other direction. He wouldn't even speak to her again for many years. That was the first time that Mr. S showed a side that frightened me. It proved to be an early warning sign of the volcanic eruptions that were on the way.

5

Camelot

MR. S had entertained so many gangster types in his Palm Springs compound that I assumed the wiry, freckly bespectacled man who spoke in long A's was another pillar of the underworld. I had met Italian gangsters and Jewish gangsters. Why not an Irish gangster? Mr. S certainly rolled out the red carpet for him, five fantastic hookers flown down from Vegas, and a whole staff of waiters and maids in starched gray uniforms, some from Watts, others he had me round up from the Indian reservation in the Coachella Valley. We had a lot of bedrooms, though if we ever got too crowded the hookers would double up and bunk together. They'd see the guests in the guests' bedrooms, so space was never a problem. When they weren't "in session," the girls would swim in the pool, work on their tans, eat and drink like any other guests. Mr. S wouldn't stand for orgies on his property. He was too much of a neat freak. The orgies he left to Jimmy Van Heusen. Let the girls destroy *his* place, that was Sinatra's attitude. We treated them as honored guests, not hookers. They just got paid when they went home.

The hospitality that was laid out on that weekend was truly extraordinary. Even Sam Giancana didn't get this kind of treatment. Nor did Mr. Sam *give* the abuse this seventy-year-old guy, whom Sinatra called Mr. Ambassador, heaped on all of us. He not only told nigger jokes throughout the meals, he'd call the Indians "savages" and the blacks "Sambos" and curse the hell out of anyone who served him from the wrong side or put one ice cube too many in his Jack Daniel's. "Can't you get any *white* help?" he'd needle Mr. S. "Aren't they *paying* you enough?" After one day, only the hookers remained, except for one the abusive bastard tried to brand with his Cohiba. Mr. S had me give her five hundred dollars for her trouble and let her go. The blacks went back to Watts, the Indians to the reservation. Leaving me to be the sole whipping boy of the man who may have held a Harvard degree, but was a disgrace to it, cruder and meaner and, alas, proving crime *does* pay, more successful than any of the street mobsters that Mr. S ever hosted. Such was the father of our country's most captivating president. Mr. Ambassador, if anyone had the guts to spit in his face, a bravery that my boss sadly lacked, should have been called Mr. Asshole.

Joseph Kennedy was, if anything, crueler about Jews than he was about blacks. As a guy who once owned a Hollywood studio (RKO), he must have had a tough time with his competition. To him they were "Sheenie rag traders." He referred to the august Louis B. Mayer as a "kike junkman." The Jewish jokes didn't stop. The worst one I can recall: "What's the difference between a Jew and a pizza? The pizza doesn't cry on its way to the oven." Poor Mr. S, having to sit through this, having to force a smile when he should have thrown the guy out to the coyotes. The antisemitism was shocking, yet it was nothing new. I was too young to remember Joseph Kennedy's craven appeasement of Adolf Hitler when he was Franklin Roosevelt's ambassador to the Court of St. James's, a position, like every other, he was said to have bought. I was even younger when he had made his illegal fortune as a bootlegger in Prohibition and as an insider trader on Wall Street before it was illegal and, ironically, before Roosevelt made him head of the Securities and Exchange Commission.

Because everybody loved JFK, we have mythologized his family into our American aristocracy and our image of Joe Kennedy is that of a Boston Brahmin patriarch. That's about as far off the mark as saying JFK was faithful to Jackie. Joe was mobbed up to his fancy collar pins, with Sam Giancana at the Merchandise Mart in Chicago, the world's biggest building that he owned; with Meyer Lansky at the Hialeah racetrack in Miami; with the one-armed bandit Wingy Grober at the Cal-Neva Lodge in Tahoe. If anyone's fortune was tainted, it was that of Mr. Ambassador, whose name was a joke, in that his term in London had made him the disgrace of the diplomatic corps. His bet on Hitler was the wrong horse of his lifetime, derailing and making a mockery of his ambitions to succeed his money beneficiary Roosevelt as president. But Joe Kennedy knew Americans had short memories. He still wanted that top office. If he couldn't buy it for himself, he would buy it for one of his sons. And, in Mr. Ambassador's octopus-like master plan, that's where Mr. Sinatra came in. In view of Kennedy's Midas touch in business, in view of his endless triumphs, Mr. S worshipped Joe Kennedy's brute force. He could be a shitheel, because, as Mr. S said, he'd "earned the right." His money was fuck-you money. Old Joe said fuck you to everyone. Sinatra respected his arrogance. Here was a poor Mick, a street guy who had "passed" for class, getting into Harvard, buying his way into government, laundering his entire image. He was the embodiment of the

Great American Success Story. Kennedy was a drug dealer of the high known as success, and Frank Sinatra was a hardcore addict.

By 1958 Frank Sinatra was so successful in movies and music, that even taking control of the business side of show business looked as if it might be too limiting to the juggernaut he was on. What else could there be for the Man Who Had Everything? The answer was power, political power, and crafty old Joe Kennedy knew just how to play to Mr. S's vanity, as well as to his massive insecurity. The road to power would be his road to respect, and that road was the road to the White House in 1960. He dangled ambassador to Italy, he threw out the idea of senator from Nevada. These were the days when the only song-and-dance man to hold major office was Gentleman Jimmy Walker, the mayor of New York (who was forced to resign in a massive corruption scandal). This was before George Murphy, before Ronald Reagan. But to his credit, Joe Kennedy saw it coming. And even if he didn't he was a brilliant enough salesman to put a restless and ravenous Frank Sinatra under his Harvard-cloaked snake-oil sell.

The seeds of Mr. S's interest in politics that Joe Kennedy so cleverly cultivated had been planted in him as a boy by his mother, Dolly. "If you serve your country, you serve yourself," Dolly said while explaining to me why she got involved in local government in Hoboken. Right after she married Marty and before Frank was born in 1915, she became a ward heeler in Hoboken's Third Ward, rounding up Democratic votes from new Italian immigrants in return for Dolly's help with papers, welfare, whatever the government could do for them. Dolly was a natural for this because of her great language skills. In addition to her perfect English, she spoke numerous Italian dialects, from her own Genoese to Marty's Sicilian. She also spoke good old Jersey "fuck-ese." I've never heard a woman curse like Dolly. "Fuck you, you fucking asshole son of a bitch fucking bastard motherfucker," was a typical Dolly sentence. It probably came in handy when she needed to muscle up votes or favors.

Quickly Dolly became indispensable to the Irish politicians who ran the town. They even got her a job as the official court interpreter for the off-the-boat Italians, whom she would then convince to vote the Democratic ticket. Dolly loved her political work so much that, even after Frank was born, she continued to do it full-time, not to mention her after-hours midwifery, which she also translated into still more Democratic votes. Little Frank would be left in the day care of Dolly's Old World mother. He often spoke to Dolly fondly of Grandma, which might explain his own Old World courtliness to the fairer sex. His mother's absence on behalf of the Democratic Party had made a big impression on little Mr. S. He would not forget it, hence his near-religious admiration for Franklin D. Roosevelt, whose signed photo held a place of honor in the Bowmont house. There was thus an actual tradition of the Sinatras and the Irish working together for the Democratic cause. What Mr. S would now do was to elevate this tradition from the slums of Hoboken to the White House.

By 1958 Mr. S had pretty much played out his hand in movies. After winning his Supporting Oscar for *Eternity*, he hoped to go all the way and get the Big One, but it didn't happen. His best effort and best shot was playing the junkie gambler Frankie Machine in *The Man with the Golden Arm*. He got a 1955 Best Actor nomination but lost to Ernest Borgnine in *Marty*. He couldn't hold it against Borgnine, Borgnine had played Fatso, who had killed Maggio in *Eternity*, and by doing so won Sinatra's character the sympathy that resulted in the Oscar. "He won me one, he lost me one." Mr. S tried to be nonchalant, but it hurt. His major cinematic satisfaction was his showdown with Marlon Brando in the big-budget extravaganza *Guys and Dolls*, whose Damon Runyon dialogue about heat and lettuce and markers and action and broads was the inspiration for the future gangsterese Rat Pack-speak. Sinatra loved the idea of being in the movie, based on one of the best shows ever to hit Broadway. It was an honor, a prestige production all the way, starring not one but two Oscar winners, and directed by the great Joe Mankiewicz, who made *All About Eve*. The only problem was that Sinatra wanted Brando's role, which was bigger and required more singing. The producer, the all-powerful Sam Goldwyn himself, leaned on Mr. S to roll with the punches. After all, Brando's *Waterfront* Oscar was for Best Actor, not Best Supporting Actor, Goldwyn reminded Mr. S, as if he needed to be reminded. Bottom line was that even Frank Sinatra didn't say No to Sam Goldwyn.

The shoot was a horror show. I would come to the set frequently, to do errands for Mr. S, and the tension was as thick as poisoned molasses. Everyone was just waiting for things to blow up, and they often did. Sinatra called Brando "Mumbles." Brando called Sinatra "Baldie." (A word Brando would come to eat.) Although Brando had the romantic lead of Sky Masterson, Sinatra relished Brando making a singing fool of himself, totally unable to carry the tune of "Luck Be a Lady Tonight." As Nathan Detroit, Sinatra sang the wonderful title song and felt he had blown the great Brando off the screen. "He and his Actors Studio can fuck themselves," Mr. S gloated. While Goldwyn bribed Brando with a new black Thunderbird to do publicity, and gave nothing to Sinatra, Mr. S was so competitive that he carefully calculated that he had bedded more of the spectacular chorus line known as the Goldwyn Girls than had the despised Mumbles. Mr. S's revenge came in many forms.

He had great expectations for his tribute biopic of his friend Joe E. Lewis. *The Joker Is Wild* was wall-to-wall with references to mob brutality in the music business, which proved to be a turn-off to a Pollyanna public. It flopped, despite "All the Way" winning the Oscar for Best Song. So did *Johnny Concho,* a Western that was the first film Mr. S produced himself. He had his dream, costarring with two of his idols, Bing Crosby in *High Society* and Cary Grant in *The Pride and the Passion,* which Mr. S called "the cannon movie," and was embarrassed by. He was more embarrassed that he had used the film as an excuse to be in Spain (I stayed at home for this one) and chase Ava Gardner one more time, and had failed dismally in the process. He couldn't compete with Spanish matadors, Italian film studs (Walter Chiari), unknown black jazz musicians, or, most difficult of all, his own shattered past with Ava. He was so distracted romantically that he spent no time at all with Cary Grant, who under normal circumstances he would have loved getting to know. He was also ashamed to face Cary after his endless tantrums on the set, taking out on the film the frustration he felt toward Ava, made him seem like a prima donna. If anyone had the right to be the prima donna it was Cary, and Mr. S knew it. Yet Cary was a total pro, and Frank a total brat. A few years later, Cary came up to the house for some dinners, and *Pride* never once was mentioned.

On the record front, his 1958 Nelson Riddle-arranged *Only the Lonely* album was one of his best, the pinnacle of a prodigiously productive relationship with Riddle. The immaculate, Dutch Reformed-reared Riddle may have resembled a square accountant, but he was a musical genius whom Frank treasured every bit as much as Dean Martin or Jimmy Van Heusen. Sinatra *worshipped* Riddle, who added his swinging strings to Sinatra's emotional ballads, making them wonderful to listen to without sacrificing their romantic intensity. Their new sound together at Capitol Records, beginning in 1954, helped recharge Mr. S's singing career. Yet, for all their affection, Frank and Nelson rarely hung out on the Toots Shor carousing circuit. Nelson had too many problems at home. That's why he always seemed sad. His wife, a devout Catholic, had flipped out on a guilt trip over an abortion Nelson pushed her into early in their marriage. She became an alcoholic, and an even worse one when their little girl died of asthma when she was six months old. The only person Nelson was more devoted to than Mr. S was his poor wife, though even that got so much for him that he broke down into a drunken, guilt-filled affair with Rosemary Clooney in the early sixties. If Sinatra had a lot of romantic pain to draw from in his music, so did Nelson.

Mr. S couldn't read a note of music, but he knew greatness when he heard it. He was truly the Man with the Golden Ear. For the technical side of music, and it is extremely technical, he relied entirely on Nelson, whom he often called "Maestro." He never misbehaved around Nelson. Even though I would come to many of their recording sessions at the studio on Franklin and Vine as the designated bartender, Mr. S laid down a law, which applied to himself as well, that no one could take a drink until after the session was completed. It was strictly tea with honey, followed by an endless supply of Luden's Cough Drops. Once, when we were doing a session with the all-black Count Basie Orchestra, we ran out of Luden's. I gave Mr. S some licorice breath drops that turned his tongue black. "What is this shit?" he barked. "If you're gonna work with spooks, this'll help you sound like them," I joked. Liquor or none, we had fun.

If Nelson Riddle seemed on the surface too square for Mr. S, Mr. S himself may have been getting too square for America. He was beginning to feel the greasy shadow of Elvis Presley. Elvis outsold Mr. S, and that bugged him. He denounced the King of Rock n' Roll as degenerate and vicious. In fact, Sinatra was treating Elvis the way Washington was treating another rebellious upstart from the south, Fidel Castro. To Mr. S Elvis was another "Mumbles," the Marlon Brando of music, and what could be worse? "If I want a nigger I'll get a *real* nigger," he said to anyone who'd listen, including me and Sammy. It didn't offend either of us, because it was Mr. S's attempt at

Don Rickles-type humor, and we all knew that comedy was not Sinatra's strong suit. Sinatra did, too. His idea of a great comic was Danny
Thomas, who was perhaps the top laugh draw in Vegas. Mr. S would
like to sit in on Danny's shows, incognito at a back table, trying to
analyze what made a joke work.

By the same token, he wanted to analyze what made Elvis work.
Mr. S hated Elvis so much that he'd sit in the den all by himself at the
music console and listen to every new track over and over, "Don't Be
Cruel," "All Shook Up," "Teddy Bear." He was trying to figure out just
what the hell this new stuff *was*, both artistically (though he'd never
concede it was art) and culturally (though he'd never concede it was
culture). Why was the public digging this stuff? What did it have?
What was the hook? These questions got the better of Mr. S. I knew
he was in trouble when he said he preferred Pat Boone. I secretly
loved Elvis. I bought all his records. My wife dug him as well. But I
didn't dare tell Mr. S. It was like reading heretical books during the
Spanish Inquisition. He would have burned me at the stake, or at
least fired me as some pervert. So I just lied to keep the peace. Sometimes all you can do is lie.

I never lied about how I felt about Joe Kennedy. Mr. S felt the same
way about the old man, but he did like the boy. He believed in the
"product" the old hustler was pushing Mr. S to not only promote but
also take a piece of. It was the best investment, the ambassador
hyped, that Sinatra could ever make. Mr. S had a lot to overcome. He
had an instinctive hatred of the Irish from Hoboken, when the
Shanty gangs were the Dago gangs' worst enemies, never to be
trusted. Mr. S had an immediate mistrust of Joe's son Bobby, though
he hadn't met him in person. How could he trust a nasty kid, a street-
fighter type, forget the Harvard sheepskin, who could be working for
Joseph McCarthy one day chasing Commies in Hollywood among
Mr. S's friends, then the next day be working for another kind of

witch-hunter, Sen. John McClellan, the phony devout Southern Baptist, chasing Teamsters in Chicago, again among Mr. S's friends. What was worse was Bobby's efforts to humiliate Sinatra's most sacred cow, Sam Giancana. When Bobby subpoenaed Mr. Sam before him, the polite don took the Fifth, and always with a smile. "I thought only little girls giggled, Mr. Giancana," Bobby insulted the owner of Chicago on national television. "Can you believe this little weasel?" Mr. S shouted when he saw it. "Can you believe how crazy this goddamn Mick is!"

If Mr. S didn't naturally cotton to the Irish, he had even more reservations about the English. Poor English, Cockney English, East Enders, they were fine with Mr. S, who had always been wonderfully received in Britain and, besides, was a born champion of underdogs, wherever he found them. But English aristocrats, whom he had not exactly encountered in the Hoboken gang wars, he feared as much as Sam Giancana on a deadly rampage. "Never trust that fancy accent," he warned me. "They're the most treacherous bastards you'll ever meet." I don't know on what these attitudes were based. The only high-toned Englishmen he saw often were David Niven and Cary Grant, who only were acting the part. There was Mike Romanoff, who spoke with a plummy fake British accent. There was the hated Sam Spiegel, who used London as home base but was beyond borders. And then there was Peter Lawford, who was the fanciest Englishman in Hollywood, as close to an aristocrat as we had, who just happened to be the showbiz link to the Kennedys. Making things harder for Joe Kennedy to enlist Mr. S into his crusade was the fact that Peter Lawford embodied every treachery and bad trait Mr. S ascribed to the lords of that Sceptered Isle. Maybe it was the Slimey Limey himself who brought Mr. S so down on his people to begin with.

Cheap, weak, sneak, and freak were the words Mr. S most often used to describe Peter Lawford. The two had met in their early days in Hollywood on the MGM lot in 1946, when they costarred with Jimmy Durante in *It Happened in Brooklyn,* a musical about a sailor played by Mr. S who tries to get into show business. As far as movie stardom went at that point, both young men might as well have been in Brooklyn, the brass ring seemed that far away. To Mr. S, however, Peter Lawford, with his British accent and worldly upbringing as the son of Sir Sidney Lawford, a British general who traversed the empire from Europe to South Africa to India to Australia, was one of the "classiest" guys he had met. Peter had the added polish of having been a child star in England, but he also had the added pressure of having to support Sir Sidney and his pushy stage mother, Lady Lawford, who had pushed her husband into some shady investments that had fizzled. Young Peter was the cash cow, or calf, and he would always be under the gun, whether from his family or from the Kennedys.

Because Lawford was an eligible bachelor in the swinging late forties, Mr. S, still married to look-away Nancy, brought him into his circle of musical swingers, including Jimmy Van Heusen, Sammy Cahn, and Jule Styne, who wrote the score for Sinatra's *Anchors Aweigh* and later for Marilyn's *Gentlemen Prefer Blondes.* Peter Lawford, like these other guys, preferred hookers. Peter was whips-and-chains kinky, and not the slightest bit ashamed of it, at least around me. He told me how his mother used to dress him up as a girl, then beat him with a hairbrush if he became a mischievous boy while in little lady drag. His remembrance of things past would get him going. "Let's go buy some puss, old boy," was his call to action. Alas, his expensive tastes were not matched by his struggling thespian pocketbook, and he got a reputation for stiffing working girls. That was a real no-no among the Mr. S group, which had deep respect for hookers, and treated them with gallantry. Sinatra often said to me he preferred an honest hooker to a conniving starlet. Honesty was a key virtue to Mr. S. Although he was one of the last romantics, sometimes Mr. S just wanted it His Way, and fast, and he valued the service and fair exchange the best call girls provided. As he said, "a pro is a pro."

Lawford became a self-parody of the high-class tightwad by never once picking up a check, for anyone else, or his own. Lawford's cardinal sin, however, was that of disloyalty. Sinatra had confided to him, and to anyone else who might listen, about his heartbreak over Ava. At the depths of Mr. S's miseries, in 1953, Ava had returned to L.A. from Rome from filming *The Barefoot Contessa* with Bogart. There she had spurned Mr. S's attempts at reconciliation for the gossip columns of the world to read. Aware of all this, Lawford still took Ava on a date to an Italian place called Frascati in Beverly Hills the first night she was back in town. Having died by the swords of the gossips myself, I am fully aware how mistaken they can be, and even more aware of how unforgivingly judgmental Mr. S could be. It's entirely possible, probable in fact, that nothing happened. Lawford was sneaky, while not suicidal, and while Ava had many types, she had told me Peter was not one of them. She preferred Latins and blacks, she liked strong men, and she detested cheapness, though not poverty. That all left Peter out. Furthermore, Sinatra's temper was already world-famous for his punching out (rather having his bodyguards punch out) columnists, parking attendants, whoever done him wrong or rubbed him wrong, although I had not at this point seen him or his crew hit anyone. But he certainly had a fear-inducing aura. Whatever did or didn't happen, the Ava-Peter date was itself a fact, and Hedda, Louella, Sheilah Graham, the whole lot, went wild with it. Just as he would later dump Lauren Bacall for getting his name in the papers, Mr. S dumped Peter Lawford. I never once heard his name until Joe Kennedy began putting the arm on Mr. S around 1958.

Mr. S was so down on the guy that he might have shunned Lawford forever had Old Joe not put his daughter Pat on the case. After highly publicized romances with a number of other heiresses, fortune hunter (by necessity, as the movie parts weren't doing it) Peter had married Pat Kennedy in 1954, in one of the society weddings of the year. Now, propelled by this front-page marriage, he was the star of *The Thin Man,* a sophisticated detective comedy that had made him the Cary Grant of the small screen, the smoothest, slickest guy in America, debonair, English, a Kennedy, a star. He had it all. Except the acknowledgment of Frank Sinatra, which at this point was in Hollywood what a "By Appointment to Her Majesty" tag was in Britain.

It was at an A-list party at the Gary Coopers' in Holmby Hills where Pat, who had had an admitted crush on Frank since his crooner days, accomplished a feat of social engineering. She got Rocky Cooper, the tall blond patrician and sporty, totally *Town and Country,* wife of Coop, who preferred working on cars in overalls to black tie, to invite her and Peter under the same roof as Mr. S. Of course, the way to Mr. S's heart was through his libido. Pat turned on the charm. Although she was obviously pregnant at the time, Mr. S smelled a potential seduction of one of the most high-profile "super-broads" in America. Sinatra had few scruples regarding a gentleman's honor toward some English snob who had already tried to stab him in the back. The prospect of Pat Kennedy opened Mr. S's eyes to the even more exciting prospect of John Kennedy. Presto, the grudge against Peter Lawford disappeared.

Soon Pat gave birth to a daughter, Victoria Francis, whom the Lawfords said they were naming after their dear friend, Francis Albert. Talk about flattery, and Mr. S ate it up. With Mr. S's eyes trained on Pat, Peter became his new best friend. It was as if the old times had never existed. Lawford overnight became one of the "Clan." Sinatra cast him in his new war movie with Gina Lollobrigida (Gettalittlebitofher, Sinatra droolingly renamed her), *Never So Few.*

They drove twin Dual Ghias, a supercool Euro-style roadster produced by Chrysler on a Dodge frame. I think they got them free, for the publicity. Mr. S even partnered with Lawford on an Italian restaurant, called Puccini, after Mr. S's favorite composer. Naturally cheapskate Peter didn't put up a cent. He was getting the free ride of all time, his tightwad dream come true. What did the ultimate Italian restaurant guy need an *English* partner for, anyway? Why not Dean? Why not Vic Damone? Because they weren't married to Kennedys, that's why. Another deal they had together was the production of the Vegas heist movie *Ocean's 11,* a script Peter and Pat paid their own money to option, ostensibly for Peter to star in, but it also brought them closer to Frank. I don't know why Pat's name never showed up on the credits as producer, but she deserved it.

Even after the rapprochement with Lawford, it wasn't always smooth sailing. Some time after they had made up and Pat had given birth, Mr. S took them out for dinner. For the first time since they had met, plain Pat was all dolled up and looking foxy in a black low-cut dress, you could see she had a body. Suddenly Mr. S could not only be snowed by her status as an American Princess, he could also lust for her. After dinner, around midnight, he suggested they all drive down to Palm Springs together, which was not at all unusual. Peter couldn't, because he had a *Thin Man* or something to shoot, which Mr. S may have known. It may have been part of his strategy. In any case, Mr. S suggested he just take Pat. She could use the sun and fresh air. He said I could drive her back the next day. There was a lot of discussion, back and forth, should she or shouldn't she. She seemed as if she wanted to. But somehow she didn't go, and Mr. S blamed Peter for spoiling his party.

The Lawfords were so at home with us in the new house on Wonder Palms Drive that they left lots of golf and swimming clothes in the closet of the bedroom they used. When a clearly frustrated Mr. S and I got to Palm Springs that morning, about five A.M., after driving for hours without saying a word, he went right into that closet, tore the clothes off the hangers, threw them outside, and tried to set them on fire with his cigarette lighter. The flames went up, but when the cushions of the pool chairs caught fire, we risked burning the whole house down. So Mr. S and I pushed everything into the pool to stop the blaze. You see, Mr. S didn't like to be frustrated in any way. It interfered with his "art." He always liked to get laid the night before a recording session. Unlike boxers, who like to conserve their precious bodily fluids before a fight, Sinatra believed that sex made him sing better. It made him looser, more confident. Actually, come to think of it, he liked to get laid *every* night, recording session or not. The next day after his failure with Pat, he had a new hooker sent over to take the edge off.

Somehow, the Lawfords didn't get mad about their clothes. We told them there was an accident. Actually, I felt Mr. S could have burned down Pat's *house*, and she wouldn't have cared. At the Sands, when he was singing something like "I've Got the World on a String," and she was sitting at the front table, and he'd come up and train his blues right on her, as if he were serenading her, she was *gone*. I could just feel it. I don't know exactly what went on between Pat and Mr. S, but they spent a huge amount of time together, both in L.A. and in Palm Springs, and Peter, who never lost his penchant for hookers and walks on the wild side, often was missing in action. However, if anything happened between Pat and Mr. S, I never saw a trace of it. In Palm Springs, she always went to bed alone, in her own guest room, and always woke up alone, bright and early and cheerful, but not the-earth-moved ecstatic.

One arena where Lawford was clearly ahead of the curve was drug use. Drug-hater that he was, Mr. S would have cut Peter dead if he had known about his enormous ingestion of cocaine, not to mention a level of pot smoking that would have impressed the hippies in Berkeley nearly a decade later. I feel bad about it because I was something of what the folks in AA now call an "enabler." I would go with Peter on coke runs to Watts in a nondescript Chevy that he owned for his maids to use. It was the only time I ever saw him spend his own money on anything. No wonder he was so cheap; he had an expensive habit to support. He figured that, being a "brother," I would run interference for him if his deal went bad. It was funny, watching this English fop doing business in rat-infested slum cottages with ghetto boys. He was, however, just as smooth as he was on *The Thin Man,* so I suppose Peter wasn't as bad an actor as everyone said.

I also sat, or babysat, him many times when he got high. He talked about sex, about celebrity body parts, almost as much as his brother-in-law. To Jack's delight, Peter had actually *been* with some of the stars he described, hence tales of Lana Turner's perfect breasts, Judy Garland's perfect blow jobs, Judy Holliday's perfect ass, before she got fat. For all his stars, however, Peter said flat-out that he preferred whores. I can see how he and JFK bonded, over pussy. Peter had a special thing for black girls, not mulattos like Lena Horne but jet-black pure African types, who were not seen on the silver screen in those days nor were readily available through Hollywood madams. It was often back to Watts for this sex safari, and again, I was Peter's guide to the jungle. Call me Bwana. Sometimes Peter would get paranoid that I would "rat him out" to Mr. S. I wasn't that stupid. For Mr. S hookers were a way of life, but drugs were a guaranteed way of death. My job was to keep Mr. S's friends happy, not to pass judgment, and never, ever to spy. In all my years with him, Frank Sinatra never once asked me any gossipy questions about guests of his I was supposedly looking after, other than Ava Gardner. And that wasn't really gossip, that was endless love. Even though Peter would have a catty remark about everybody, he never spoke ill either about any

Kennedy or about Mr. S. I guess he was smart enough to know where his bread was buttered.

On the subject of hookers, on his visits to Palm Springs, Joe Kennedy, who expected to be serviced *gratis* courtesy of his host, took a liking to one of Mr. S's favorite call girls of the time, a wholesomely suburban Irish Catholic dark beauty named Judy Campbell. She was the perfect Eisenhower era pinup of the girl next door. That she charged for her wholesomeness was beside the point. Money was incidental to Mr. S and friends. Judy would go on to American infamy as the fourth corner of a quadrangle that included Sinatra, Giancana, and JFK. But before the son took a bite of this poison apple, the father was there first. Talk about chips off the old block. In her memoirs, Judy Campbell was one lady who did protest way too much. She insisted that she never took a penny from either JFK or Mr. Sam, that she traveled to Washington, Chicago, Vegas, Miami, wherever they were, planes, trains, luxury hotels, all at her own expense, because she *cared* so much about them. Barbara Hutton or Doris Duke could have barely afforded Judy's travel bills. No, Judy was a major player. What made her so special is that she was a brilliant actress in not seeming in any way like what she really was.

Frank Sinatra had a terrible weakness for sweet Irish rose, convent-school types. I think those were the girls from the right side of the tracks in Hoboken who would never stoop to Italian hoods like he was thrown in with. Mia Farrow was precisely the type, minus the right amount of skin on her bones. Ava Gardner was a voluptuous, glamorized version of the type, too. She had Scotch-Irish blood, and would have been raised in her father's Catholicism had the local Carolina bigots not equated "papists," as the Catholics were reviled, with blacks and Jews on their hate parade. How did Judy Campbell go from the convent to Sinatra's den of iniquity? It wasn't that unusual. Although she was in her early twenties, she was running from a bad marriage to a failed actor (What else is new in L.A.?) and, before that had run from a broken family that used to have some money, had given her the taste for the good life, and then lost it. So, as with so many other newly poor, downwardly mobile girls next door in a city that makes you crazy for all the material goodies you can't afford, Judy found herself a secret-agent madam and began turning some discreet tricks. If there was a new trickster on the block, Jimmy Van Heusen would sniff her out. That's how she got to Mr. S.

Aside from her looks, which combined a little Liz Taylor with a little Jackie Kennedy (a little Jackie would be a dangerous thing, as we would soon see), Judy had grown up in New Jersey and had thwarted dreams of being a singer. She knew all Frank's songs, and she knew a lot more about music than the typical call girl. Mr. S liked to *talk* to his hookers, and Judy spoke his language. He may have been one of the best johns in history, because he treated his whores like ladies. I'd feed them, buy gifts for them on his orders, pick them up, drive them home, take care of the money for him (a top girl would get a hundred dollars a night back then). And, if they were good, and Judy was supposed to be very good, he'd invite them back and pass them through to his special friends. It was like a hot tip on an undiscovered restaurant or hidden resort. I may have given the money, typically inside a Hallmark "thank you" greeting card, to Judy at the beginning, but once she graduated to the inner circle, she stopped charging Frank as a commission for the introductions. Sometimes Mr. S would treat his call girls so well that they forgot, as they would love to forget, how they met him to begin with. Judy may have been that way at first. But when she started making the rounds, to Eddie Fisher, and Sammy Davis, and "Cheap Pete" Lawford, who I'm sure was the one guy who got away without paying, then Mr. Ambassador and Mr. Sam and Mr. President, she knew damn well that she was not the innocent "good-time girl" she later pretended to have been at the time.

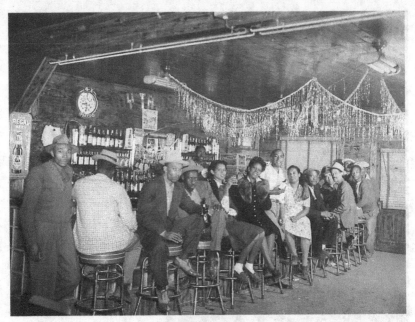

Joy Tavern, New Orleans. My father's bar and my introduction to our version of "showbiz." *(Courtesy of George Jacobs)*

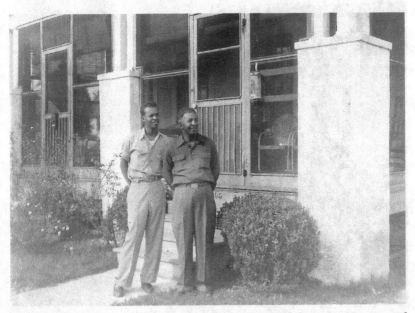

My father, George Jacobs, Sr., and I just before I joined the navy. *(Courtesy of George Jacobs)*

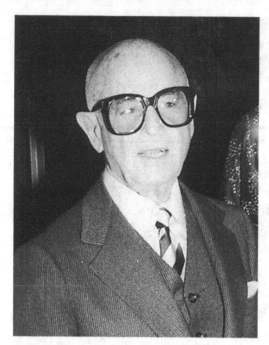

Irving "Swifty" Lazar, superagent and the biggest snob in Hollywood. Working for him made me the "hottest" valet in town. *(Photofest)*

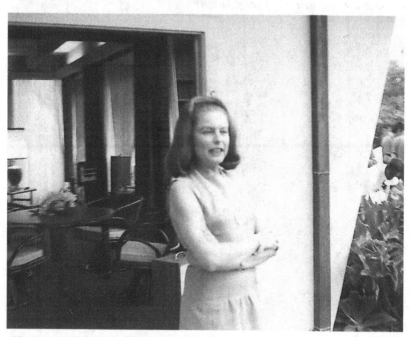

Gloria Lovell, Mr. S's devoted secretary who helped him "steal" me from Lazar. *(Courtesy of George Jacobs)*

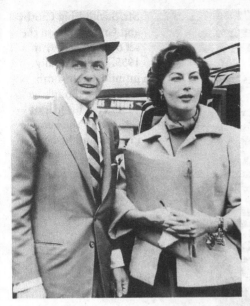

Mr. S and Ava Gardner, the unrequited love of his life, just about the time I went to work for him in 1953. The highs of his comeback didn't outweigh the lows of his failure to get *her* to come back. *(Photofest)*

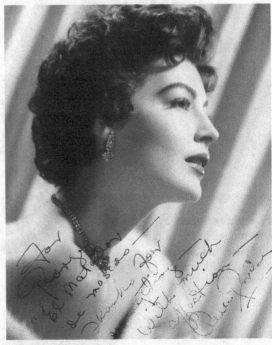

Ava. I could barely control myself when we spent our first weekend alone in Palm Springs. Her dedication to me as "El Matador de Moscas (flies)" is a tribute to my dead aim with a flyswatter. *(Courtesy of George Jacobs)*

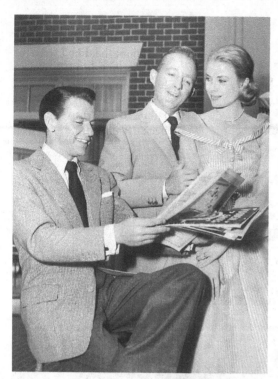

Mr. S with Bing Crosby and Grace Kelly on the set of *High Society* in 1955. He was totally intimidated by both superstars, though he conquered his fear of Grace after she became Princess and he became Chairman. *(Photofest)*

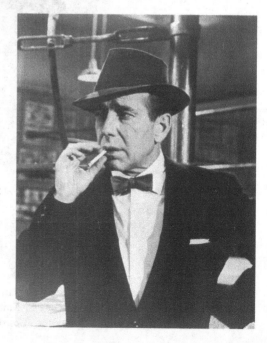

Humphrey Bogart, Mr. S's role model, in the tough-guy pose that Sinatra most admired. *(Photofest)*

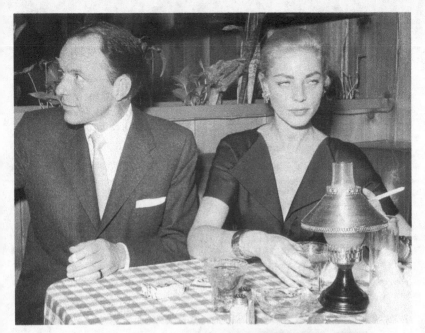

Mr. S and Lauren Bacall, during their "romance" after Bogart died in 1957. You can see that it wasn't working. *(Photofest)*

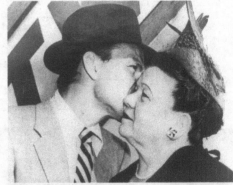

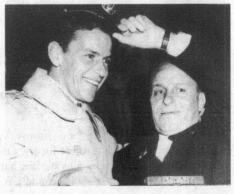

Marty and Dolly Sinatra. Mr. S's parents couldn't have been more different: Marty was the quiet ex-prizefighting fireman, Dolly the ebullient politician. Dolly called me her "Jigcilian," for black Sicilian. *(Photofest)*

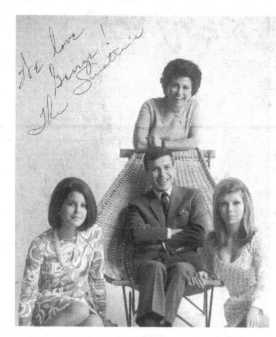

The Sinatra clan (clockwise from top): Big Nancy; Little Nancy; Frank, Jr.; Tina. There were times when I saw more of them than Mr. S did. *(Courtesy of George Jacobs)*

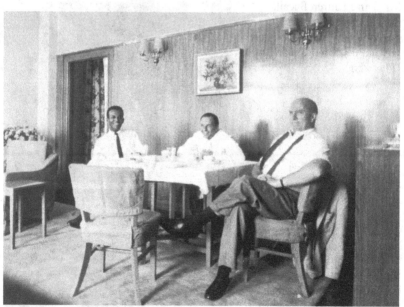

On the road with Mr. S and Jimmy Van Heusen. Van Heusen was indispensable to Sinatra not just for the Oscar-winning tunes he wrote for him but equally for the gorgeous starlets, harlots, and stewardesses he would round up for Mr. S's all-night bacchanals. *(Courtesy of George Jacobs)*

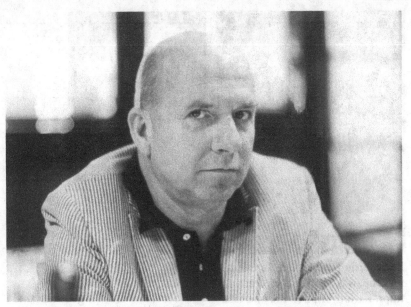

Up close with Jimmy Van Heusen. *(Courtesy of George Jacobs)*

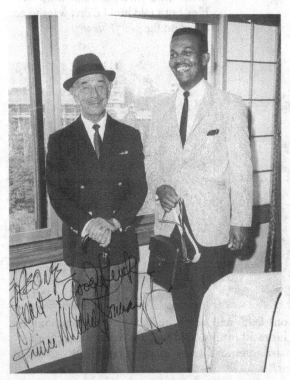

The Prince and I. With Mike Romanoff, famed restaurateur to the stars and probably the world's biggest con man. Mr. S adored him. *(Courtesy of George Jacobs)*

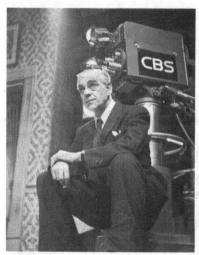

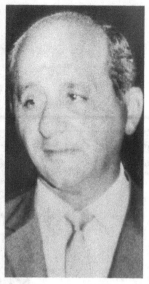

Boris Karloff, out of *Frankenstein* makeup, was Mr. S's revered acting tutor. Karloff inspired the one-take approach that made Sinatra the bane of directors. *(Photofest)*

Sam Giancana, Chicago godfather and Sinatra father figure. "Mr. Sam" begged me to leave Mr. S and come work for him, but I told him I didn't want to get killed on the job. *(Photofest)*

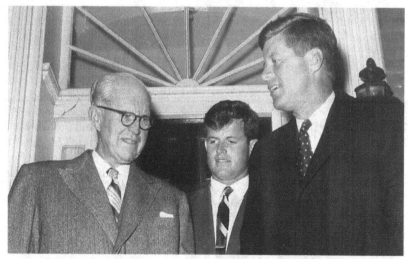

Joseph Kennedy, with sons Teddy and Jack. With his Harvard pretentions, his gangster brutality, and his racist insults, "Old Joe" was by far the unpleasant-est character in the Sinatra entourage. I was amazed that JFK turned out as nice as he did. *(Photofest)*

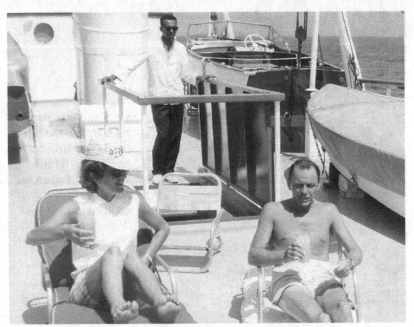

Standing by on the Sinatra yacht for Mr. S and Patricia Kennedy Lawford. She was one woman I thought Mr. S wanted to marry. *(Courtesy of George Jacobs)*

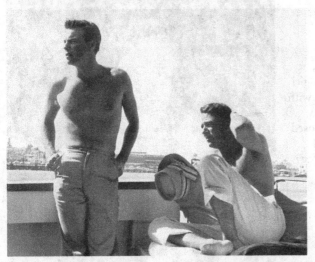

Hollywood Adonises: Robert Wagner and Peter Lawford. Wagner was one Hollywood "newcomer" Mr. S happily embraced. He only embraced Lawford after the Kennedys did. When the Kennedys dumped Mr. S, Lawford got the brunt of his rage. *(Courtesy of George Jacobs)*

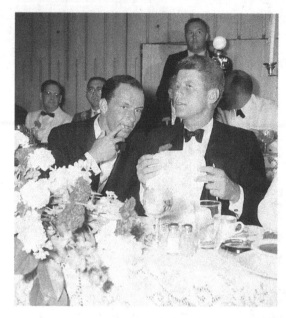

Mr. S and JFK. Putting his man into the White House was Sinatra's finest hour. It broke Mr. S's heart when the Kennedys turned against him. *(Photofest)*

Judith Campbell, Hollywood party girl who shared beds with Sinatra, Giancana, and JFK and exposed the underbelly of Camelot. *(Photofest)*

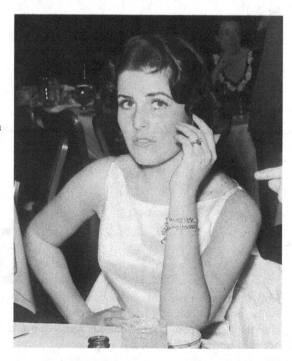

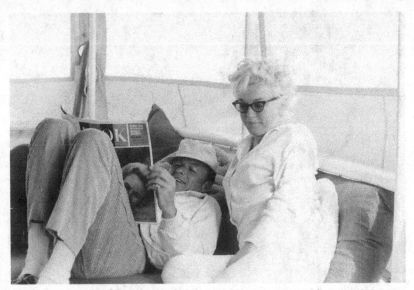

Mr. S and Marilyn Monroe. This is the girl Dolly wanted her son to marry, but Mr. S was too much of a neat freak to put up with Marilyn's nasty habits. He loved her, though, and blamed the Kennedys for her death, though Mr. S's onetime friend Joe DiMaggio blamed Sinatra as well. *(Courtesy of George Jacobs)*

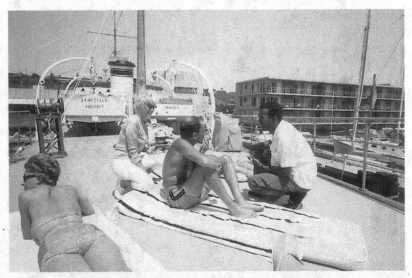

In the California sun with Mr. S and Marilyn. I was the "boy next door" to Marilyn in an apartment complex owned by Mr. S. She lived by night; it was very rare to get her outside during daylight. *(Courtesy of George Jacobs)*

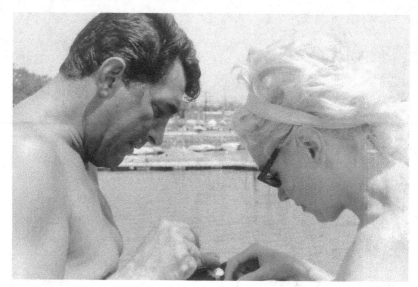

Dean Martin and Marilyn. Contrary to Rat Pack lore, aside from movies and shows, Mr. S and Dean rarely hung out together. A family man and obsessive golfer, Dean went to bed far too early for Sinatra. *(Courtesy of George Jacobs)*

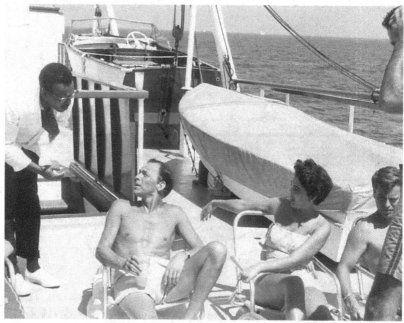

At sea with the Chairman. Mr. S hated going fishing; he preferred shooting fish with his Smith & Wesson .38. *(Courtesy of George Jacobs)*

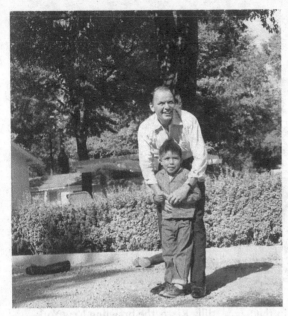

Mr. S with my son Gregory. It wasn't all movie stars, mobsters, and politicians. Sinatra treated me and my family as if we were part of his. *(Courtesy of George Jacobs)*

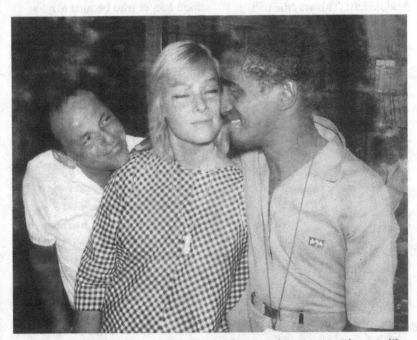

Mr. S, May Britt, and Sammy Davis, Jr. Mr. S treated Sammy much more like a son than he did Frank, Jr. I had a running joke with Sammy that I was a more authentic black Jew than he was. *(Courtesy of George Jacobs)*

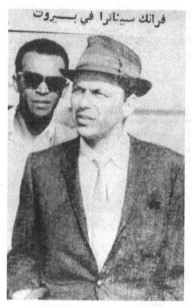

فرانك سيناترا في بيروت

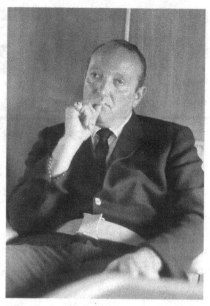

Holy Land. Mr. S and I in the Middle East. This was the trip when he got me bar mitzvahed in Israel. *(Photographer unknown)*

Jilly Rizzo, the brawling New York saloon keeper who became Mr. S's closest companion. *(Courtesy of George Jacobs)*

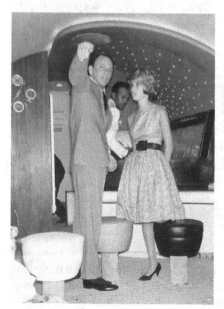

Backstage with the Chairman and pianist Bill Miller. *(Photograph by Timothy Galfas)*

Jet set. On the *El Dago* with Mr. S and Little Nancy. In an early bow to political correctness, we changed the name of the plane to *Christina*. *(Courtesy of George Jacobs)*

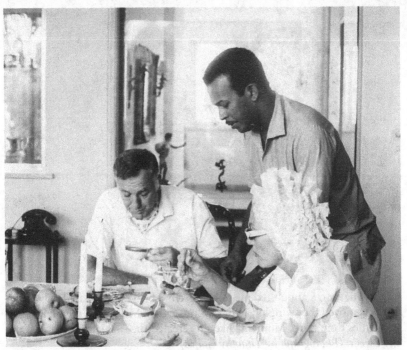

Breakfast with Jack Entratter, who ran the Sands in Vegas, and Honey Rizzo, Jilly's wife. Entratter was Mr. S's closest ally in the nightclub business until Sinatra got his teeth knocked out at the Sands by one of Entratter's lieutenants. *(Courtesy of George Jacobs)*

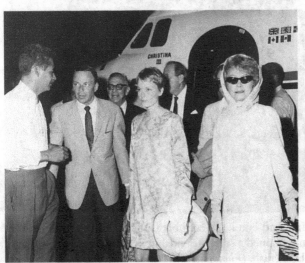

A-list. The new Sinatras, with Mia's biggest champions Bill (in glasses) and Edie Goetz (in sunglasses). The daughter of Louis B. Mayer, Edie was Hollywood's queen bee social arbiter. *(Courtesy of George Jacobs)*

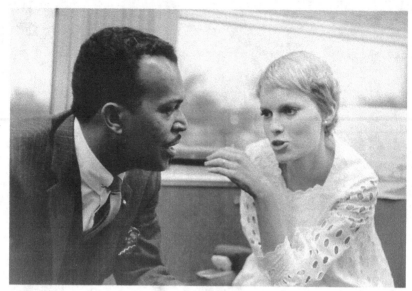

Me 'n' Mia. Mr. S appointed me to be his child bride's designated babysitter, but we enjoyed the swinging sixties far more than Mr. S, who seemed locked in a fifties time warp. Moments like this created the suspicions that cost me my career. *(Photograph by Timothy Galfas)*

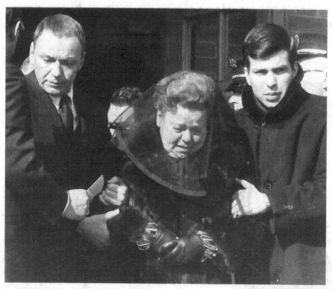

A very bad year. Mr. S and Frank, Jr., comfort Dolly after Marty's funeral in 1969. Dolly and I maintained a secret friendship in Palm Springs until her tragic death in a plane crash. *(Photofest)*

Given that Old Joe had had a long, famous affair with Gloria Swanson and that Young Jack would have a short, famous one with Marilyn Monroe, as well as flings with other stars, I was surprised that either guy would have bothered for more than a session or two with Judy Campbell. But I guess the Irish boys liked coming home to roost. Mr. Sam's "official" girlfriend, singer Phyllis McGuire, was a similar wholesome type. Her father was a minister in Ohio. Phyllis, who with her sisters had the huge hit "Sugartime," was definitely a girl-next-door type in the Judy mold, though according to Sammy Cahn, who had the best way with words of all the Sinatra friends, Judy's mold was penicillin.

As much as I disliked his father, that's how much I was crazy about John Fitzgerald Kennedy. He was handsome and funny and naughty and as irreverent as Dean Martin. "What do colored people want, George?" he asked me the first time he visited Palm Springs, not long after Mr. S and Peter Lawford became bosom buddies.

"I don't know, Mr. Senator."

"Jack, George. Jack."

"What do *you* want? Jack?" I asked.

"I want to fuck every woman in Hollywood," he said with a big leering grin.

"With a campaign promise like that you can't lose, sir."

"You're my man. Jack."

"No, it's George, sir."

"Who's on third?"

"Pardon me, sir?

"Jack, goddamn it. Call me Jack. Or I'll send you back to Mississippi."

"Louisiana, Jack. They eat Catholics in Mississippi. They hate you worse than me."

And that was the way we'd go on, giving each other shit all the time, no master-servant games. He and Mr. S got along great. They had everything in common, charisma, talent, power. They were about the same age, but JFK seemed much younger. He was handsomer, sportier, wittier, vastly more cultured. After all, like his dad, he was a Harvard Man. *And* a war hero. *And* a Pulitzer Prize-winning author. *And* a senator. Mr. S, dropout 4-F Hoboken Man that he was, stood in awe of JFK and his Ivy slickness, his heroics, his national acclaim. Yet JFK was far more in awe of Mr. S than Mr. S was of him. Because Frank Sinatra controlled the one thing JFK wanted more than anything else: Pussy! Mr. S was the Pope of Pussy, and JFK was honored to kiss his ring. The pontiff could bestow a Judy Campbell, or, if he was feeling magnanimous, he could bestow a Marilyn Monroe, such was his beneficence. Marilyn was actually Mr. S's celebrity version of Judy. He had brokered assignations not only between her and JFK, but also Giancana and Johnny Rosselli. I saw father Joe pinch her ass many times, but that may have been as far as it went, though with Marilyn it was hard to tell. She was the ultimate Girl Who Can't Say No. In view of a deeply unloved childhood, if a man showed interest (it was rarely mere interest; it was usually rabid passion) she was so flattered that she thought it would be terribly rude to turn him down. Marilyn was nothing if not polite. So here was Mr. S, the big Hollywood matchmaker, the Hello Dolly of Sunset Boulevard. As far as he was concerned, he was just as happy to fix his friends up with the girls of Hollywood than have them himself. It was a case of been there, fucked that. Ironically, while Jack Kennedy had his horny eyes on Mr. S's girls, Mr. S had his ambitious eyes on Jack's sister Pat. He felt it was a matter of time until she and Uncle Scrooge Lawford would self-destruct.

"Do you find Pat attractive, George?" Mr. S asked me.

"She's a lovely lady, Mr. S."

"Are you saying she's a dog, George?"

"No way, Mr. S. How can a Kennedy be a dog?"

"Be honest, George. Don't shit me."

"If she wore some makeup, did her hair . . ."

"You wouldn't fuck her, would you, George?"

"I'm a married man, Mr. S."

"I suppose you wouldn't fuck Gina [Lollobrigida] either?" Mr. S gave me a gotcha smirk.

"What do you want from Pat, Mr. S? She's crazy about you."

"That's the rub, George."

I couldn't believe Mr. S was asking my opinion of Pat, but sometimes he would if he was totally confused about a situation. Pat was an outdoor girl, a far less pretty version of Rocky Cooper. Sports were her thing, a Kennedy thing, but somehow I didn't see Mr. S playing touch football in Hyannisport.

I don't think Jack had a clue about Frank's potential interest in his sister. Jack didn't worry about things like that. For all his charm, he was one of the most self-centered guys I had met. He focused on what was essential to him. That, I suppose, is how he got the job done. I am, however, fairly amazed he got anything done politically, given his endless obsession with sex and gossip. In the latter category, he was like the women at the beauty salon. He wanted to know all the Hollywood dirt, who was a drunk, who was a junkie, who had black lovers, all that jazz. Maybe it was because being with Sinatra was a holiday for him that he showed so little enthusiasm for politics. I would ask him about Castro or Khrushchev, but he wanted to know if Janet Leigh was cheating on Tony Curtis or what was going on with Eddie and Debbie. He read every issue of *Confidential* magazine. To him, that scandal sheet was a lot better than *Foreign Affairs*. He would have been a terrific talk show host, with all his *Entertainment Tonight*-type questions. But the world wasn't ready for prime time dirt. Instead he became president.

Aside from gossip and scandal, JFK was obsessed with Mr. S's love life, past and present. Because Mr. S wasn't a kiss-and-teller, JFK figured he could get the real skinny out of me. He loved massages when we talked, and he claimed I gave the best rubdowns outside of the Senate gym. JFK did live with enormous pain. He wore a kind of stiff girdle to support his bad back, which must have been hell to get in and out of for all the quickies he was supposed to have gotten. I would work on his back for a good hour, all the while being peppered with prurient questions about his favorite topic, celebrity "poontang," as he liked to call it.

"George, does Shirley MacLaine have a red pussy?"

"I've never seen her pussy, Jack."

"Come on. Isn't she here [Palm Springs] all the time?"

"She's never here. Why would she be here?" I asked JFK.

"To fuck your boss."

"They're not doing anything."

"Can't be. They were in *Some Came Running*, they've got *Can-Can*," JFK puzzled, trying to figure it out.

"It's not happening, Senator. No red puss from Old Shirl."

"Then why in blazes did he cast her, for Dean?"

"Her acting, Jack."

JFK roared. "You kill me, George. George, tell me something."

"What?" I asked.

"If she's not doing Frank, and she's not doing Dean, who *is* she doing? Korshak?"

"Maybe she's doing herself, Senator."

"I like that, George. I like those legs of hers, don't you?"

"They are good, yes sir."

"As good as Cyd Charisse's?"

"Never saw them up close, Jack."

"What about Dietrich?"

"Hard to beat, even now," I answered.

"She stroked my dick once, George."

"Good for you, man."

"It was in the South of France. Hotel du Cap. I was visiting my father for the summer from boarding school. I think she may have been fucking him. He may have put her up to it."

"Where did she do it, Senator?"

"The whole thing. Up and down . . ."

"I mean, in your room, the pool?"

"Grand ballroom. I think it was Cole Porter. Begin the Beguine. It was dark and hot, lots of candles. She smelled like a French whore, George, this terrific perfume. She was leading me, holding me so tight and then she slipped her hand down my trousers," JFK was getting into some heavy nostalgia. "Can you imagine what that was like for a goddamn teenager?"

By the time I rolled him over to do his trunk and thighs he had an enormous erection. He turned beet red, but he didn't ask me to stop, or to stop talking. "We better get you laid, Jack."

"You darn well better," he insisted. "There's something about this desert air."

Even after John F. Kennedy declared for the Democratic presidential nomination I never heard him talk about government or the plans for his New Frontier. I didn't expect him to talk this stuff with me, except maybe as an ear to the black community, of which I was not really a part. I did, however, assume that he and Mr. S would have a lot of politics to talk about. After all, Mr. S did have that framed and signed photo of FDR in a place of honor on the wall, and I figured that once he agreed to board the Kennedy campaign train, he would get deeply versed in politics. But, no. Here Mr. S was with the man who was en route to becoming the great leader of our time and what do I hear them talk about? Juliet Prowse's shaved *mons veneris,* what we now call a bikini wax. A lot of dancers and showgirls were shaved, but few normal women were, and JFK was intrigued by the whole thing, pushing Mr. S to arrange for him to meet some dancers, for the sake "of scientific curiosity," as the senator put it. "Naked lunch," was what he said he wanted. Mr. S didn't get the joke. JFK had to explain his reference to the title of the hip heroin novel by William Burroughs. Mr. S said he'd never heard of it. Why the hell would a guy like the senator be reading about heroin? Sometimes Mr. S could be incredibly funny, usually at someone else's expense, and sometimes he could be square as a Dubuque Rotarian. Where the pop culture was concerned, if *he* himself wasn't the culture, he didn't want to know about it.

The other thing he didn't want to know about was JFK's drug use. On several occasions in Palm Springs I was there when Peter Lawford and the future president did lines of cocaine together in Lawford's guest room. The first time it happened Jack must have seen the shocked look on my face. "For my back, George," Kennedy said to me, with his bad-boy wink. Peter was more direct. "For God's sake, George, don't tell Frank," he beseeched me with a serious look. But to his brother-in-law, it was all one big lark. "National security," he added, laughing, then offered me a line. Just as I kept the secret from Mr. S about Peter's drug obsession, I wasn't about to break the bad news about Jack, whom Mr. S put on such a pedestal. Sex and alcohol may have made Jack a better man in Sinatra's sight. Cocaine was a different story. The leader of the free world with his finger on the trigger and a straw up his nose? It was an image that I didn't want to contemplate.

While Mr. S and JFK kept their dialogue to affairs of the flesh, whenever Sinatra was with Sam Giancana, their former long sessions on the casino business now gave way to talk about politics, handicapping the odds whether Kennedy could beat Nixon, and whether or not it was a good idea. Mr. Sam preferred Nixon. He would have preferred Harold Stassen, because he had a blood rage against Bobby Kennedy. Even though Sam and Joe were brothers under the skin who had done big deals together, Sam now distrusted Joe as having come too far from his roots, of getting "uppity," as Sam called it. With Joe there may have been distrust; with Bobby there was dead certainty. "Bobby's the fruit that poisons the whole tree," Sam summarized his deep misgivings. Sinatra did his best to pacify the Chi Man, to assure him the nasty little brother was chump change. "Jack's the candidate, not the weasel," Mr. S hard-sold the kingpin. "Jack's our friend." I am certain, however, that had Mr. Sam not given Mr. S his blessing, Mr. S and company would have never devoted most of 1960 to getting the Kennedys their impossible dream. But given how much Mr. Sam distrusted Bobby, he had to have expected some serious tit for tat.

The first tangible token of Mr. Ambassador's gratitude was the Cal-Neva Lodge, a rustic wigwam-inspired fishing-gaming retreat straddling the state line on the shores of Lake Tahoe. The Kennedys had been coming to this Alpine paradise since the Roaring Twenties. Every year, the lodge would cut and ship the Kennedys the Christmas trees for their assorted compounds. Because of its unique situation halfway in anything-goes Nevada, the lodge had been a haven for gangsters from its earliest days. Pretty Boy Floyd, Baby Face Nelson, and other bullet-ridden legends had played there. The Kennedys loved the place. So did Sam Giancana. For the Kennedys, it was a kind of Western White House before they took power. For Giancana, it was also a Western White House, or big house, to use prison jargon. There were secret underground passages, endless safe rooms, private cabins in the deep woods that made it an ideal hideaway and getaway.

In the late fifties the nominal owner of the lodge was "Miami hotelier" (short for Meyer Lansky lieutenant) Wingy (because of his missing arm, perfect name for a slot machine guy) Grober. Mr. S liked Wingy, who cozied up to the Sinatra crowd by bringing out Sinatra's dear friend Skinny D'Amato from Atlantic City to run the place. Wingy was just a front man for the ambassador, Mr. S said. In 1960, before the election, Grober "sold" a half interest in the lodge, for hundreds of thousands of dollars, a fortune back then, to a consortium of Sinatra, Dean Martin, Hank Sanicola, and Peter Lawford, who were fronting for Sam Giancana. They *had* to be fronting for Mr. Sam, because Peter Lawford never paid for *anything*, except drugs, with his own cash. However they got it, Mr. S and his guys now had a piece of the rock, Joe Kennedy's rock. At last Sinatra was in business with big business, and he hoped this was just the beginning.

The Rat Pack was how the public came to know the crew that made *Ocean's 11* based at the Sands in 1960. The real name the guys used for themselves was the Clan, but that sounded like the Ku Klux Klan, and Jack Kennedy already had enough problems in the South being a Catholic that he didn't need this rainbow coalition of showbiz minorities giving themselves an inflammatory name. They were inflammatory enough on their own. That was the point, to use these hip Hollywood Unsquares to play at being cool mob/Vegas types and get a young and changing America to vote for JFK and against the ultimate square Dick Nixon. If the whole *Ocean's 11* experience was something of a subliminal long liquor ad, the famous Vegas shows at night during the filming were an equally subliminal, and frequently direct, plug for the Kennedy campaign, as key to JFK's image as the Broadway musical *Camelot*. You didn't see Nixon at the Sands, but Kennedy was right there at the A table, for the country to ogle. The way the Rat Pack was utilized to sell the president, including the Sinatra-sung, Cahn and Van Heusen-written campaign song "High Hopes," was all the brainchild of the Godfather father, Mr. Ambassador. He was evil, but he was a strategic genius. He had fucked up on Hitler and was going to make up for it now.

Dean Martin had nothing but contempt for Joe Kennedy. Dean

was totally apolitical, and, because he knew about JFK's bad habits, he thought that any country that had to choose between Kennedy and Nixon was in bad shape. He resented being used as a Democratic shill, but, pro that he was, he did his shows, he shot his scenes, and then he golfed. Not that Dean was a saint. Despite his big and happy family, he loved the whores as much as Mr. S. He just loved them for a shorter time, so he could get to bed and get up early to be on the links. If Mr. S was respected and feared in Vegas, Dean Martin was *adored*. Whenever he came to town to do a show, before or after *Ocean's 11*, the showgirls and cocktail waitresses at the Sands would have a lottery to see what lucky lady would have the honor of giving Dean his welcome-back blow job.

The Sands girls that Mr. S fancied fell into two extreme categories. The first were the most drop-dead gorgeous showgirls, the newest of whom would be dispatched to the Sinatra suite by Jack Entratter at four A.M. after the show as an on-the-house "nitecap" for Mr. S, who, it must be remembered, was a significant shareholder in the Sands, and not just a VIP. These beauties worked for him, and they were plenty afraid of their temperamental boss, who might have them fired if he didn't like the way they did their hair or wore their costume. That was Frank the Tyrant. The other category of Sands girl who appealed to the *other* Frank, Frank the Samaritan, was the sweet and needy cocktail waitress, the one with the sick baby or the troubled marriage. Mr. S got an erotic charge in rescuing a damsel in distress. The affair might not have lasted long, but the gratitude did. He paid the college tuition of several of the coffee shop girls, and the medical bills of many more. Moreover, as he strode through his domain, if he ever heard a customer abuse a waitress, he would be down the lout's throat in a split second. "Get this bastard off *my* property!" the Chairman would declare. At the Sands, the customer wasn't always right, not if he happened to cross swords with the Main Event.

During the Kennedy campaign, I had never seen Mr. S happier since I began to work for him. He was in even better spirits than when he won the Oscar. Now he had a purpose, a higher purpose than Hollywood stardom. "We're gonna take this mother, George," he'd say constantly, as if he were going to win one for the Gipper. Except that the Gipper here was no saintly Knute Rockne, but the devil himself, Joe Kennedy. Despite JFK's decadent playboy indulgences, I never sensed that Sinatra was personally troubled in any way by the character of "his leader." Nor did he seem repulsed by the repulsive behavior of his leader's father. That is, not before two occasions during the run for Washington when Old Joe made Mr. S feel lower than Lew Wasserman or Sam Spiegel ever had.

The first was when he was trying to put a movie together based on the book *The Execution of Private Slovik,* about a soldier who was executed by the U.S. Army for desertion. Mr. S was planning to direct it, his first effort behind the camera. It was a total downer, but, as Mr. S put it, "You don't win Oscars for comedies." He still really wanted that Oscar. He hadn't given up on being taken seriously as a filmmaker, and he knew that *Ocean's 11* wasn't going to do it for him. *Ocean's* was for the Kennedys, the campaign. *Slovik* would be for him. But he made a fatal mistake. In trying to get a great script, he hired an old friend he thought was a great writer, Albert Maltz, who had scripted such films as *This Gun for Hire* and was known as a master of "message" movies. Unfortunately, Maltz was better known as one of the Hollywood Ten. Blacklisted in the McCarthy witch-hunts as a "Red," Maltz had fled to Mexico. He had not had a screen credit, at least not under his own name, for years. Mr. S was giving him a chance at a comeback. That was something Mr. S loved to do.

But not Joe Kennedy. Sinatra's movie plans hit all the papers, and Joe freaked out over what he read. "What is this commie Jew shit?

You stupid guinea!" the ambassador unloaded on the Chairman over the phone, and Mr. S took it. Of course this was after half the country had been whipped up into a red scare by the press over the issue. In Hollywood, John Wayne had come out against poor Maltz. Mr. S had told the press to fuck themselves, he told the Duke to fuck himself, took out ads in the trade papers asserting his right to free speech, his right to make his own movies. But he didn't say fuck you to Old Joe. He said, "Yes, sir." And that was it. This shows that politics were more important to Mr. S at this point than Hollywood. If winning an election meant dropping a film, so be it. JFK was considered left enough, compared to Nixon. Mr. S justified dropping Maltz (he paid him in full) and the project on the grounds of helping Jack, but it still killed him to have to eat Joe's humble pie and give up his own dream. He went on a three-day Jack Daniel's binge and totally destroyed his office at the Bowmont house. "Who gives a shit? I'm outta this fucking business!" he screamed, ripping up books and scripts, hurling over bookcases. This time I felt his rage and frustration were understandable.

Although Mr. S would never talk back to Joe Kennedy, he soon vented his spleen on Teddy Kennedy, who showed up at a campaign appearance in Honolulu with three of the cheesiest-looking bimbos. You couldn't find junkie hookers this low in the worst part of Times Square, but somehow Teddy had dug deeper and hit paydirt. Even if they weren't hookers, they *looked* like hookers. Mr. S had a strong sense of decorum. He was outraged that Teddy could do something that would make his brother look bad. But I think he was really reacting to Joe's abuse of him. If he had to fire Albert Maltz for the sake of appearances, he wasn't going to let this big spoiled drunken Harvard brat get away with a far worse appearance. So he reamed Teddy out, cursing him at the top of his lungs, right in the hotel suite in front of dozens of high-level campaign workers and donors. Teddy got scared and disappeared. I think he flew back to the mainland that night. And Teddy gave Mr. S a wide, wide berth after that.

The second time Joe Kennedy rained on Mr. S's parade was at the biggest party Mr. S ever threw, the inaugural party for John F. Kennedy in January 1961. Mr. S was so crazed then that he had forgotten his specially made striped tuxedo pants that were to go with his big-night outfit, which included a cape. I told him he looked like Dracula. "Shut up, or I'll bite your neck," he gave it back to me. I was with him in D.C. when he discovered that he had packed the wrong pants. He could have blamed me, but he knew he had done the packing of this precious costume. I had to fly back to L.A. in a massive snowstorm to get the right pants, then fly back the same night into the same snowstorm. Friendly skies, my ass.

Nothing, however, got Mr. S more crazed than Old Joe's edict that Sammy not be allowed to perform at the inaugural. Sammy was the ambassador's sum of all fears. He was black, he was Jewish, he was married to a blond Aryan, he was a superstar. That drove Old Joe crazy, that Sammy had beaten all the odds. But he wasn't going to beat *Joe's* odds. Joe had absolutely no gratitude for the indefatigable campaigning Sammy had done for Jack as a key pillar of the Rat Pack. To him Sammy was just a pushy nigger who could only give his son a worse name in the throwback places like the South where he already had a bad one. Sammy had had to eat a lot of shit during the campaign, jokes like was he going to be JFK's ambassador to Israel or to the Congo. He also had postponed his wedding to Swedish goddess/star May Britt until after the election, so as not to turn off voters at the last minute. This was done by Sammy as a huge favor to Mr. S, who was to be Sammy's best man at the Jewish ceremony, which took place in mid-November, once the White House was in Jack's bag.

Mr. S had asked me to counsel Sammy about being married to a Scandinavian, but Sammy had dated more blonds than I could dream of. All I could do was to say how well my own marriage was going (a big lie at the time) and how indifferent Nordic people were to color (and to everything else, which was one of my big problems, though I didn't share this, either). Sammy didn't need my wisdom. He did need Mr. S's approval. Desperately. So it was brutal when Old Joe put his jackboot down on Sinatra's fingers one more time and, in a dictatorial telephone conversation with Mr. S, barred Sammy from this Show of Shows, a cavalcade of America's greatest talent. If anybody belonged in the program, front and center, it was Sammy. Mr. S begged him, but Joe said No. Ella Fitzgerald was okay, so was Mahalia Jackson, Harry Belafonte, Nat King Cole. But to Joe, they were "nigger niggers." They knew their place. They kept in their place. But "the nigger bastard with the German whore," as the presidential patriarch referred to America's most controversial "fun couple," that was beyond the beyond. Not at his son's debutant ball for the world to see. At the pinnacle of his new power, the master of ceremonies of the coming out of the New Frontier, Mr. S, in all his glory, could only see an Ugly Past, of the bigotry, prejudice, and elitism that, minus a few breaks, could have mired him forever in the slums of Hoboken. He looked like the King of the World, but all he could taste were ashes. It was a foretaste of worse, far worse, to come.

6

Flirting with Disaster

MR. S's philosophy was that bad things only happened to good people. If someone was bad enough, he somehow had a natural immunity to disaster, at least in this lifetime, which is the only one Mr. S could count on. There was no day of reckoning for the bad guys. The meek would inherit nothing, and Sam Spiegel and Lew Wasserman would live forever. Thus it was a terrible shock to Mr. S's system when the baddest guy of all, the guy who had taken all the marbles, his way, was felled by a massive stroke on the golf course in Palm Beach. It was 1961. Old Joe would live another eight years, but he would never speak again. Mr. Ambassador had become a vegetable. Mr. S found out from Peter Lawford by phone. He was shocked, as I said, but he wasn't sad. He was just amazed, for he thought Joe Kennedy was beyond the long arm of God. He called the president with his condolences, sent flowers to the hospital in Palm Beach, but he didn't go to visit. Yet in time, a short time, he would come to regret the incapacity of Joe Kennedy. Without the dictatorial restraint of his father, little Bobby, "the weasel" as Mr. S contemptuously referred to him, was now free to unleash the rabid contempt he had for Mr. S.

Bobby wasn't the only Kennedy who didn't approve of Frank Sinatra. Jackie couldn't stand him. She hated him without really knowing him, refusing to visit Palm Springs out of hand, though I'm sure Jack was relieved, so he could have his fun. Jack hardly ever mentioned Jackie to me, except in regard to big family gatherings. She was pretty much a ceremonial figure to him. Jackie's dislike of Frank may have been on account of her natural suspicions that Mr. S was leading her husband down the primrose path to perdition. Or it may have been that she believed that her own sister, Lee Radziwill, had fallen prey to the crooner's charms during the campaign. Mr. S did flirt with Lee; he might have nailed her just to get prissy Jackie's pedigreed goat, but I'm not sure if anything transpired. Sinatra was outraged by what he regarded as Jackie's anti-Italian (specifically poor Jersey Italian) prejudice, and he had a big thing against prejudice. "I'd like to fuck that bitch," he'd say whenever he'd see her on TV. Given Sinatra's innate courtliness to women, that was as nasty a comment as he could make. He'd have *never* said that about any woman he *liked*.

Jackie felt Mr. S was beneath her dignity and that of the White House; Bobby felt Mr. S was beneath the dignity of the *country*. Jackie's repulsion was that of an uptight socialite; Bobby's was that of a holier-than-thou crusader. Bobby was out to get Mr. S in a big way. He saw Frank as Al Capone, all sex and crime, and he saw himself as Cotton Mather, all fire and brimstone. His liberal, Puritan, Yankee zeal was made more poisonous by his own weakness for and attraction to the carnal pleasures of Hollywood that Mr. S embodied. There was going to be a whole lotta shakin' goin' on.

The troubles for Mr. S started even before Bobby went on the attack. The "tragic decade" that the sixties were for Sinatra actually began for him in late 1959 with the death, at forty-four, of Billie Holiday, who had been a tremendous influence on him. Mr. S didn't cry for Joe Kennedy. He didn't cry for Humphrey Bogart. He didn't cry for much. But he cried for Billie Holiday. Mr. S had tried to save her life, or at least to help her with her pain. We had been in New York, and had gone to visit her on her deathbed uptown in the run-down Harlem Metropolitan Hospital. There was a line of picketers outside with placards reading LET LADY LIVE. There was a huge controversy going on over Lady's right to take illegal narcotics in the hospital.

Lady was dying *of* cirrhosis; she was dying *for* heroin. The New York police had raided her room and found heroin in her pocketbook. The attitude of the hospital, and the law, was how can we cure this patient if she's shooting up. But Billie Holiday didn't care. She wanted her smack more than she wanted to get well. She had been on it for years, done time for it. She wasn't about to quit now. Three cops were stationed at her door when we arrived. A beautician was doing her hair and nails, and she was smoking outside her oxygen tent and begging the nurse to get her a beer. She'd say catchy things like, "Don't trust that bitch. She can take the gold outta your teeth while you're chewin' gum." While Lady's spirit was ever feisty, her body was defeated. Her once plump frame was wasted away. She was skin and bones, and barely that. The hard life that made her music so great and true had literally eaten her alive. All the booze had rotted out her insides. Still, she was thrilled to see Mr. S. He was very positive, telling her how much he loved her last year's album, *Lady in Satin*, and kept trying to get her to talk about future projects. He told her, showing her off for my benefit, how much he owed to her for teaching him how to phrase when he was starting out with Harry James. "I may have showed you how to bend a note, Frankie, that's all," Lady said. Then she leaned over to him and whispered so the cops couldn't hear, "Will you cut the shit, baby, and get me some dope?"

Lady Day begged Sinatra to get her a fix of heroin. Begged him. As much as he hated drugs, and hated what they had done to this genius of the blues, Mr. S tried to get her what she wanted. Mr. S offered money to the top doctors at the hospital, but they were terrified that Mayor Wagner, who was on a campaign to rid New York City of drugs, would cut off their funding if they got caught. He made some calls to try to get to the mayor, but struck out. Frustrated at the front door, he tried going through the back. Sinatra went out and used all his connections to find the biggest dealer in New York. He gave him a big wad of cash, and put him to the task.

But the cops were staking out Lady Day's room night and day. The dealer couldn't get through to deliver Mr. S's gift of mercy. As he was trying, Lady Day's liver failed, she went into a coma, and died. Mr. S beat himself up for letting her down. What good was all his power if he couldn't help a friend? He locked himself in the Seventy-second Street penthouse and wept for two days, playing her songs like "Autumn in New York," drinking, and crying. I had never seen him hurt so much, even for Ava, but, then again, who else could match this horrible waste? Mr. S told me something she had said, that you don't know what enough is until you've had more than enough. Now she knew, but it was too late, and it killed him a little bit as well.

Billie Holiday's death intensified the midlife vulnerability Mr. S had been starting to feel. He was forty-four, the same age as she. And she was dead. Mr. S was awash in fame and now power, but what, he asked himself, did he really have? Aside from myself, there was nobody even there to comfort him when Billie died. What about the basics of life, the stuff that mattered to a real guy, a guy like his father?

He had a family, whom he rarely saw. He had more sex than Hugh Hefner, more than Casanova, but where was the love? He hadn't been in love since Ava, but Ava was a lost cause. Most of his crew were now married. Even Sammy had bitten the dust. Now it was just him and Jimmy Van Heusen and their legions of hookers. Oh, he had plenty of dates, but he wasn't crazy about anyone, and Mr. S had to be crazy to be alive. His most recent consort was Dorothy Provine, a blond rising star on a show called *The Roaring 20s*. She was gorgeous, but not exciting. Mr. S called her "Deadwood," after her birthplace of Deadwood, South Dakota. The only woman Mr. S had any real interest in was Pat Lawford, though that was probably as much a political fantasy as it was a romantic pipe dream. After JFK was elected, the notion that she and Peter would break up proved to be nothing but wishful thinking. Although she and Peter were estranged by now, there could be no cracks in the perfect façade of America's First Family. Pat had learned about the hookers and the drugs and had retreated to her own room. But they were forced to "play house" for the world, and that house was a worse prison for Pat than it was for Peter, who was a master of façades. "Brother-in-Lawford" could have his whores, just as did Pat's father and brothers, but taking the cue from endlessly suffering Mother Rose, the unbreakable rule for the Kennedy women was Stand by Your Man.

The big problem for Mr. S was that there wasn't anybody good enough for him. Mr. S, beneath all the tough guy Jersey stuff, was as big a snob as Old Joe. He was the King. He felt he was entitled to a Queen. A sparkling commoner like Dorothy Provine, adorable as she was, didn't have the right stuff. There was someone, however, who just came back on the market after the election. She was as big as Frank, larger than life, the most famous woman in America, probably the world. And she loved Frank Sinatra with all her heart. On paper, at least, Marilyn Monroe was the perfect match for Mr. S. After the debacle of *The Misfits,* Marilyn, because of her endless takes, lateness, and fuckups on the set, was blamed for giving Clark Gable the heart attack that killed him. In turn Marilyn blamed her distress on her imperially detached husband, Arthur Miller, who, she would tell me, made her feel like "the stupidest woman in the world" and thereby destroyed the self-esteem she was seeking by marrying a genius. Marilyn divorced Miller and returned "home" to Hollywood and to Mr. S, who stepped up to the challenge that had defeated such previous champs as DiMaggio and now Miller.

While a Monroe-Sinatra match would have been a bigger royal wedding than when Grace Kelly married Prince Rainier, bigger than Mary Pickford and Douglas Fairbanks, Mr. S had a ton of misgivings about Marilyn. She was a total mess. She was usually drunk, which he could deal with. She was also usually filthy, which he couldn't. She was frequently too depressed to bathe or wash her hair, she ate in bed and slept among the crumbs and scraps, she would wear the same stained pants for days. She was too miserable to care. Furthermore, she was usually fat, twenty pounds overweight, which she would lose on mad crash diets right before starting a film, like drugging herself into a near coma for a week at a time so she wouldn't eat.

The image was glorious; the reality was squalid. Mr. S claimed he didn't even want to sleep with her. Of course, that rarely stopped him from doing it. If Marilyn Monroe wanted sex, and she did constantly to make herself feel desirable, Mr. S would play Sir Galahad and rise to the occasion. He would rarely turn a good friend down. He called them "mercy fucks," and it fit in with his *padrone* self-image to give rather than receive. Aside from Marilyn, Peggy Lee was the occasional beneficiary of Mr. S's largesse. So was Judy Garland, who, at her lowest depths, made major sexual demands on Mr. S, showing up on Bowmont Drive at all hours of the night for a shoulder to cry on and his manhood to pacify her. We wanted to rename the street

*Blow*mont. Frank had had an affair with Judy in the late forties, when she was one of the biggest stars at MGM and he was just getting started. Then she was adorable. By 1958 she was not.

Judy had just returned from a London engagement that was a sell-out triumph, except for the vicious English press attacking Judy's appearance as pudgy, dumpy, chubby, bloated, how many ways can you say fat. Judy was also having money troubles as well as hubby troubles with former test pilot turned horse-breeder/producer Sid Luft. Whenever she and Sid were separated, which was often, she would descend on Bowmont, drunk as a skunk. (Like Billie Holiday, Judy would get cirrhosis of the liver.) She wanted Mr. S to hold her, to love her, to make her feel beautiful again, and he did. Sinatra had the highest regard for Judy and her talent. She had one of the biggest personalities in the business, all charisma. That had turned Mr. S on, even if her physique hadn't. But now he loved her the way he had come to love Big Nancy. Judy, however, was not self-effacing like Nancy. She would never settle for "just friends." She had to have sex, and even when Mr. S couldn't force himself into the mood, she'd unzip his pants right on the orange couch in the den where they'd listen to records and create the mood she so desperately needed. These confidence-building sessions would continue for years, until the early sixties.

Because of Marilyn's nasty habits, such as never using sanitary napkins or tampons and bleeding all over her bed, Mr. S did not take her into the Bowmont house to live with him, as she would have liked. Instead of a ring he gave her a poodle, which she promptly named "Maf," short for Mafia, just to annoy him for not loving her enough. And instead of spending the time with her she madly desired, he dumped her on me. He put us both into an apartment house at 882 North Doheny Drive, between Sunset and Santa Monica on the border of Beverly Hills and an area then known as Boys Town, and now as West Hollywood. The building was called "The Sinatra

Arms," because in addition to Marilyn and me were Sinatra's secretary Gloria Lovell and his longtime on-off bedmate Jeannie Carmen, who became Marilyn's best girlfriend.

Mr. S would sometimes live there himself between houses and women. I was living there because after a decade of marriage, my wife Sally and I were splitting up. Given the job I had, both of us were amazed we lasted so long. I could blame the divorce on Mr. S, but I've tried not to. But the beginning of our end came just as his romance with the Kennedys started. We had kept our personal lives completely separate. I was there for him, he paid me handsomely, that was that. I wasn't trying to be part of the Clan. One weekend, however, he insisted I bring my wife and kids down to the desert. He had just bought the new compound on Wonder Palms, off the fairway of the Tamarisk Golf Club. There was lots of room, and he was one of the most generous men alive. But his eyes popped out when he met Sally. She was good-looking, in a Nordic way, but I probably had taken her for granted by then. "Hey, hey, hey, George," he said when she put on her bathing suit and got into the pool. "What the hell did you do to deserve *that*?"

"I work for you, boss," I joked. "All good things come to those who stand and wait."

"You've been holding out on me, playboy."

"I had to marry the dame to get her, Mr. S," I told the truth. "Ain't no play in this boy."

"You spooks are such fucking studs. You kill me, George."

"If all men are created equal, we have to even it out somewhere, Mr. S."

From that day on, he would insist Sally and the boys come down whenever they wanted, which turned out to be about once a month in the season. And he treated us like all the guests, inviting us to the table for dinner with the Lawfords, Van Heusen, even David Niven and his family. Instead of the servant, I would be served, by Sinatra's other maids and houseboys. Mr. S, who was big on a man's dignity, wanted me to look good in front of my wife and family. He had one maid there just to look after our kids. I only began getting suspicious when he would send me on long errands, like to Vegas to pick up financial documents from the Sands or back to L.A., to get clothes or art, whenever Sally came down. When Sally began listening to Sinatra music all the time, and reading fan magazines, which she never before had done, I got even more suspicious.

I knew Mr. S's mentality when it came to the spouses of some of his friends, Lawford, Bogart, Romanoff. He liked their wives, plain and simple. In his religion, he was capable of suspending the commandment about thy neighbor's wife. As the King, his subjects owed him more than total loyalty; they owed him their families. Yet what was I going to do, accuse my wife of fucking my boss, or vice versa? Lie in wait and try to catch them in the act? I was getting jealous of my employer, which is about as bad an occupational hazard as you can have. I tried to put it out of my mind, and I tried to limit Sally's visits, but I couldn't do it to my boys who had this fabulous country club for themselves. Mr. S was great to the boys. He bought them all BB rifles, and they immediately proceeded to shoot out half the windows of the Palm Springs house. Mr. S didn't get mad; he thought it was hilarious. That was *his* kind of prank.

Maybe I was being paranoid, being unfair to Mr. S, who had been nothing but good to me. I had done enough damage of my own to Sally by being gone so much. I was married more to Sinatra than I was to her. Nevertheless, the poison had gotten into the system. As did Sally's conversion to becoming a Jehovah's Witness. She'd stand on street corners handing out *The Watchtower* and other religious propaganda, and she had our little kids out there with her handing out the stuff. That got me crazy. I wasn't pushing for them to be Jews or anything else, but I didn't want my kids out in the street pushing, be it faith or drugs. Within a year or so we got separated, then divorced. Sally met a rich white businessman, not a Witness, dropped the religion bit, and took the kids to live with him in Hawaii.

Our divorce was extremely ugly. Even though she had found a cash cow in Honolulu, Sally decided to milk me as well. She found a lawyer who dragged me into court looking for big support payments. Their claim was that I was making thousands monthly in undeclared tips from the friends of Frank Sinatra. So here I was up on the stand, being bombarded with questions about how much money has Sam Giancana given you. I didn't like *my* name being dragged out in public. I could imagine how Mr. Sam felt. I was worried I'd get a bullet in my head to keep me from testifying, but Mr. S assured me not to worry. After the press, Mr. S's least favorite group of people were lawyers, and he stood in my corner, got me a top lawyer, though he avoided coming to court. Every day, if they weren't nagging me about Giancana, it was Dean, Ava, Sammy, Bob Wagner, Sam Goldwyn, Yul Brynner. Mentioning Yul showed how ridiculous the whole thing was. Yul wouldn't tip a scale. The truth was *none* of them gave me tips. That would have been insulting both to me and to Sinatra, who, his friends all knew, paid me plenty. I wasn't a bellboy. I got so mad that, after court one day, when a press photographer was hounding me, I picked up a big trash can and threw it at him. The picture made all the papers. Mr. S loved it. "Who do you think you are, Spook?" he asked. "Frank Sinatra?" In the end Sally got nothing more than the normal support I had offered to pay her. Mr. S took me to Romanoff's to celebrate the court victory.

My consolation prize was to move in with Marilyn Monroe. Well, it was next door, but we were together a lot of the time. Not "together" together, mind you. I was a caretaker for Mr. S, so I tried to be professional. But Marilyn didn't want a servant, she wanted a friend, needed a friend. I could have stayed with Mr. S at the Bowmont house. I had my own room there by the pool. But I needed a little space all to myself, and if I had stayed there, there would have been no such thing as off-duty. So it was off to Doheny.

Marilyn's apartment was hardly the lair of a superstar. There were three rooms, one bedroom, with hideous white, Maf-stained shag carpet that must have been there since she first rented the place in 1953 while DiMaggio was courting her and her star burst onto the screen in *Gentlemen Prefer Blondes*. There was a badly out-of-tune piano, a few ratty chairs and couches, a fireplace that took me a week to clean out so "we can live like Connecticut," as she had with Arthur Miller. This place was a long way from Connecticut. There were no posters, few books, a small television, a lot of records, Sinatra records, which made me sad about my wife. One of Marilyn's few big luxuries were thick curtains, a double set on each window, so she could sleep all day. She was a much worse night owl than Sinatra. I used to call her "Drac" because she kept vampire hours. Her other indulgences were full-length mirrors in every closet, every room, "so I can see how disgusting I am."

Marilyn may have been a space cadet about many things, but she was an absolute virtuoso about projecting her own sexuality. Bloated, pimply, filthy hair, broken nails, Marilyn could still get any man and she knew it. That's why she had those mirrors, to flaunt herself, half naked, or fully naked, to whoever happened to be around. In a way, she was like Mia Farrow in reverse. Mia would always say I'm so skinny and flat, who would look at me? Marilyn would say, I'm such a fat pig, who would look at me? Marilyn, however, was masochistic. She would *get* fat just to see if men would still like her, just as she would put on black wigs and glasses and go down to the bars on Santa Monica Boulevard, just to see if she could fail to be picked up. When she did fail, she would come home and get drunk and cry for hours, or worse, she would pop a bunch of sleeping pills. That's why Mr. S put me there, to prevent these bouts of self-loathing from turning into self-destruction. Mr. S instructed me to look in on her (he gave me a key) before I went to sleep—to make sure that if she were asleep she was breathing normally, and if she was awake that she wasn't drugged out to a danger point. If possible I should sit with her until she went to bed safely.

"Nobody even looked at me. Not once all night," she moaned to me after an abortive bar hop.

"What do you expect? They're all queers where you went," I told her.

"Oh."

"Why didn't you just go to Chasen's?" I asked her. "Play some Ping-Pong." They had a table in a back room that was one of the town's best pickup spots.

"No, George. They'd know me there."

"Are you looking to get laid or to get rejected?"

"I'm looking for love. I'm looking for someone to like me for *me*, not some stupid movie poster," Marilyn said, popping open a split of champagne. Her refrigerator was full of them, and little else. "Here's to love, George. True love."

We clinked glasses. "Who's gonna like you in that ugly wig? You look like a cross between a witch and a telephone operator."

"That bad, huh?"

"I think you're going overboard not to be you."

Marilyn ripped off the wig, took off the glasses, unzipped the dowdy cocktail dress. As usual, she had nothing on underneath. I went to get her a robe. "Aw, do I *have* to? It's so hot."

"I'd better be going," I said.

"Chicken!" she taunted me and put on her robe. "What if you didn't work for Frankie?"

"Then I'd be on welfare."

She started to laugh. "What's our boy doing tonight? Does he have a date?"

"With his Vicks Inhaler," I told her. Mr. S had a cold. Jimmy Van Heusen had sent him an additional remedy, a redhead sinus clearer. I didn't tell Marilyn this. Mr. S had given me strict orders, under penalty of God knows what, to tell Marilyn nothing of his private life. He knew any other woman would make her insanely jealous and potentially self-destructive.

"Do you think he'll ever settle down, George?"

"Do you?" I tried to avoid all diplomatic confrontations by letting her answer her own loaded questions. If I said what I thought, that Frank wouldn't settle down, not now, it might have extinguished Marilyn's hopes and made her suicidal.

"Don't you think he and I should both throw in the towel and get married? He doesn't want any more kids. I'm perfect for him."

"You're bigger than he is."

"Not in his elevators." Marilyn giggled.

"I mean your career. Look at Ava. Two stars under the same roof . . ."

"Frankie can be the star. He can be two stars. He's so sad these days. All I want to do is make that poor boy happy. Help me, George, pretty please . . ."

Who could say no to Marilyn Monroe? Then again, who could say *anything* to Frank Sinatra? Even if Marilyn cleaned up her act, I knew she was as unlikely to give up her career for love as Mr. S would be. She had fought like a dog, fucked like a dog, to get to the top, suffering the grossest indignities Hollywood could throw at her. She had posed for cheesecake, turned tricks, slept with studio ogres, did bad movies, got bad money, yet she had made it to Queen of the World, just as Mr. S was King.

Marilyn talked the talk of standing by and behind her man, but she wouldn't walk the walk. Also problematic for Mr. S was that there was another famous man (and no one loved famous men more than

Marilyn) she was interested in standing by, and possibly two, and they were both named Kennedy. Thus Mr. S was in the awkward position of being in a romantic *mano a mano* with the last man in America he wanted to compete with, President Jack Kennedy (whom Mr. S began calling "TP" after he became the president), and with the man in America who hated him the most, Attorney General Bobby Kennedy. Only that master strategist Old Joe could tell Frank how to sort this out, but by now Old Joe wasn't talking. What a can of worms!

Marilyn would tell me breathlessly about Jack, though she never mentioned Bobby. Most of the stories involved how sexually obsessed Jack was with her, how many times and where they had made love, from suites at the Plaza in New York to broom closets at the Sands. I knew how horny Jack was, so nothing she said surprised me, except her belief in his promises that he would leave Jackie and that she would be his First Lady for his second term. That guy would say *anything* to score!

Marilyn may have been talking about JFK to make Mr. S jealous. When it came to men Marilyn was a shrewd card player. Yet I didn't go gossiping back to Mr. S. You know what they say about killing the messenger. Nor did I want to burst Marilyn's bubble about how mad about her the president was. I had spent enough time with the man to know that no woman, not even his wife, was sacred to him. His need was like that of Alexander the Great, to conquer the world. To him, Marilyn was one more conquest, a trophy, maybe the Great White Shark of Hollywood, but still a record, not a romance. Marilyn did concede that the president was not a great lover. His biggest problem, she told me, was premature ejaculation. She tried to take it as a positive, evidence of how she drove the president out of control. "Jesus, George, he's got a *country* to run. He doesn't have time for that mushy stuff," she said, further rationalizing JFK's amatory haste. Frank Sinatra, on the other hand, *made* time for the "mushy stuff."

"He's the best," Marilyn frequently swooned. "Nobody compares to him," she would say, then wink. "And *I* should know."

Marilyn's L.A. sessions with the president would never take place in the apartment, but at the Lawfords' beach house in Santa Monica. In the "Gold Coast" strip of mansions on the Pacific Coast Highway, near where Cary Grant and Barbara Hutton lived when they were married, the Lawford compound was redubbed "High Anus Port" by one of the Rat Pack wits, probably wordsmith Sammy Cahn, because of all the wild sex that went on there. "Poor Pat's so out of touch," Marilyn commented. "She probably thinks we're playing football." I'm sure Pat was not clueless. She was just resigned. One person who did not party, at least sexually, at the Lawfords' was Mr. S. He had too much respect for Pat. Which was more than her own brother had. Peter told me Pat knew exactly what was transpiring between Jack and Marilyn. Pat must have hated feeling that her house was being used as her brother's brothel.

Moreover, while Marilyn liked the idea of Frank being jealous, she didn't want him to see what she was doing with JFK. Mr. S may not have cared what the president was doing with Judy Campbell. Marilyn Monroe was a different story. Mr. S may have played Cupid in getting them together. He was doing it to show off. But he felt like a pimp. He also felt jealous, but maybe not in the way Marilyn intended, which was to make him sweep her away to the altar, away from the competition. If he were actually thinking about marrying Marilyn, how could those thoughts not be clouded by his lover's escapades on the Gold Coast, at the Carlyle Hotel in New York, wherever the leader wanted to swing on a star. When they played "Hail to the Chief," what was Mr. S thinking?

In the first year of the JFK presidency, 1961, Mr. S felt that giving his girl to the Chief was the price you paid to be that close to power. To that same end, he spent most of the year redoing the Palm

Springs compound clearly with the president in mind, new cottages, new phones, new furniture, walls of photos of Frank, Jack, Peter, and Pat, even a plaque in the bedroom where Jack had screwed so many whores reading JOHN F. KENNEDY SLEPT HERE. This was going to be Jack's West Coast crash pad, White House West, and Frank was going to be Host with the Most, for all the world to see. But when Joe Kennedy had his stroke in late 1961, the tune changed overnight. Bobby, the Puritan, and Jackie, the snot, took over and decreed that Mr. Sinatra was Not Our Kind. All of a sudden, the Irish eyes stopped smiling. And Mr. S went from being the First Friend to just another greaser from Hoboken.

Mr. S's total humiliation occurred in early spring 1962. JFK was planning a high-profile visit to Southern California that would inaugurate our new Palm Springs digs. We worked for weeks getting everything perfect, planning parties, doing guest lists, trying to include everyone and not piss anybody off. Then, at the last minute, Peter Lawford, who had set up the visit to begin with, calls from L.A. to tell Mr. S that Jack isn't coming. At first Sinatra assumed the trip had been delayed, some political crisis. Then Lawford says, totally sheepishly, well, he's still coming, but he's not coming *here.*

Lawford first tried to blame the Secret Service, saying it was a security issue, then he finally admitted that it was a *Frank* issue and that Bobby was the mastermind behind it. Mr. S smashed the phone he was talking on against the wall. He went into another room and was able to get Bobby on the line in Washington. "What *is* this shit?" I remember him repeating. Unfortunately, this shit was all coming down on Mr. S. Bobby basically told him we can't have the president sleeping in the same house where Sam Giancana slept. And Mr. S said he's *already* slept here, so what's the big fucking deal. Bobby played hardball. He said it's *my* deal now, and Jack ain't sleeping there and hung up. There went another phone, smashed to smithereens. We were lucky to have had all those extra lines installed. I felt sorry for Mr. S. He was like the girl who got stood up for the prom, all dressed up with no place to go. He had spent a fortune on the house, just for JFK, and now the house was off-limits. It wasn't fair. And the house was just a symbol of all he had done for the Kennedys. How could they treat their friend this way, he wailed to me, like a little kid and nearly in tears.

He called Peter again to try to figure out some other way to fix this. Frank appealed to Peter desperately, saying flat-out he could not lose face this way. And then Peter came out with the worst news of all. There *was* no other way. They already had new lodgings for JFK. So why didn't you tell me this on the first call, Sinatra asked Lawford, his face getting redder and redder. Peter claimed Frank had cut him off without giving him a chance. So where, where, Sinatra pressed. There was an endless silence. Then Mr. S simply dropped the phone on the floor. He stood there staring out at the desert, as if someone had told him his folks had died. It took about five minutes before he could tell me. Guess where the president was staying instead? Bing fucking Crosby's! That was the cruelest blow of all. Bing Crosby was a Republican! He was an Eisenhower, Nixon guy. He represented old-guard, old WASP Palm Springs, the community that looked at Sinatra as a "there goes the neighborhood" kinda guy. Or, as he put it, losing all of his normal control, "like a fucking nigger." He and Crosby were superficially buddies, Crosby had been an idol, a king who had surrendered his throne to Sinatra. And now here he was taking it back.

Yet Sinatra didn't blame Crosby. He didn't blame Bobby, because he had no way to get at Bobby, not yet at least. He didn't blame Jack, who didn't even call to apologize. Mr. S felt so betrayed, he had no idea how to deal with Jack. Instead he blamed it all on Lawford, his once-dear "Charley," the one guy close at hand he could vent his wrath upon. Fuck him. Once the import of the last call to Lawford had sunk in, Mr. S went on the most violent rampage I had seen. Lawford's clothes were ripped out of the closets, ripped personally to shreds. His golf clubs were bent in half. Pat's makeup and perfume kit was crushed under foot. I followed Mr. S around the house on his search-and-destroy mission, just to make sure he didn't die of a cerebral hemorrhage, his blood pressure was so off the charts. I didn't dare try to stop him, or even say, "Cool it, boss. This ain't worth it." He probably would have killed me.

My main job was to take all the stuff and throw it into an off-site garbage dump a few miles away "to destroy the evidence." I left thinking the rampage was over. But it wasn't. When I got back, I found the whole compound was a sea of glass shards. Mr. S had smashed every Kennedy photo. He had also kicked the bedroom door in, but somehow he couldn't pry the KENNEDY SLEPT HERE plaque off of it, and it would remain as a bitter reminder of how he had been used and dumped. "Now I know how whores feel," he confessed to me in the week or so afterward that it took him to calm down. No one came near him during this period. Who knew what to say? Any sort of condolence would have been seen as pity, and it would have been better to shoot Mr. S than pity him. Press coverage of JFK's change of plans didn't help things. Each article was salt in Sinatra's wounds. As punishment, Peter was immediately excommunicated by being cut out of the two upcoming Rat Pack movies *Four for Texas* and *Robin and the Seven Hoods*. Lawford, and his career, never recovered.

At the same time Mr. S was getting the brush from the Kennedys, he was getting the squeeze from the mob. Sam Giancana was giving him the old "I told you so." But Mr. S knew that Mr. Sam never stopped at mere scolding. Sam made Sinatra nervous, especially now that he realized he had made an error of judgment. Fuck-ups, in *this* world, were not well tolerated. "Why, oh why," Sinatra asked himself aloud over and over, "did Joe get that fucking stroke?" "It's gonna give me one," he declared. The minute Old Joe hit that wheelchair, Bobby unleashed the dogs of J. Edgar Hoover on organized crime in general, and Sam Giancana in particular. That winter Mr. Sam came out to Palm Springs to play golf. Mr. S had been anxious about Sam's arrival, buying brand-new Italian linen sheets for his bed, a silk robe from Sulka, the best caviar, going more overboard than usual to make him happy. I was relieved that, once Giancana arrived, relations between the two, at least on the surface, were exactly as before.

One morning, Mr. S called me into Mr. Sam's room, and they showed me all these expensive golf clothes. "Put them on, George," Mr. S told me. "Let's see how they look."

"But I'm no golfer," I said.

"You are now," Mr. S ordered.

It turned out that I was about the same size as Mr. Sam. I needed a tight belt to hold the pants up, and the sleeves were a little short, and I had to use a pair of Mr. S's golf shoes. I was still totally confused. Then they put a wide-brimmed golf cap on me and sent me outside. There was a black car waiting with three other golfers, other guys from Chicago who barely spoke to me. We were driven off to a golf club, the one where Mr. Sam came to play. What was going on was that I was being used as a decoy for Sam Giancana. The FBI was tailing him and bugging him everywhere he went, including the links. That day, however, I was the missing link. Sam loved his golf so much that he went to play somewhere else. Meanwhile, I went to his club and shot the highest score ever recorded. Every ball went into the rough, a lake, a sand trap. The Chicago boys were pissed, but they were under orders from Sam. Still, they gave me a hard time. "Golf was not designed for niggers," they ribbed me, saying I should stick to caddying, and I couldn't disagree with them at the time. I wonder what these clowns would have to say about Tiger Woods. I was a little pissed myself, but who was I to get pissed at Sam Giancana? I felt as if

I was in that Jerry Lewis movie *The Caddy,* and I tried to look at the whole episode as one big joke. I'd live longer that way.

Just as Frank Sinatra blamed Peter Lawford for his fucking over by the First Family, Sam Giancana blamed Frank Sinatra. But Mr. Sam, unlike Mr. S, knew how to keep his temper under control. World-class killers, which is what Sam was reputed to be, were like that. Never show emotion. I don't know what happened in the election, but Mr. Sam often mentioned "the marker" and how the Kennedys were welching on it. I do know Skinny D'Amato did get invoved in the key West Virginia primary, and Skinny wasn't your typical campaign volunteer. His prison time had left him well connected, but how that translated into votes, I'll never guess. I also know Sinatra was on the phone to Giancana dozens of times on election night, while he was anxiously watching the televised returns that had Nixon ahead. "It's gonna turn, it's gonna turn," Mr. S would reassure Van Heusen and Sanicola and some other Dagos, who were watching the returns with us. Van Heusen had a bunch of hookers on hold to celebrate with, but the contest was so tight, they never showed. By morning, Illinois, the state that Sam owned, *had* turned. "Ye assholes of little faith" was all that Sinatra could say, with a weary victory smile. Now the Kennedys were trying to handcuff the hand that had elected them, and Mr. Sam was pissed.

Mr. Sam was always offering me a job, ever since we first met. It was a running joke between him and Sinatra. I was never sure whether he really meant it or not. "Come work for me, George," he'd say.

"Mr. Sam, I couldn't do that."

"Why not?"

"I don't wanna get killed."

"Sinatra never hit a fly," Giancana said, scoffing at the notion of Mr. S as tough.

"Not by him, Mr. Sam. By these G-men who want your scalp."

He laughed his high-pitched chuckle, the sound that Bobby Kennedy drew eternal wrath for by likening it to a little girl's giggle. "You're more likely to get hit in Hollywood than Chicago," Sam said ominously. "At least I can protect you." From whom, I wondered, and actually had a twinge of fear for Mr. S's life.

There have been lots of rumors that while the FBI was pursuing Sam Giancana to put him in jail, the CIA was also pursuing Giancana to kill Fidel Castro. America had been humiliated by the failed Bay of Pigs invasion. The mob had been deeply damaged financially by losing their Havana casinos. Thus there was a unity of interest in seeing Castro disposed of. Also, as we have now seen, the FBI and the CIA are rarely on the same page, often at deadly cross-purposes with each other. Many times I heard Sinatra and Giancana talking about the "good old days" in Havana, where I regretted that I had never gotten to go. They would have loved to reclaim what was theirs, but no one could hate the "G" (for government), or the "feds," more than Sam Giancana. I can't imagine him getting in bed with them, not with Bobby K running the Justice Department. It would have been more likely for Mr. Sam to get in bed with Castro to retaliate against the "Ks." He gave them the office; all he wanted in return was a little peace and quiet. Couldn't they give him a fucking break?

Judy Campbell continued to spend an occasional evening with Mr. S at the same time she was seeing both JFK and Mr. Sam. She thought she was pretty hot shit at this point, playing Mata Hari with two arch-enemies. By now, Mr. S's loyalties were squarely with Giancana, and against the Kennedys. He was always Sam's man (once in, never out), but he was trying to have his *tiramisù* and his Irish stew at the same time, and that was one food combination that would prove toxic. I'm sure Judy was giving more information to Sam about JFK than she was giving JFK about Sam. JFK couldn't have cared less about the spy stuff; he wanted sex. Like Marilyn, Judy may have been momentarily deluded that Jack would leave Jackie for her, also like Sinatra may have been deluded that Pat would leave Peter. But those dreams died fast, and Judy, like Frank, realized that Sam was the more dangerous figure to trifle with. The little giggler scared the devil out of all of us.

Not that the Kennedys were pussycats. Mr. S found one more reason to hate them on his suspicion that they killed Marilyn that awful summer of 1962. On the other hand, he needed to believe in this sort of conspiracy theory. If he didn't he might have had to blame himself. Marilyn loved him, more realistically than either Kennedy. He was her guardian, her lover, her friend, her soul mate. She trusted him more than anyone else in her life, except her shrink. Mr. S had his own conspiracy of control over Marilyn. Her beloved shrink, Ralph Greenson, was the brother-in-law of Sinatra's lawyer, Mickey Rudin. The men's wives were sisters. Mickey, whom Frank met through Judy Garland, would give his life, and anyone's else's, for his cash-cow client Mr. S. There was another strong medical tie: Marilyn's gynecologist was Red Krohn, who also treated the doctor-phobic Mr. S and performed all necessary abortions whenever Sinatra knocked someone up (never stars, but mostly one-night-stand waitresses and showgirls). Dean Martin was the costar of Marilyn's final film, *Something's Got to Give*. I had been Sinata's surrogate watchman over Marilyn until she moved to the little house in Brentwood where she died. She almost OD'd at Sinatra's Cal-Neva Lodge coming up to watch him sing a week before her final tragedy. And it was Sinatra himself who had pushed her into the clutches of the Kennedys. It reminds me of *Rosemary's Baby*. Every road Marilyn took led to Frank. And to oblivion. Talk about guilt and dirty hands.

Mr. S also felt bad that he had used his affair with Juliet Prowse to "punish" Marilyn for her affair with Jack Kennedy. (If he believed the affair with Bobby to be true, she would have been beyond punishment.) Juliet was the South African dancer whose shaved pussy was such a curiosity to Jack Kennedy. It must have been special to Mr. S as well, for she went from conversation piece to fiancée in about a year. She wasn't a superstar, but she was different from the other actresses Mr. S had been seeing. First of all, she was exotic, born in Bombay, raised in South Africa and had that classy English accent Mr. S was a goner for. He was also a leg man, and hers were state-of-the-art. She was a top ballet dancer before being discovered for Sinatra's *Can-Can*, where she also caught the eye of Soviet premier Nikita Khrushchev, who was visiting the set. Sinatra put her in the Kennedy inaugural, in shows at the Sands, and at Cal-Neva.

He even took a break from his concert tour in Germany and went to Johannesburg, South Africa. He took me along. There were a lot of houses in Johannesburg that looked like Tara in *Gone With the Wind*, and had as many servants. This was during apartheid, and the rich whites in South Africa lived in a style resembling that of the old plantations on the River Road outside New Orleans, much grander than anything in Beverly Hills and with far more help, all black. From the little we saw of it on our weekend trip, it seemed as if the Old South had risen again down there in South Africa. The black people I saw appeared very downtrodden to me, with no spirit whatsoever. I was depressed for them, but not in a there-but-for-the-grace-of-God-go-I way. I knew those people would rise up eventually; there were too many of them not to take control of their country. Mr. S, who was the archenemy of racism, disagreed with me. He said the situation looked hopeless, too hopeless even for him to try to remedy, that the ruling whites were too entrenched. I'm sure he was thrilled when those walls were finally torn down. I got funny looks at our fancy hotel, but not *too* funny because I was in the room next to Mr. S. I guess I got to go where few other black men had been in that country, but that was the story of my life. I wanted Mr. S to take us on safari, but he had bad associations with wild animals after having dejectedly followed Ava Gardner to Africa when she made *Mogambo*. Instead he sent me to the Johannesburg Zoo.

We met the Prowses, nice, middle-class people, lacking Juliet's upper-crust accent. They lived in a modest suburban house, with no servants. I sensed Mr. S was disappointed. He may have been expecting a South African version of the Kennedys. The most memorable part of the trip was Mrs. Prowse's gift to me. She gave Mr. S a lionskin rug. She gave me a *spear*. Ungawa! I wanted to shout and do a rain dance, but I bit my tongue. I did show Mrs. Prowse the switchblade I carried, just to make her a little nervous about this "savage" she had in her home. Mr. S almost lost it, he was so cracked up. The minute we left, he was crying, he was laughing so hard. This was Mrs. Prowse's culture, so I couldn't hold it against her, but talk about being put in your place. A spear!

I showed the spear to Marilyn, who missed the joke. If Mr. S wanted to hurt Marilyn, he succeeded. The Sinatra-Prowse "engagement," which lasted about a month, drove Marilyn up the wall and out of the Sinatra Arms to her own place in Brentwood on Fifth Helena Drive. It also drove her to the mirror. That Juliet was a decade younger than Marilyn was bad; that her legs were perfect was worse. Both Marilyn and Ava were ridiculously insecure about their legs. Too short, too fat, was the whine. Marilyn must have stayed in front of the mirror for days, trying on a hundred pairs of high heels, asking me and whoever else she could grab which ones made her legs look the best. That she was usually naked in the heels made it hard to focus on the legs, but that was Marilyn. Even after Frank and Juliet called the whole thing off on the grounds that she wanted a career and he didn't want any wife of his to have one, Marilyn remained in pain, even though Mr. S was seeing her once again. No one took rejection harder than Marilyn. She would see rejection where someone else would see acceptance, she was that sensitive. Because Jack

Kennedy was a better bullshitter than Mr. S (after all, JFK was the ultimate politician), he got Marilyn to believe, as she frequently said to me, that she had a better chance to marry him than she had with Sinatra. One more reason why Mr. S came to hate "TP," the guy he once loved.

I never saw Marilyn alone with Bobby Kennedy. Our neighbors at 882 North Doheny did tell me that Bobby had come to the apartment and that he and Marilyn were having some kind of sexual thing. The Weasel definitely wasn't her type, which ran to Italian macho-Dago types like Mr. S and Joe DiMaggio, who never stopped seeing her, though his paranoia about showbiz and its toxic shock to her kept them from settling in again. But type never stopped Marilyn from fucking someone who was nice to her. It's hard to imagine Bobby being nice to *anybody*, and it's hard to imagine Jack *not* being nice. Yet at some point, Marilyn may have gotten too needy with Jack, and because of her fame, Jack got worried that if she went public about their romance, the world would have complete sympathy for her as the woman scorned. So he may have sent Bobby as his reverse Cupid, to get Marilyn off his aching back. Bobby always did Jack's dirty work. Once Bobby showed up, his own weakness and weaselness may have lured him into Marilyn's bed. Or Marilyn may have lured him herself. Just to show "TP." Or just for the fuck of it. With Marilyn, anything sexual was possible, and usually probable.

The bottom line on August 5, 1962, was that Marilyn was dead, and Mr. S was devastated. When the cops said it was an overdose, he had no doubt about it, nor did I. We had both seen her pop pills galore, and mix them with booze, cursing the life that the rest of the world would have done anything to have. She was a walking pharmacy, an overdose waiting to happen. It was only later when the autopsy revealed no residue of pills in her system that we got curious. Mr. S began to suspect Lawford and his brothers-in-law of possible foul play, but since at that point he would get suspicious of them for a rainstorm, I didn't put much stock in it. What was very sad about the whole thing was that Joe DiMaggio wouldn't allow Mr. S (or me) to come to the funeral. The two Dagos both loved her in good ways and could have been so helpful and supportive to each other. But DiMaggio held a grudge the way he held a bat, as tightly and viciously as Mr. S. Their friendship was never again to be.

The day Marilyn died was a horrible, and horribly sad, moment not only for me and Mr. S, who both felt we had failed in our efforts to protect her from herself, but also for Hollywood and the country, who had lost one of the prime symbols of what makes America great. Here was this poor, abandoned girl with nothing but liabilities, who becomes the biggest star of the big screen. If that isn't an American Dream Come True success story, what is? Her death was a bigger blow to the image of Hollywood than James Dean's. It was one thing to crash a Porsche, quite another to die of an overdose with the president and attorney general of the United States standing in the shadows. If Hollywood had an innocence to lose, it lost it on that August 5.

Marilyn gave the whole world hope. I certainly identified with her, another poor person from nowhere who had made it in Hollywood. If Marilyn could be a star, if I could be the right hand of Frank Sinatra, this was indeed the land of opportunity. Marilyn was one of Mr. S's favorite people. He loved how much she loved him. Without that love and admiration she constantly showered onto him, he was deeply wounded. The healing of that wound made him harder and colder than ever before. Aside from all the symbolism, I personally grieved for, and missed, Marilyn the woman. Nobody could be as miserable as she was in such a loving, good-natured way. No matter how sad she may have been, she was never mean, never lashed out at me. Instead she just wanted to hug me and have me hug her and tell her it was all going to work out. That it didn't broke my heart.

Given Mr. S's turn of attitude toward the Kennedys, I can see *The Manchurian Candidate*, which went into production in early 1962, just after Joe Kennedy's stroke and in the midst of Bobby's anti-Frank rampage, as less than a love letter to the family. "I hope it pisses the shit out of them," Mr. S said. The Kennedys were anything but closet Communists, as the villains in the movie were, but a lot of the country, particularly the South, *thought* they were. So Mr. S took pleasure in sticking it to them, the whole hypocrisy bit, the idea of this rich political dynasty controlling their hero son, using him as a charming puppet. Sinatra had absolutely no idea, however, how hideously prophetic the whole assassination theme would be.

My main job during the filming was avoiding the advances of the dashing British star Laurence Harvey, who was such a sensation in *Room at the Top* in 1959. Women adored him, but he adored men, even though, as a career move, he married the beautiful young widow of Columbia mogul Harry Cohn, whose insane temper finally gave him a fatal heart attack. Echoing the future *Forrest Gump*, Larry would say to me, "You're like a box of chocolates, George. I'm *dying* to take a bite." It made my skin crawl, but after dodging the likes of Noël Coward and Cole Porter with Swifty Lazar, I knew all the right moves to keep Larry at bay without insulting him. Even though Mr. S was a dyed-in-the-wool homophobe, he was crazy about Larry, as well as in awe of Noël Coward, who had become a great fan of Sinatra. He couldn't understand why such brilliant men could be "assfuckers," as he derided them, yet "as long as they don't try to play drop the soap with me," he relished having them around. They were superb conversationalists, and he needed people "for the ladies to talk to" while he and his Dagos debated boxing and set off cherry bombs.

The subtle jibes of *The Manchurian Candidate* went right over the heads of Sam Giancana and his mobster friends. Even though Mr. S was being trashed by the Kennedys the same as they were, Mr. Sam didn't think Mr. S had shown the proper respect to him, and the proper disrespect to the Kennedys, for fooling the dumb Dagos into betting on the wrong horse. Mr. Sam would have liked the head of that horse to wind up in Bobby Kennedy's bed. Short of that, Giancana leaned on Sinatra to make a declaration of independence from the Kennedys. To that end, Frank enlisted Dean and Sammy to go on the road and perform, for free and very publicly, for the very gangsters Bobby Kennedy was denouncing to America and the world. In your face, Weasel, was the idea. The Clan, delightedly rid of the dead weight of Peter Lawford, did a week of shows at Skinny D'Amato's 500 Club in Atlantic City, which was dying at the time because gambling was illegal and everyone was flying to Vegas. I was there, and there was *more* gambling in Skinny's back room than on the floor of the Sands. It was as if Mr. S was daring the law to try and bust him. They didn't.

There was even more illegal gambling, and whoring, a few months later in November when the boys, plus Eddie Fisher and Jimmy Durante, played Giancana's own club, the Villa Venice, in the Chicago suburbs. It was flashier than a Hollywood premiere, with the guests here being a Who's Who of Illinois mob royalty. Foreshadowing the Bellagio and the Venetian by four decades, Mr. Sam had gondolas ferrying the guests to the entrance, with gondoliers singing "O Sole Mio." There was also an adjacent den of iniquity called the Quonset Hut where huge amounts of money were won and lost at Vegas-style and -level games of chance. The "Summit," as the Rat Pack engagement was called, was said to have grossed many tax-free millions for the Giancana outfit. Shortly after the summit, the Villa Venice, for all its elaborate new trappings all set up for Mr. S's appearance, burned mysteriously to the ground and was never rebuilt. "Dago lightning," Jimmy Van Heusen explained the conflagration.

The biggest red flag to the FBI bulls of Bobby Kennedy was the Cal-Neva Lodge, which, ironically, his now-speechless father had put into the mob/Sinatra's possession. To Bobby every song Sinatra sang hit the sourest of notes. To keep sticking it to Bobby, Sam Giancana loved going to see Sinatra perform at Cal-Neva, despite the fact he was on the Nevada state blacklist, forbidding the gangster's supposedly dangerous presence. It was hard to exclude the guy who secretly owned the place, especially when his girlfriend Phyllis McGuire and her sisters were on the bill. The idea of Nevada enforcing such laws against the gangsters who built the place seemed particularly ridiculous to the two Misters, S and Sam. Mr. Sam was there the weekend before Marilyn's death and spent her pre-overdose evening at her lakeside bungalow. Because Johnny Rosselli was also there that weekend, there was talk of an S&M Mafia orgy to teach Marilyn a lesson for bestowing her famous favors on the Kennedys. She was *their* girl, not those Micks'. But I was the one who drove Marilyn to the plane that would take her back to L.A. In the car, the thing that bothered her most was that her drugged-out behavior had offended the strait-laced Mr. Sam, who was united with Mr. S in a hatred of drugs (this despite the mob's supposedly making a fortune in the narcotics trade). Marilyn had total respect for Sam, and he always treated her like a lady. That was his Old World style. To her Sam was no fearsome killer figure but a statesman of his own peculiar country. She liked him a lot.

Even though on stage at Cal-Neva, Mr. S looked great, everything else about the place, and his fronting ownership of it, seemed terrible. In addition to Marilyn's overdose and Giancana's illegal visits, there was a big investigation of a prostitution ring being run out of the front desk, and there was the mysterious death of a Nevada sheriff who had taken a punch at Frank for fooling around with his wife, who worked as a cocktail hostess at the lodge. The sheriff was driven off the road one night by a speeding convertible that caused a fatal crash. The convertible was never identified. Of course, the connection between the mob and Sinatra caught the imagination of the yellow press. It was too much for Hank Sanicola, who had been inseparable from Mr. S since the thirties. Hank was a nominal coowner of the lodge. Now it was getting too hot, even for a tough old Dago like him. He wanted to sell his share of Cal-Neva. Mr. S went ballistic at Hank. For him it was "All or Nothing at All." How, he railed to me, could Hank be such a Judas, especially now that the homeboys were being besieged by the Kennedy Gestapo? This was the time to rally round, not break ranks. But there was to be no dialogue with Hank, no debate. The second Hank expressed doubt, he was Out. If you don't fit, you must quit. Mr. S bought out Hank's share in Cal-Neva. From thirty years of brotherhood to zeroness in one split second. As with Lawford, he never spoke to Hank again. That was the Sinatra Silent Treatment. As I said, I never thought it would happen to me, but that's what we all said.

7

Jet Set

𝓘 N the face of his humiliating public rejection by the Kennedys and his equally public association with gangland, there were basically two things Frank Sinatra could do in 1962. One was to rehabilitate his tarnished image. The other was to get out of town. Mr. S took full control of the situation by doing both. Instead of being ridiculed as a political bag man or a mob puppet, Mr. S decided to become a *philanthropist*. The singing philanthropist, Rockefeller with a tune. He spent a lot of time with Hollywood public relations people and with his lawyer Mickey Rudin, and this was the best they could come up with, a three-month around-the-world concert tour that would benefit underprivileged kids. He had just wrapped *The Manchurian Candidate*, he had just broken up with Juliet Prowse, Marilyn was obsessed with "TP," Bobby was obsessed with Sinatra. There was absolutely nothing to keep Mr. S in Hollywood.

The only problem with this proposed Great Escape was that Mr. S had no interest in travel. To him travel was work. He had a plane now, the El Dago, which was like an airborne bachelor pad, but he was always nervous about flying. He would triple-check the weather along his route before taking off. If there was the slightest storm, or even possible turbulence in the forecast, we wouldn't go. Mr. S had lots of Sicilian superstitions, one of which was that flying was tempting fate. It was for the birds, and for that nutcase daredevil Chester, his name for Jimmy Van Heusen. Mr. S was supposed to have gone on the plane with flamboyant Broadway and Hollywood impresario Mike Todd that crashed in 1958. The plane, *The Lucky Liz*, named after Todd's wife, Elizabeth Taylor, was bound for a Friars Club affair at the Waldorf-Astoria to honor Todd, the Oscar-winning producer of *Around the World in 80 Days* (with a script by Mia Farrow's father), in which Sinatra had a cameo as a Wild West saloon piano player. *The Lucky Liz* went down in an icy New Mexico cornfield. Mr. S had backed out at the last second on account of some music crisis. He talked about it for years. Now he was on borrowed time. If he had to fly, it had to be essential to be worth the risk. He didn't trust commercial flights. That was his control factor. He would be more careful than TWA or Pan Am. And he was.

The other problem with traveling for Mr. S was his total lack of curiosity about the outside world. For all his shelves of biographies, for all his hours in the dictionary, geography, history, and culture left him totally cold. He was a homebody, not an explorer. He had done other tours, and they had felt like onerous tours of duty. He vastly preferred Little Italy to the Big One, Hoboken to Hong Kong, Las Vegas to Monte Carlo, Palm Springs to Marrakech. Again it was the control factor, more than being an Ugly American. Here he was the Chairman, there he was just another rich tourist. Not even the most imperial suite at the Ritz or the Savoy could compare with his Bowmont Drive digs. Besides, where would he get the Campbell's Franks and Beans?

This time, kicking and screaming, Mr. S agreed to go. It was an essential career move. This time, however, he would bring his friends to insulate himself from the local traditions. They could take the boy out of Palm Springs, but he wasn't about to let them take Palm Springs out of the boy. I was thrilled to be included. I loved traveling from my Navy days, and this would be for me a sentimental journey to a lot of old haunts. It was also a good time for me to get out of town. Sally had left me and taken the kids, and I was feeling down. There's nothing like a trip to change your outlook, and there would be nothing like *this* trip in the annals of travel.

In addition to me, the Sinatra entourage included his banker Al Hart, his restaurateur Mike Romanoff, his sports guru Leo Durocher, and his whoremeister Jimmy Van Heusen. Van Heusen came along as a total civilian. He didn't play piano, write music, nothing. He was simply there for the ride, for the inspiration, for the girls. Romanoff's purpose in being aboard was twofold. The old con was, for all his lies, the most worldly man in Hollywood. He had fleeced aristocrats around the globe, and they loved him for it. His address book was unequaled. Also, he was tight with all the other great restaurant men. He would secure the red carpet and best tables at places like Tour d'Argent and Maxim's. Because Mr. S was very insecure about status matters, Mike was the perfect guy to play his traveling concierge. The second reason Mr. S took Mike was that he liked being around Mike's beautiful, clever, and much, much younger wife, Gloria, who ran the restaurant for him. Sinatra was often asking me if I thought Gloria had eyes for him. He thought she did, and he certainly had them for her. I wasn't sure, though I suggested he invite her on the journey so he could find out. What could be more romantic than being in all these exotic locales? Mr. S thought this was a brilliant idea. He relished the challenge of an intrigue along the long way.

Mr. S's other potential conquest was fifty-eight-year-old Leo Durocher's gorgeous twenty-something blond date, by far the most beautiful woman on the tour, or whom we even *saw* on the trip. The only catch, and it was a big one, was that she was a devout Jehovah's Witness and a committed virgin. Durocher had met her, I think, as a shopgirl in some Beverly Hills boutique. She certainly appeared to be the picture of sophistication. Was *that* look ever deceiving! The goddess carried a large Bible with her and read it constantly. Poor Leo was in an agony that became a three-month running joke. Durocher was a totally cool guy. I could see why Sinatra loved him. Not only had he been a great shortstop, but he was an even greater manager, cultivating Willie Mays and leading the Giants to their 1954 World Series championship. He was also a famous wit. "The Lip," as he was known, was more often quoted than Yogi Berra. His most famous saying was, "Nice guys finish last." He also had such immortal lines as "God looks after drunks and third basemen," and "As long as I've got a chance to beat you, I'm gonna take it." Leo loved Hollywood. He had been married to the beautiful actress Laraine Day, who starred in *Mr. Lucky* with Cary Grant and in Hitchcock's *Foreign Correspondent* (Leo had an eye as well as a lip), and liked ladies of pleasure almost as much as Jimmy Van Heusen. This hypersexed Wizard of the Polo Grounds couldn't have picked a more inappropriate companion. "Maybe if I steal the Bible, you can get a blow job," Mr. S teased Leo. It never happened.

Al Hart was there to talk business, which at this point had eclipsed sex and sports as Sinatra's favorite topic. Mr. S had broken with Capitol, over the one-sided (their side) deals he called artistic slavery, and had started his own record label, Reprise, in 1961. He was insulted that Capitol wouldn't finance his own company in return for a 50 percent ownership stake. Capitol argued that if they did this for Sinatra, they'd have to do the same thing for their other great, Nat King Cole. As much as Mr. S admired Nat, he insisted on being "special" and regarded Capitol's refusal as a sign of deep disrespect. "I'm gonna tear that fucking tower down," he said of the landmark circular Capitol Records Building in Hollywood, which had been built "on my back," he insisted, in 1956.

Mr. S also didn't like the technological direction in which the record business, and Capitol, were heading, with too many overproducing, meddling technicians. This was shorthand for not wanting to be forced to stay in the studio for days instead of hours. Mr. S was a great believer in spontaneity and not beating a horse, or a song, or a movie line, to death. Because Sinatra was Reprise's own cash cow, he could use the label to discover other singers, like Trini Lopez, whom he met in the men's room at P.J.'s, a club on Sunset, where Trini was struggling; or to give his less fortunate friends, like comedian Joe E. Lewis (on whom *Joker Is Wild* was based) and singer Jimmy Witherspoon, the fair deals the big record companies would not. The revolutionary hallmark of the Reprise contract was that rights to the master recording reverted to the performer, who could "reprise" them. There was also another meaning. Sinatra purposely mispronounced the name of his company "re-prize," as in reprisal, against the now-hated Capitol, which itself had rescued his career in 1953.

Despite being unable to bring Nelson Riddle with him at the start (Nelson was under an unbreakable contract to Capitol until 1963), Mr. S worked with other top arrangers—Billy May, Sy Oliver, Neal Hefti—and Reprise was big out of the gate, just by recording Sinatra as well as Sammy and Dean, who had left their previous labels for him. But Mr. S wanted it to get a lot bigger. His goal was to become an entertainment mogul on a par with Harry Cohn and Jules Stein, and Al Hart was his numbers man. His first Reprise album, *Ring-a-Ding-Ding*, sold huge numbers, and the two men had endless financial discussions on upcoming albums and films, as well as casino interests, that kept them away from most of the tourist highlights, like Mount Fuji or the Eiffel Tower. "Who gives a shit?" was the way Mr. S saw it. Since he had given me a chunk of stock in the new company, I was perfectly happy that the boss was taking care of business, keeping his blue eyes on the bottom line. (By the way, ring-a-ding-ding, which became Sinatra's swinging watchword, was taken straight from the prologue to Cole Porter's sly ode to sex, "Let's Do It": "When the little bluebell, in the bottom of the dell, Starts to ring: 'Ding, ding!' Such are the roots of cool.)

Our first stop was Tokyo, where we stayed at the New Japan Hotel. The whole city was so alien and confusing to Mr. S that he didn't want to leave the hotel, not even to see the nearby Imperial Palace and the famous cherry blossoms that were just starting to bloom. "The only cherries I want to see are the geisha girls," he decreed and Van Heusen rounded up some in-suite entertainment. When the girls refused to kiss him, Mr. S threw a tantrum. "You eat sushi but you won't kiss my lips?" He felt seriously insulted until our translator explained that kissing was not popular in Japanese culture. "You call that culture?" he snickered. We played a huge, packed arena at the Mikado Theatre, and Mr. S was given a solid-gold key to the city, which softened him up a bit to a country that he continued to distrust as a World War II enemy. "How the fuck can you trust *anyone* who eats raw fish?" he defended his position. Still, his generosity toward any needy soul was immune to any tinge of chauvinism or racism.

One thing Mr. S did religiously was read the local English-language newspaper. On our first day in Japan, he saw a story about a group of struggling, nearly starving Buddhist priests in a remote mountain monastery near Mount Fuji. He decided he would help them. He chartered a helicopter to fly up to see them. When the fog was too heavy to reach them, he gave the helicopter to me and some others to tour Tokyo. Even though I had no idea what the signs said or what anyone was saying, my ignorance was bliss. I loved Japan. Tokyo was vast, but very serene, with lovely temples and gardens to punctuate the urban sprawl. There seemed to be no noise, no honking horns, no sirens. It was clean, polite, civilized. In New York the people were pushing one another off subway platforms to get on a train, and here they were bowing to each other. Mr. S barely saw the city, but he did bring the priests down by train, hosted them at the hotel for a week, and made a major donation to the order. It was weird, priests by day, geishas by night. He didn't go so far as to mix these two constituencies, though he did proudly play his records for the priests and had the translators explain the lyrics to them. The religious guys seemed to dig the songs, as did everyone else in Japan. Probably the biggest kick Mr. S got in Japan was learning about a school that gave a course in English to corporate executives that consisted of playing his records and having them sing along. Sinatra was their model of perfect enunciation. What better compliment could a singer have?

We then flew to Korea, which was run-down compared to Japan (its economic miracle was yet to happen), then to Okinawa to entertain the troops at our military bases there. Mr. S were worried that the GIs were all "Elvis guys," and that they wouldn't dig him. He was completely wrong. Sinatra had made peace with Elvis by putting the King on his 1960 ABC television special when he got out of the service in Germany. The show got monster ratings, because of the King, better than any the Chairman had ever gotten on his own. Hence it was a bittersweet triumph, but a hit was a hit and Mr. S just accepted it. He had even let Little Nancy go on some dates with Elvis, who was reputed to be a tad twisted with the ladies, the white cotton panty fetish, hangups from his Memphis boyhood. He turned out to be a perfect Southern gentleman. "I didn't want to get killed," the King told his friends. Now Nancy had married another, Elvis-like Deep Southern rock singer, Tommy Sands, who had had a gold record with "Teenage Crush" and was total crush material himself. Their romance was a version of *Guess Who's Coming to Dinner* with a rocker instead of a black man. Like Spencer Tracy in the movie, Mr. S got over it. There was simply no getting away from the new pop sounds. The one "pop" he couldn't bear, however, was being Nancy's "pop." Her growing up, wanting to be a star herself, a rock star, made him feel old for the first time. Thus when the GIs in Okinawa went as wild for him as those Paramount teens in the forties, it gave him back his youth and a lot of the confidence the Kennedys had recently cost him.

Next stop was Hong Kong, where we stayed at the legendary Peninsula Hotel, where the uniformed bellmen pad around the colonial lobby with signs paging MR. SINATRA. He stayed out of the lobby, but loved the opportunities it provided for practical jokes. He'd page guys like Durocher, have him go back to the room, where a cherry bomb would explode when he opened the door. He had a guy page Van Heusen saying he was some big pimp and he had this incredible brothel in the Walled City of Kowloon, which was so dangerous that it was off-limits to the cops. But there were no risks Van Heusen would not take for the sake of sex, and he went on a wild-goose chase that nearly got him mugged by pickpockets. Mr. S thought this was hilarious. "Some guys have an Achilles' heel. You've got an Achilles' dick," Sinatra roared at him. "Chester" didn't get pissed off. It wasn't in his nature. He could take the pranks as well as he could dish them out.

The other thing Mr. S liked about Hong Kong was the overnight custom tailors. He had a dozen orange blazers made, and custom elevator shoes in alligator and snakeskin. Why so many coats? Mr. S wasn't like Jerry Lewis, who would throw a jacket away after wearing it once. He just liked to travel light, and he could afford it. He wanted one blazer for L.A., one for Palm Springs, one for New York, one for Vegas, one for the road, and some backup. That was all. Who was to argue that people were freezing in Siberia? Mr. S was nice enough to let me get a bunch of outfits made for myself.

In addition to his jackets, Mr. S had at least two dozen pairs of fine wool slacks made up. As far as he was concerned, he couldn't have too many trousers. He was embarrassed by any creases, thought they looked slovenly. He would often change pants if he sat down once. That's why he was forever pacing. He may have seemed wired and edgy, but the reality was that this vain fashion plate didn't want to wrinkle his trousers and spoil the perfection. Mr. S did love clothes, and the richer he got, the more clothes he would buy. Despite living in Palm Springs, he abhorred the notion of casual, both for men and women. Casual was for golf courses, and swimming pools, and that was it. One of the reasons Marilyn Monroe drove him so around the bend was that she didn't like to dress at all, much less dress up. To Mr. S, the more elegantly, more formally, a woman dressed, the better. Expensive jewelry was a fetish item for him. He would have liked living in the court of Louis XIV, when women spent hours making themselves out of this world. As for ladies' dress colors, for Mr. S black was most beautiful. He hated orange on women. Orange was for him, and him alone.

Mr. S couldn't resist a prank with the Hong Kong tailors. He bribed Mike Romanoff's shirtmaker to sew on the sleeves so that one would quickly fall off. By the time we got to Paris, all of Mike's lovely new shirts had fallen apart. He was completely mystified, which gave Mr. S a bigger kick than a screaming crowd. I do think he would have been content being the host of *Candid Camera*. The tailors were meticulous craftsmen, and they had an appreciative customer in Mr. S, who had no patience for shoddy work or less than a 100 percent effort. "I dig these coolies, George," he said. "I may have to replace you."

That was typical of his sense of humor, always a little nasty, always containing a threat that would make you slightly insecure, then the laugh that said it was all a joke, that Sinatra really loves you, baby. You hoped and prayed. I never answered him back. I would just wait for the punch line, which was the laugh that always came. If it hadn't come, I'm sure I could have gotten an A-list Hollywood job if I had wanted one. There was a lot of status attached to having worked for both Lazar and Sinatra, and status was all the A-list was about. However, I had no desire to work for anyone else, even the Bill Goetzes or the Jules Steins. The Sinatra job was unique, and because there would be nothing to replace it, I couldn't help but feel a twinge of anxiety whenever he threatened me, even in jest, with losing it.

The only time Mr. S lost his temper on the trip was at his concert in the Hong Kong City Hall. On his closing number, "One for My Baby (And One More for the Road)," the spotlight was supposed to keep getting smaller and smaller until it went black and Sinatra would disappear. The Chinese camera operator forgot to turn off the light, ruining the dramatic fadeout. Mr. S went crazy, smashing up not only his dressing rooms, but also his Peninsula suite. He didn't need Jack Daniel's to stoke his incompetence rages, though the Jack did add fuel to the fire. They said rock bands were hard on hotels, but Mr. S was worse, both foreign and domestic, wherever mistakes were made, whether on the stage, as in Hong Kong, or overcooking a room-service steak in Chicago. "Fucking slant-eye Chink bastards," he'd shout and rip up a priceless antique screen or shatter a Ming vase. The guy got off on breaking things, as if it were sex. The only good part for me was that I stopped worrying about being replaced by a coolie. I'd just stand back with my mouth shut, watch this private version of Demolition Derby, and help the chambermaids pick up the pieces when it was over. Telling Mr. S to calm down would only make things worse, like showing a red flag to a bull.

After our week in Hong Kong we flew on to Israel. Mr. S adored Israel, and Israel adored him right back. Here was a whole country of underdogs and survivors, the people Sinatra respected most, people like himself who had beaten the odds. He was so awed by the place, so respectful, that he didn't tell a single one of his beloved "Uncle Scrooge Cheap Jew" jokes the whole time we were there. These weren't the Beverly Hills fat cats who had treated him so badly, hence his bitter humor. These were battling pioneers. He was genuinely ashamed to have put them all in the same category. Oddly enough, the two cheapest people Sinatra knew were the Anglo Peter Lawford and the Russian/Mongol Yul Brynner, hardly Bev Hills Jews. The King of Siam was such a penny pincher that he actually made the Thin Man seem like a big spender. Peter could be shamed into paying but not Yul, whom I never saw pick up a check.

We were in Israel in early May for their Independence Day celebrations, and Mr. S was welcomed to the reviewing stand with Prime Minister David Ben-Gurion and Gen. Moshe Dayan as if he were secretary of state. We stayed at the King David Hotel, which had been blown up in 1946 when it was British military headquarters in Palestine. The violence drove the British out of Palestine and led to the creation of the State of Israel. We also went to the Wailing Wall, the Via Dolorosa, and other shrines—most movingly for both Mr. S and me, the Yad Vashem Holocaust Memorial on the Hill of Memory, where all the trees had been planted in memory of the victims. This was a stunning and solemn place. The external beauty of the land of milk and honey contrasted with the horrors shown within, particularly the underground Children's Museum, where each of the more than one million tiny lights represented the life of a child that had been snuffed out. Afterward Mr. S said the visit had made him feel rotten about not fighting in World War II and that Israel was a wonderful country "worth dying for."

Israel was the only place on the whole tour where Mr. S took a real interest in the country as anything other than a concert stop. He wanted to see *everything*, and Israel rolled out the red carpet. When he wanted to cross the Sea of Galilee and see the Golan Heights, the Israelis contacted the Syrians to tell them that our long convoy was not a troop movement and to hold fire. The sundown on the Sea of Galilee was beautiful. "Another few days and I could become a believer," Mr. S half-joked.

After dedicating a youth center he endowed in honor of his friend Jack Entratter's late wife, we chartered a yacht and cruised the Mediterranean to Athens. There he performed in an ancient Greek theatre, one of the oldest in antiquity, in the shadow of the Parthenon. Mr. S couldn't have cared less about the history. He couldn't wait to get back to his suite at the Grande Bretagne Hotel and see what brothels Van Heusen had excavated. The whores Chester found were even better than the one Melina Mercouri had played in *Never on Sunday*, and treated Mr. S like Zeus on Mount Olympus. Two of them even came back with a giant moussaka they had made in his honor. When the trip was over, he pronounced the Greek hookers his favorite of all the international damsels he had sampled, not necessarily for their looks but for their warmth and hospitality. Sinatra had no need to beware of Greeks bearing gifts. Nor did he beware of social diseases. He never once asked me to buy him condoms, on this trip or any other. He hated the idea of condoms, though this was way before AIDS or even herpes had become scourges. He was so fastidious about cleanliness, body odors, excess perfume, dirty nails, smudged makeup, any hint of less than immaculate grooming, that he prided himself on his personal radar detector of potential contagion, which would call for the instant dismissal of a dangerous candidate. "If I have any doubt, I'll let *you* test them for me first, George," he'd tease me. It never happened, nor did I ever know him to get a dose of anything.

Wherever we went Mr. S kept reading the papers. In Greece he found a story about a poor kid who needed open-heart surgery. He paid to have the boy brought to Athens for the operation, and he insisted on no publicity. He was like the benefactor on the TV show *The Millionaire*, which, not surprisingly, had supplanted *Amos 'n' Andy* as his favorite program. From Greece, we sailed back to Israel, then flew to Rome. Until then we had been flying on chartered planes. The *El Dago*, a DC-6 prop, with a classic Sinatra orange interior, wouldn't have made the long distance ocean routes. But the plane was waiting in Rome for the rest of our European hops. Except now it had a new name, the *Tina*. The purpose of the trip was to rehab Mr. S's image. Somehow his handlers figured out that the name *El Dago* might not play in Italy. Mr. S was glad to see the plane. He was getting homesick, and the *El Dago* was a slice of home. It had a terrific sound system and all his records, a projector for most of his films, as well as the latest studio offerings, a great bar, of which I was the barman of the skies. I was also chef of the skies, but because the galley was so small, I mostly made sandwiches of the best bread, prosciutto, cheeses, and salmon I could find in whatever city we were in. I served lots of caviar, too. The flights were great, a true movable feast. It was a flying cocktail party. There was a bedroom in the back of the plane, but, to my knowledge, Mr. S never joined the Mile-High Club. He was too superstitious about flying in sin, worried that going down on *El Dago* might might make *El Dago* go down.

Mr. S didn't play particularly well in the land of his ancestors. To begin with, he had no interest in visiting the Sicilian village where his father was from, or even his mother's legendary Genoa. The people in the street loved him, every guy trying to get close to him and claim to be his long-lost cousin. On the other hand, the richer people who could afford the tickets to his shows in Rome were rude, shouting "Ava, Ava." It could have been that some of the Italians felt Sinatra wasn't excited by his homecoming as they thought he should be. I attended all the concerts on the trip, and for whatever reason the Rome shows were the least inspired. Mr. S threw a minor fit when the people at the Perugina chocolate company, for whom he was filming a commercial, asked him to do a second take. We were at the RCA studios, and the ad people requested that Mr. S say the three words, "Buy Perugina Chocolates." It didn't seem like much, but he turned beet red, went over to the camera, and had the operator remove the film and destroy it. "It's not in the contract," Mr. S seethed and left. The spot never was redone. Even the food in Italy turned him off. At the Principe di Savoia in Milan, we had a kitchen in the suite, where he had me cooking night and day, Hoboken style. Talk about carrying coals to Newcastle, but that was His Way, and you just didn't argue. You would only lose.

His only joyous moment in Italy that I ever saw was, on a brief tour a few years before, returning to his suite at the Excelsior in Rome and finding Charles "Lucky" Luciano, who was living outside of Rome, sitting in the pitch-black room waiting for him. At first I thought it was going to be a mob hit, especially when Luciano got up and kissed Sinatra. I assumed that was the kiss of death. But it was the kiss of friendship. Sinatra had met the head of Murder, Inc., in the forties in New York, before Luciano was deported to Italy. The Rome reunion was old-home week. They sat up until morning talking about the glory days. It was sheer nostalgic bliss for Mr. S.

Italy was so bad that England seemed like a homecoming for Mr. S. We took over several floors of the Savoy Hotel, where the waiters and bellmen, all Italians, treated Mr. S far more reverently than the people in Italy. At the Royal Festival Hall, we had a terrific concert, with young kid performers singing with Mr. S, who had dinner afterward with Princess Margaret, who was extremely good-looking and flirtatiously sexy, especially for a member of the famously unsexy female half of the British Royal Family. Mr. S said he loved her ass. The princess had admitted to her American best friend, Sharman Douglas, the daughter of Harry Truman's ambassador to the Court of St. James's, that she had held a crush on Sinatra for years. Mr. S in turn had learned this from Sharman's boyfriend, Peter Lawford, when he and Mr. S were still MGM buddies. The princess's supposed obsession had stuck in Mr. S's mind for over a decade. Late at night after the concert, Sinatra and "the guys" all speculated on how hard it would be to fuck her, how he could get into Buckingham Palace or Windsor Castle and get into the royal bed. If Mr. S had really been serious about the exercise, he would have never discussed it with anyone.

On the tour Mr. S took special care of his voice. He only drank tea with honey the day before concerts, and the glass he carried on stage that everyone thought was his trademark Jack Daniel's was actually Lipton's. He also swore off milk and cream. He believed that all dairy products caused phlegm, the bane of any singer. Nor did he ever touch soft drinks. The carbonation caused gas and bloating, and Mr. S was horrified by anyone who belched, especially himself. I never ceased to be amazed at how polite Mr. S was to strangers, and not only royal ones. At a cocktail reception, he would put out his hand and say, "Frank Sinatra. Nice to meet you," even though he knew he needed no introduction. He didn't like the way Hollywood stars took their fame for granted. He had almost lost his once, and his downplaying his fame was one more superstition that he hung on to.

We had our most fun in Paris. There were hordes of waving Frenchwomen as we tooled around the City of Light in a caravan of Chrysler convertibles. The most beautiful of these were the Bluebelles, the chorus girls of the Lido on the Champs Élysées, where Mr. S performed. A lot of them came for a big after-party in our suites at the Georges V, which was the Hollywood headquarters in Paris. We saw Darryl Zanuck in the lobby, but Mr. S made a point of ducking him. The idea was to get away. Mike Romanoff took us to all the famous restaurants. He knew Claude Terrail of Tour d'Argent, who had been married to Jack Warner's daughter Barbara. The restaurant, maybe the most elegant in the world, overlooking Notre Dame, was renowned for its wine cellar and its pressed duck. However, Mr. S was uncomfortable around Terrail, a dashing world-class polo player and playboy, who had had affairs with *everyone,* including Ava and Marilyn. Mr. S drank tea, ate a steak, and left early. I had found him some Campbell's Franks and Beans at Fauchon, a luxury grocery store that stocked American treats. I'll never forget his opening a can at five A.M. and feeding it, forkful by forkful to two visiting Bluebelles. He didn't get any action from the showgirls, however, prompting Mr. S to complain how the Bluebelles had given him blue balls.

Through Romanoff, we also saw another superstud, Porfirio Rubirosa, the polo-playing Dominican Republic diplomat whose first wife was the daughter of the dictator Trujillo, who had just been assassinated in 1961. Rubirosa had gone on to become the ex of superheiresses Doris Duke and Barbara Hutton. Because of this high-stakes conjugal double play, Rubirosa had developed a reputation as the greatest playboy since Casanova. He was famous for having the biggest cock in the world. French waiters called their peppermills "Rubirosas." Mr. S wasn't interested in the competition. He was polite to "Rubi," but kept his distance. Surprised that Sinatra wasn't interested in his hospitality, Rubi, who was then fifty-three, took me under his wing. He took me back to his art-filled apartment and cooked me rice and beans. He was from the Dominican Republic and part black. I think he was sick of all the polo-playing aristos and liked the idea of having a black buddy. He also took me to meet Madame Claude, the world's most famous madam, who lived in a fancy apartment near the Eiffel Tower. It wasn't a bordello. It was more like a salon. Madame Claude was a tiny birdlike woman who resembled a banker more than a madam. She spoke no English, but welcomed me as if I were royalty. If I was Rubi's friend, I had to be okay. When he told her I was Sinatra's right-hand man, she lit up and begged me to bring him over. It would be her honor to service him, she told Rubi, who said she serviced everyone from the Rothschilds to Lord Mountbatten to the shah of Iran to Picasso. There were five girls there when we arrived, two tall American cover girls, the others diamonds-and-pearls European upper-crust types. That was Madame Claude's specialty, arranging for her clients to have affairs with "normal" girls who would never turn a trick except for huge money. A lot of her girls had married Wall Streeet and Hollywood tycoons. She was very tight with Zanuck. When I told Jimmy Van Heusen I had met her, he told me he preferred the street girls of Pigalle, the Irma la Douce-types. Madame Claude, to him, was a rip-off, "You're paying for class, not ass," he said.

At that point it was class that Mr. S was really looking for. He found the embodiment of class at our next stop, Monte Carlo, in the person of his Dream Girl, the princess of Monaco. Or as he called her, "Gracie." She called him "Francis." He and the fake prince Romanoff visited the real prince and princess at the royal palace, and got the grand tour. Francis had been crazy about Gracie since he'd first gotten to know her on the set of *Mogambo* and later as her costar in *High Society.* But because first Ava Gardner and then Bing Crosby were looming heavily over Mr. S in those two productions, he had been too self-conscious about making a play for the actress he viewed as the screen's most elegant. Now that Gracie had retired from the screen, and now that Francis had no powerful presence to inhibit him, he was ready to make his big move. But what about the powerful presence of the prince of Monaco? That's where I came in.

To achieve his goal of spending some "quality time" alone with Grace, Mr. S concocted a plan worthy of his Italian forebear Machiavelli. To begin with, he sent me back to the palace with a case of special bonded Jack Daniel's for Prince Rainier. The prince received it, and me, personally. The prince had a funny little moustache that made him remind me of a stocky version of the actor Vincent Price, who was so "Euro" in his demeanor. Although the prince was a bit portly, the minute he started moving he could have been Fred Astaire. He handled himself with total aplomb, effortlessly switching between five fluent languages. He was the nicest guy, much less "princely" than the pompous Mike Romanoff. He loved jazz, and he loved cars. He took me down to the royal garage and showed me his collection, which included Bugattis and old Daimlers, and grand prix Ferraris. He took me for a spin in the hills in his Facel Vega, which reminded me of Sinatra's Dual Ghia, but was even more expensive.

Mr. S was so happy that the prince and I had bonded, he sent me back with more gifts. He was also using me as a decoy, I believe, just as Sam Giancana had used me with the FBI. When they were alone on the balcony of the palace after a reception there, I had overheard him and Gracie make elaborate plans to meet at some villa near the David Nivenses at Cap Ferrat. When I went to the palace and was served a fabulous lunch in the state dining room, the prince said that the princess was at the flower market. I was told by Mr. S to say that he was rehearsing. I knew he wasn't. But he never did tell me what went on. All the hypothetical arrangements he talked about for Operation Princess Margaret may have been put to work with Princess Grace, while the prince and I were listening to his Count Basie and Duke Ellington collections and talking about how seeing Josephine Baker dance had changed his life. I felt bad being part of any plan to deceive this good guy, but they say the French are "sophisticated" about things like this.

All I know is that Mr. S had such a grand time, he began returning to Monaco every summer to be the star of Gracie's Red Cross Ball, and to do God knows what else. On this and later trips, we stayed at the Hotel de Paris across from the casino, which Mr. S declared "a joke" compared to those of his beloved Las Vegas. He got a special kick hiding on his balcony and lobbing cherry bombs and eggs at the snooty black-tie couples going in to gamble. He even got dressed up himself, went in and won thousands of dollars without breaking a sweat. At the roulette wheels, he would bet either on red or on black, and he would win. Afterward, we would all drive in a caravan down the coast to a restaurant called Le Pirate, which was a simple outdoor grill place, but for billionaires. Even though it was totally French, it had adopted the Greek tradition of smashing plates after dinner, maybe because the place was a favorite of Aristotle Onassis, who had bailed out Prince Rainier when his kingdom was in financial trouble. Mr. S and his party immediately got into the Greek swing of things, breaking every piece of china and glass in the house before the dawn rose over the Mediterranean. He paid for the damage with his casino winnings. "That's what all this play money's for," he said.

After Monaco we returned to England to record an album of British love songs, such as "A Nightingale Sang at Berkeley Square," and then we all flew home. I hadn't seen Mr. S so exhilarated and positive since "TP" won the election two years before. He immediately began talking about going back, especially to Monaco. This world tour had finally made him worldly. It had cured him of his reluctance to trot the globe. Like many glamorous people with the advent of the 707 jet plane, Mr. S began to look at Europe as another playground with infinite possibilities. He was now forty-seven, and he wasn't feeling his age one bit. If Rubirosa could swing the way he did at fifty-three, Sinatra was, relatively speaking, a mere kid. There was nothing unseemly to Mr. S for "a man his age" to live it up globally. The best was yet to come. It was too bad that he had to return to the midst of all Marilyn Monroe's troubles, as well as new ones of his own. Being squeezed at one end by Bobby Kennedy and at the other by Sam Giancana, Mr. S had nowhere to hide except in his music and in the enormously successful business that his music had become. Between 1962 and 1963 Sinatra released at least six new Reprise albums, all great: *Sinatra and Strings, Sinatra-Basie, The Concert Sinatra, Sinatra's Sinatra,* a collection of Broadway hits, and more. He also starred in the movie version of the Neil Simon Broadway smash *Come Blow Your Horn,* in which he played a playboy, but the role was getting tired, just as it was in real life. It wasn't age so much as sheer repetition.

The truth of the matter was that Mr. S had been seriously looking for love, thus far in all the wrong places, such places being anywhere in the glare of the Hollywood spotlights. He said he didn't want a woman with a career, so why was he dating the likes of Dorothy Provine and Juliet Prowse? Quietly, secretly, or at least as secretly as Frank Sinatra could be, he began throwing a wider net. As I have said, he was looking for "class." His first serious nonshowbiz candidate was a woman he met at George Raft's Colony Club, a gambling den in Mayfair, on an English concert tour in 1958. Her name was Lady Adele Beatty, and while she sounded terribly English and had been married to, and divorced from, a Lord of the Admiralty or something, she was in fact a country girl from Oklahoma. She had climbed up the social ladder, first rung in Dallas, where she modeled at Neiman-Marcus. Next stop Beverly Hills, where she married a prominent lawyer, whom she dumped for Lord Beatty, whom she met while he was visiting Southern California and moved with him to England.

Lady Beatty's goal had been to reinvent herself in Europe as a full-scale aristocrat. She had done it well. Tall, skinny, chic, sporty, a real Jackie Kennedy-type, Lady Beatty was considered one of the top partygivers in all London. When the party king arrived in town, she descended on him, and, well, ring-a-ding-ding. But there was more Hollywood in Lady Beatty than met the eye. She missed a lot of what she had left behind in Beverly Hills. She ultimately left Mr. S and married the director Stanley Donen, whom Sinatra resented for giving him second billing to Gene Kelly in *On the Town.* Ava couldn't stand Lady Beatty, whom she saw as a phony social climber. Of course, even while courting the lady, Sinatra was trying, as usual, to get Ava back. He had given her an expensive ten-carat "reengagement" ring from Bulgari in Rome, where Mr. S was pursuing Ava while Ava was pursuing the comedian Walter Chiari, known as the Danny Kaye of Italy. In addition to being funny, Chiari was incredibly handsome in a chiseled, muscular way, as perfect a man as Ava was a woman. Understandably, Chiari was the rare male who made Sinatra insecure. When Ava found out about Lady Beatty, she left Sinatra's ring with the concierge at the Hassler Hotel, where he was staying, with instructions to give the ring to Lady Beatty. By then, however, the lady had chosen Donen over Mr. S.

The next socialite on Mr. S's marriage prospect list was a Southern belle from Kentucky named Josephine Abercrombie, who was no relation to the store Abercrombie & Fitch but equally posh. Blond, voluptuous, an accomplished equestrienne, Josephine was a horse-breeding heiress who had been married five times when she met Sinatra in her midthirties. Her father, "Big Jim" Abercrombie, who made his fortune inventing oil-drilling equipment, was one of the richest men of the Bluegrass State. Mr. S had met Josephine on a jet-set blind date in Jamaica and had pursued her from Breakfast at Tiffany's to supper at Saks. I've never seen him give a woman so many gifts, diamonds, furs, a Cadillac convertible. She gave him just as much in return, things such as the finest crystal, china, porcelain, linens, and somehow turned on this boxing fan to the nuances of domestic luxury. "She's going to turn you into an interior decorator if you don't watch out," I warned him. "Who's the fag, now?" I had been with him long enough to feel at ease ribbing him about any personal subject, except his hairpieces and his makeup.

"If fags could get ladies like that, they wouldn't be fags," Mr. S closed the subject. The catch with Josephine was that she was so far out of show business, she wasn't sufficiently impressed with Mr. S's accomplishments. Her father was even less impressed. Big Jim saw Little Frank as another greasy Yankee Dago. Mr. S's pursuit lasted over a year. He never took me with him to Lexington, Kentucky, where she lived on a plantation/horse farm. "I don't want to get you lynched," he teased me. Apparently Josephine had an army of "slaves," as Mr. S called them, and he didn't want me to feel like one of them. I doubt that Josephine would have let that happen. I had met her when she came to Los Angeles and Palm Springs. She was a real lady, a Dixie belle. Josephine was no breathless fan who wanted to meet the Rat Pack. She genuinely liked Mr. S for himself and preferred being alone together with him, taking long walks or, better yet, getting Frank up on a horse, which I told her was not going to happen.

I think Mr. S was more intimidated than he needed to be by Josephine's grand lifestyle and was overly nervous about how bringing me might play in Kentucky. This was one relationship where he couldn't run the show, and that was ultimately no good for him. They broke up on her last visit to Palm Springs. They had a big fight over Sinatra's level of commitment. Josephine wanted to be the One, not one of many. Sinatra seemed as though he was making up by treating Josephine to a complete hairdo and beauty treatment at the town's top coiffeur. After the beautification, however, Mr. S handed

her a first-class ticket back to Kentucky, saying she was too demanding for him. A limo he had called for her was waiting outside.
Josephine totally shocked Sinatra by throwing the ticket back in his
face. She was one step ahead of him. Her own private jet was already
waiting at the airport. She had wanted out before he did.

Mr. S wasn't very good at breaking up with women. Just look at his
split with his once-beloved Betty Bacall, whom he dumped over the
phone. He hated face-to-face partings. Normally, he would disappear
and stop calling the girlfriend. She would call, and either Gloria
Lovell or I would make up something about Sinatra being in the studio, traveling, whatever. A few of those responses and the lady got the
message. If she didn't, and kept trying to reach Sinatra, Mickey Rudin
would step in and send out one of his scary cease-and-desist legal letters. "Hit the road, Jack!" was his attitude, over and out. The message
was clear. None of his exes stalked him. The only breakup he was sentimental about was Ava.

After Josephine Abercrombie, Mr. S made a try for Merle Oberon,
who had a house near his in Acapulco. The elegant Indian-born
actresss had been married to Bruno Pagliai, one of the richest indus-
trialists in Mexico. Like Princess Grace, she had left cinema for high
society, *real* high society. Now she looked down on Sinatra as someone she'd hire to entertain her guests at a party, like a flamenco
dancer. His good-neighbor policy approach couldn't even get him a
Margarita. Mr. S had nowhere to go at the moment but back to the
starlets. He spent some time with a beautiful, WASPy actress named
Nita Talbot, who looked more aristocratic than Grace Kelly. In real
life her name had been Anita Sokol and she was a nice Russian girl
from the Bronx, sort of like Betty Bacall. After Betty Mr. S had rarely
dated Jewish girls, except for Jill St. John, whom he might have been
even wilder about had she not been so ambitious about her career at
the time. Having cut her teeth on her neighbor George Raft, she

could be fluent in the underworld lingo Mr. S loved to speak. He did all he could for her, casting her in two films, *Come Blow Your Horn* and *Tony Rome*, but he always assumed he couldn't compete with the powerful Jewish father figures like Sid Korshak whom she was attracted to. Imagine his surprise when she wed his acolyte, singer Jack Jones, who won Grammys in the early sixties for "Lollipops and Roses" and "Wives and Lovers."

I never saw Sinatra get involved with a black girl, though he often requested black hookers. "Trade you two vanillas for one chocolate," he'd say to Van Heusen. He talked about a brief fling with Billie Holiday in his crooner days in the forties and his desire to love and learn from the woman he considered the Queen of Song. Mr. S was attracted to Nancy Wilson, but she was taken and let him down without making him feel rejected. Not so with Lena Horne, for whom he did try to make a big play. It failed, and afterward he often dumped on her, which was strange for the normally gracious Mr. S. In a long interview in *Life*, he trashed her singing as "mechanical." I never heard that before. But when a lady said "no," hell had no fury like Sinatra scorned.

When all else had failed, Mr. S would go over to Big Nancy's for a home-cooked meal, memories, and television, like a normal guy. Little Nancy was married, Frank Jr. was at a prep school in Idyllwild, in the mountains above Palm Springs, to keep him away from the "spoiled Jew brats" of Beverly Hills, whom Mr. S saw as a worse influence than drug pushers in Watts, and Tina was off being a teenager. So it was just him and Nancy, for old times' sake, though I'm sure nothing sexual happened. He often said that was long over. Yet sometimes he'd seem so happy there that I'd ask him why he didn't just pack it in and go home to the one who really loved him. "Cause I'm not a quitter, that's why," he'd say. It was a strange response, viewing that kind of a reconciliation as quitting. But what he meant, I guess, was that as a true romantic, he wouldn't give up until he found Miss Right, or Miss Right II, since Ava was always going to be Number One in the romance sweepstakes. As with his music and everything else, he was a ruthless perfectionist. It was the same with love, even if the dream girl turned out to be only a dream. The man would never compromise.

I asked Mr. S once if he had never met Ava, did he think he would still be with Big Nancy, and he said no. Maybe if he had never come to Hollywood . . . But he did admit that if he had never met Ava, he might have had a lower standard, and would not have been alone as he was. Whatever the reasons, he could never rekindle the fires with Nancy. He simply couldn't get past the old Italian mother/whore split. And since he was adamant about no more kids, plus obsessed with class and status, finding a goddess/princess who didn't want children was a tall order, even for Mr. S. On many nights, the playboy of the western world would fall asleep watching TV on Big Nancy's couch. All by himself.

From the summer to the end of 1963, Sinatra had no time for anyone. He had some major fires to extinguish. His biggest problem was the Cal-Neva Lodge. Mr. Sam had done it again. Even though he was technically barred from the premises, Sam saw himself as above the law. Always the gentleman, he also wanted to be front and center for his girlfriend Phyllis McGuire's shows, to cheer her on. However, one night after a show, when they were unwinding in Phyllis's cabin on the lake, Phyllis's manager made an insulting comment to her. The normally calm Sam leapt up and attacked the manager, who was bigger than he was. Sinatra had the cabin next door, just a few feet away, and we heard the awful ruckus. I ran over there immediately and found Sam and the manager wrestling on the floor. Phyllis was pounding on the manager's head with her high heel. I tried to pull them apart, but before I knew it Mr. S had grabbed me from behind.

"Are you crazy? Are you fucking crazy?" he screamed at them, but they didn't listen and kept slugging.

Sinatra yanked me away and out into the night. "Don't touch them!' he insisted. "We can't have anything to do with this shit!" We called some guards from the lodge to break it up, and Mr. S had me drive Mr. Sam out of Tahoe and back to Palm Springs in one of our low-profile station wagons. On the ride, Giancana mostly slept, but when he was awake I found it unusual that he made no reference whatsoever to the brawl. He talked about getting some new golf clubs in Palm Springs. Mr. S hoped this mess would go away, but it didn't. The manager, whose eye was nearly put out by a blow from Sam's diamond ring, went to the authorities and claimed both Giancana and Sinatra had made Mafia death threats to him (I never heard them). True or false, his complaint opened up a massive can of worms. The Nevada Gaming Commission got into the act, and Mr. S, who believed he had *created* Nevada, told them to go fuck themselves. Alas, at the same time of the Sinatra-Nevada shouting match, another of the Hollywood moguls, who were the perpetual bane of Mr. S's existence, began making his own Mafia-style threats to Sinatra. This was Jack Warner, an old-timey tough guy.

I had met Jack Warner in the early fifties with Lazar, and was flattered that this great mogul would remember my name whenever he saw me. "Hey, Jacobs, look sharp," he'd always greet me, echoing the Gillette razor slogan of the times, "Look sharp. Feel sharp. Be sharp." Warner, who prided himself on being sharp, was fascinated that a black guy would have a Jewish name, though he did everything he could to downplay his own Jewishness, from his English clothes, to his interest in polo, to his plantation-style estate on Angelo Drive in Benedict Canyon, to his wife Ann, who was from Louisiana, to his starlet mistresses, whom Warner liked to take to the dive Barney's Beanery, where James Dean and other bohemian actors hung out. I used to see Warner there and be surprised. The bartender told me he brought his own steaks for them to cook. He liked the atmosphere. In keeping with his flight from his Judaism, Jack Warner was fanatically pro-American and anti-Communist. He could be funny like Leo Durocher, though not as prolific with his one-liners. When he met Einstein, he told him, "I have my own theory of relativity. Never hire your relatives." He was thuglike in his insistence on wielding his immense power, as Mr. S would find out.

Sinatra was now trying to merge Reprise Records into Warner Brothers, as part of an ambitious business move in which he might eventually take over the entire studio. The last thing law-and-order-loving Jack Warner wanted was *any* association with Sam Giancana, right or wrong. Just as Joe Kennedy made Sinatra back down on Albert Maltz, Jack Warner made him back down on Sam Giancana. It was a big pissing contest, and I guess Jack Warner had the bigger dick. He also gave Sinatra millions of dollars, a huge suite of offices on the Warner lot, and a rich movie production deal to make his point. All Sam Giancana had to offer was fear, but that wasn't anything Mr. S could sneeze at. Smoking and drinking much more than usual to relieve his stress, Mr. S gave up his share of Cal-Neva as well as his big piece of the Sands. In doing so, Sinatra's silent partnership with gangland came to an end, as did his relationship with Sam Giancana, who would never forgive Mr. S for choosing Jack Warner over him. A Hebe over a fellow Dago? What kind of heresy was that? The Hebe did give Mr. S a down-payment certified check of a million dollars which he didn't cash for a week, flashing it to me and all his friends. This was true "fuck you" money. The only problem with it was that it said "fuck you" to Sam Giancana. Mr. S never met with or even called Mr. Sam to tell him he was going the Warner route. He just stopped talking to him. He was dumping Sam the same way he dumped his mistresses. Unlike with the girls, he *wanted* to talk, he *planned* to talk to Sam, but it didn't happen. I'm sure it was because Mr. S simply didn't know what to say or how to say it to Giancana. It was a measure of the heat Bobby Kennedy was putting on Sam, the nonstop surveillance, that he didn't do something unspeakable to this son who had spurned him.

The unspeakable happened anyway. First, there was the JFK assassination in November. Mr. S was at Warners in Burbank shooting *Robin and the Seven Hoods*, which was ironically conceived as an *homage* to Chicago ("My Kind of Town," the song, came from here) and to Mr. Chicago, Mr. Sam. He was in such shock, he shut down the production for days. It was one time when he simply couldn't work. We retreated to Palm Springs, where he holed up in his bedroom, watching the assassination circus, freaking out along with the rest of the world when Ruby shot Oswald, eating nothing but occasional fried-egg sandwiches, and drinking vast amounts of Jack Daniel's. He called Pat Lawford in Washington to express his regrets, though he still refused to speak to Peter. Nor did he telephone Jackie or Bobby, who, he said "wouldn't return my calls." He sent an enormous floral display instead. For all his hatred of Bobby, for all the pain "TP" had inflicted upon him by cutting him dead, Mr. S would never say one unkind word about the man he once loved and continued to admire as a leader, if not as a man. "I really liked Jack," I told Mr. S. I'd been crying. I couldn't help it. "He liked you, too, George," Sinatra answered sadly. "Probably more than me."

Among Van Heusen and his closest friends, Sinatra wondered aloud (though not too loud) if Mr. Sam, who knew Jack Ruby from the strip-club circuit, in which he had a hand, could have had something to do with it. Mr. S thought Ruby was a nut, though maybe he was a *programmed* nut, as in Sinatra's 1962 film *The Manchurian Candidate*, which he pulled from rerun distribution to avoid controversy and charges of bad taste. Sam Giancana certainly had a big score to settle, and he was nothing if not bold and decisive. But Dallas was way beyond a mob rubout. Sam had never dreamed this big before. Mr. S would have loved to hear the inside of the greatest mystery of our time, but Sam Giancana had "Lawfordized" Sinatra. The man who owned his kind of town would never speak to Sinatra again.

Mr. S had still not recovered from the JFK tragedy when, two weeks later, he received an even more brutal body blow. His son Frank Jr., who had just kicked off his own singing career at a star-studded gala in New York, was kidnapped in a Lake Tahoe hotel, not far from Cal-Neva in the northern branch of Nevada mobland. Again, Mr. S suspected his new and deadly enemy Sam Giancana, so much so that he humbled himself by calling Bobby Kennedy and asking for his help. If possible, Mr. S was even more upset at the kidnapping than Big Nancy, who was remarkably composed and resolved. I've never seen anyone so positive. "He'll be back. I know he will," she declared time and again. Mr. S was not so sure. I was surprised that he didn't sleep over with Big Nancy during the ordeal. He said he was "too nervous." He needed to be in his own place to think straight. He felt terribly guilty about neglecting his son, and was terrified that he wouldn't get the chance to make things right by "Junior," as he called him.

I had never seen Mr. S go to church since he prayed for the Oscar at the Good Shepherd Church back in 1954. Now he was back at Good Shepherd, and, once again, his prayers were answered. As it turned out, the crime had been the work, not of Giancana at all, but of some rank amateurs, who did almost more harm than the abduction itself by asserting, after they were caught, that Frank Jr. had staged the whole crime himself to get publicity for his new singing career. It was devastating to the poor kid, who had enough problems trying to follow in his father's footsteps, and it was completely untrue. Yet, because father and son had a difficult relationship that was well-known, a lot of people believed it. That kind of Hollywood gossip was lethal. Moreover, the kidnapping ordeal, which lasted a week, the longest week in the Sinatras' lives, did not in the long run bring the family any closer together. Frank Jr. remained estranged, and Mr. S remained aloof.

It should not be said, however, that Frank Sinatra did not support his son's musical career. Mr. S knew that he was the toughest act in the world to follow, yet he did nothing to discourage Junior from trying to scale this Everest of sound. Mr. S, who was musically illiterate, had deep respect for Junior's musicianship. "He's first rate," he'd say proudly. "Plays the piano as good as Nelson." As for the charge that Mr. S had hurt Junior by missing the nineteen-year-old's opening night at the Americana Hotel on Seventh Avenue in New York, Mr. S had purposely stayed away to avoid stealing the boy's thunder. He was completely aware of it, beseeching all his friends in show business to go and cheer Junior. Jackie Gleason, Toots Shor, Joe E. Lewis, all were there heeding the call of the father, who showed up a few days later, once the critics had declared the show a hit. Above all, Mr. S tried to treat Junior as a professional musician, as an equal, as a *guy*, and real guys weren't all over each other. Mr. S could be cuddly and emotional with Little Nancy and Tina, do "girl stuff" with them, but he valued his son's independence, and so did the son. Furthermore, the son lacked for *nothing*. Pete Epsteen in Chicago sent him a new Pontiac convertible the minute he could drive, his father gave him unlimited money, he had charge accounts so he could dress as well as dad, girls threw themselves at him, what *more*, Mr. S wondered, could the kid possibly need? Love? Love was for broads.

Not too long after Frank Jr.'s abduction, Tommy Sands walked out on Nancy Junior. Tommy didn't have one, but *two* impossible standards to rise to. One was Elvis Presley, the other was Frank Sinatra. As a Southern rocker, Tommy was derided as the Poor Man's Elvis. The two had both been managed by Col. Tom Parker at one point, but the colonel had dropped Tommy. I used to joke with Tommy, who like me was born in Louisiana, that the reason he wasn't as big as Elvis was that he didn't have as much black blood in him as Elvis did. The bottom line was that, blood or not, Tommy was too clean, too white bread, too Pat Boone to become the heartthrob of teenage girls who were getting a lot funkier. On the other hand, if Tommy had been any funkier, Mr. S would have never let Little Nancy marry him.

Tommy and Nancy were really nice to me. I wasn't exactly family to Little Nancy, because I was too busy with her busy dad to see her that much. We didn't have heart-to-hearts, the way I did with Ava, for example, but she knew I was there if she needed me. Once Mr. S sent me to Nashville to look after the Sandses during one of Tommy's recording sessions. The hotel in Nashville refused to give me a room, so Tommy and Nancy checked out and moved into a colored hotel so we could all stay together. When Nancy dropped her father's name at the first hotel, the manager couldn't have been less impressed or fearful that he might be the target of a mob rubout. Nancy never usually dropped her father's name, nor did her father drop his own name or the muscle attendant to it. It wasn't their style. People were supposed to *know* who they were. But not in Nashville, and Nancy was as frustrated as I was uncomfortable. "Do you know what he can do to you?" she threatened the white guy. He just shrugged and said, "He's just another Communist like the Kennedys." And that was that.

Mr. S tried to give Tommy's career a kick by putting him in his war movie *None but the Brave*, but the film bombed. All in all, the pressure on Tommy was too much. He was boxed in by these two giant walls of success, Elvis and Sinatra. He just bolted one day, and it was terrible on Little Nancy. Had it been another day, Mr. S might have ripped Tommy apart, but right then Mr. S had had most of his famous edge knocked right out of him.

Mr. S certainly missed that edge. He missed Sam Giancana and all the tough guys, all the unspoken, never-bragged-about danger and swagger and confidence that having the mob in his corner gave him. He had never been without them, and now that he was, he felt totally naked. I'm not sure that he was afraid of being without them, nor afraid *of* them, but he bought a .38 Smith & Wesson and never left home without it. He was never a good shot. He would go out on boats that he would charter and take target practice at fish, of all things, and he would usually miss. I'd tease him and call him Wyatt Earp, and he'd point the gun at me and pretend to shoot. Yet as bad as he was, he always carried the gun in a holster. It was now as essential to his "style" as his hairpieces and his makeup.

The absence of Mr. Sam created a void that was filled by one of the great male "love affairs" of Frank Sinatra's life, Jilly Rizzo. You might say Jilly was a Sam substitute, though that wouldn't be fair to either man. If Jilly was replacing anyone, it was Hank Sanicola. Giancana was too big to replace. Sam was an overlord; Jilly was a saloonkeeper, albeit a wonderful one. Jilly was the owner of a nondescript bar in New York's theatre district that had one unusual distinction: it served Chinese food, perhaps the worst Chinese food in New York. New Jersey-style Chinese food, chicken chow mein, moo goo gai pan, sweet and sour pork, totally inauthentic and not even tasty as fake food. Mr. S thought it was magnificent, the franks and beans of the mysterious East. He'd say "Let's go get some Chinks," and you knew where you were heading. A lot of Broadway chorus girls hung out here, running tabs they would never pay. That also may have had something to do with the place's appeal to Sinatra.

Jilly was a short, squat, square guy, but he was tough as nails, with a temper as quick and violent as Mr. S's. His speech was right out of *Guys and Dolls*, but much dirtier, all "dese fuckers" and "dose cock-suckers," and Mr. S liked to imitate him. "I smashed the rat bastard in the mouth and the cocksucking motherfucker went down." That was how Jilly talked. Sinatra thought Jilly was a comic genius. He laughed at all Jilly's bad jokes. Things like: "A guy walks into a bar with a duck under his arm. The bartender says that's one hideous pig you got there. The guy says, hey, that's my duck you're talking about. And the bartender says, Fuck you, asshole, I was talking to the duck." That one cracked Mr. S up. Jilly had a wife named Honey, who was Jewish and had blue hair, straight out of Miami Beach. Sinatra called her "the Blue Jew." To my knowledge, he never made a play for her, which was a token of his esteem for Jilly.

With both Sam Giancana and Hank Sanicola out of the picture, Mr. S could not live by Jilly alone. He needed a whole new entourage, and he set out to recruit it, basically along the path of least resistance, that is, the actors in his films. When it came to this entourage, for Mr. S, Size Mattered. Sensing that, now more than ever, his body could stand being guarded, he gravitated to big, burly bodyguard types. Two of his favorites were Brad Dexter, a powerful Serb, and Dick Bakalyan, an equally powerful Armenian. Both were with him in Hawaii for the 1964 filming of *None but the Brave,* and both were around for his supposedly near-death experience when an unexpected undertow swept him out toward treacherous high surf. I was there, and it was much less near to death than the press made out. The producer Howard Koch's wife Ruth was swimming on the beach in front of our rented house. The water was quite shallow very far out, so there wasn't really much risk of drowning. However, the undertow tripped Ruth up and Sinatra, who swam over to help her, got tripped up as well. Immediately a young Hawaiian surfer paddled over to help them both out. As he was helping them back to the beach, Dexter, who saw from the house that something was going on, dove in and assisted him.

They may have swallowed a lot of salt water, but neither Ruth nor Frank was in mortal danger. However, it seems as if *everyone* near the incident made it appear far worse than it was and took credit for helping save Mr. S's life. Mr. S's modest candor ("I just got a little water on my bird," he told reporters) about the incident was written off as his trying to be cool. Nevertheless, delighted that it hadn't been as bad as people thought and following his superstitions about always being grateful, Sinatra *gave* credit to everyone, including film credit. Dexter was designated a full producer (a title, like talk, is cheap in Hollywood) on a number of Mr. S's next movies, until he started believing he was a *real* producer. Then Mr. S cut him down and cut him out. The Lord giveth, the Lord taketh away.

Maybe if I had been bigger, I might have become a producer, too. But I never wanted to be one. An actor or a singer, maybe, but a producer? No way. All I had seen producers do was take a lot of abuse from stars, about everything from the nature of their role to the furniture in their dressing rooms. How many times did I see Mr. S make Howard Koch *cry*? I could easily pass on producing. Instead I just kept doing my job, which I still loved despite its having become as perpetually unpredictable as Mr. S's shifting moods. As he got older, approaching fifty, I might have thought his maturity, if not his Sicilian superstitions, would have made him kinder, gentler, more appreciative of the little things in life. Instead he got more psycho. One night in Hawaii, I was cooking a dinner for him and his guests Spencer Tracy and Katharine Hepburn. Tracy was one of Mr. S's favorite actors. One of the highlights of Sinatra's career was working with Tracy in *The Devil at 4 O'Clock,* also shot in Hawaii in 1960. Mr. S admired Hepburn, too. He also wanted to fuck her. That desire had taken him by surprise. He used to think of her as a sexless tomboy until he saw her in the see-through tank suit she wore to go swimming in the ocean at dawn, just as Mr. S was drunk and about to go to sleep. He talked about the erotic dreams he had about her, about her being the hottest fifty-something star in the business.

Mr. S's lust was pure fantasy, because no couple in Hollywood was tighter than Tracy and Hepburn, who were superdiscreet about their affair for decades. Maybe that's why they were invulnerable, even to a sexual Machiavelli like Mr. S. They never went out in public together, hence our at-home dinner. It could be that Mr. S was feeling particularly horny and frustrated, because he was extra edgy that night. When I served the spaghetti marinara, which I had made a million times for him, he tasted it, started raving that it wasn't *al dente*, and picked up the bowl and threw the pasta all over me and my white jacket. This was the only time he had ever abused me, but once was enough. Tracy and Hepburn were so appalled that they left immediately, while Sinatra cleared the table by smashing all the dishes. I left, too, trying my best to conceal the hurt and humiliation I felt. I thought about leaving permanently, for the first time in my tenure with him. Then I thought better of it. Instead, I went down to Kalakaua, the Fifth Avenue of Honolulu, and treated myself to about $2,000 worth of new clothes, and had them send the bill to Sinatra. The next day when I got back to the house Mr. S tried to treat the incident as a big joke. "You're not pissed at me, are you, Spook?" he asked, trying to make me feel like a square for not playing his party game.

"Me, boss? Pissed? Why should I be pissed?" I tried to be as cool as he was. I had vented my anger in my shopping spree, which he didn't know about yet. Mr. S never apologized, but he never complained about the bill, either. Being Frank Sinatra meant never having to say you're sorry, but it didn't mean he was without remorse. You just had to know how to read his "Remorse Code." Whenever he tried to treat a slight as a big chuckle, you knew he was trying to apologize to you.

We kept traveling and kept escaping. Aside from all the trips to Europe, one of my most memorable journeys was returning to New Orleans, which, at the time of my father's murder, I had vowed I wouldn't do. Mr. S made it easy for me. We stayed in the Presidential Suite at the Roosevelt Hotel on Canal Street. As a kid I had worked as a shoeshine boy in the barber shop there. In those days they didn't even have black chambermaids at the Roosevelt. Now here I was, all duded up in a suit and tie, and with Frank Sinatra to boot. The old-timers at the Roosevelt who remembered me as the little bootblack nearly fell over. It was hail the conquering hero. I showed Mr. S my old neighborhood, I showed him the River Road plantations that I used to run away to, I tried to get him to eat a fried oyster po'boy sandwich, but he wasn't adventurous about food. One place we didn't visit was my father's grave. Some parts of home you really can never go back to again.

We often returned to Israel, which Mr. S decided was his favorite country. Mr. S often boasted he was "King of the Jews." He donated big money to Zionist causes, and would plug the place every time he had a chance, like doing a cameo in the 1965 epic *Cast a Giant Shadow*, about the bloody founding of the Jewish state in 1948. Kirk Douglas starred, and Mr. S did a cameo as a bomber pilot. I liked Israel, too, so much that on one trip to the Promised Land I let Sinatra and Van Heusen talk me into rediscovering my "Jewish roots." Why, they insisted, should Sammy Davis be the only black Jew? They pointed to the Falashas, the black Jews of Ethiopia, who were a sect in Israel. Come on, George, they pushed me, embrace your Inner Jew. What the hell, I thought. I probably could use some faith. I had lost two families. I was alone. I may have thought I was pretty cool. I may have thought I was Frank Sinatra. I may have been crazy. Yes, a little religion might keep my life in order. So I let them find me a rabbi in Jerusalem, and after a three-day crash course, they got me a quickie bar mitzvah at a beautiful temple overlooking the ancient walls of the City of David. Afterward, to celebrate my being a man, they took me to a brothel filled with frock-coated Hasidic diamond dealers drooling after the blond Polish hookers. Then we went to a fancy restaurant and I got so drunk on kosher wine I passed out.

The next morning when I woke up, I had an instinct something wasn't quite right. I soon found out that Sinatra, Van Heusen, the entire group, had all flown back to England, a day earlier than we had planned. I also discovered that all my credit cards had been taken, and that all I had in my wallet was less than fifty dollars. This was before cash machines, and no one in this country wanted to extend credit to this black Jew. I tried calling London, but the guys had canceled their reservations at the Savoy, with no forwarding address. In L.A. Gloria Lovell was clueless. For whatever reason, she said she was unable to wire money to me in Israel. I had no family to call for help. My life had come to revolve so entirely around Frank Sinatra that I had absolutely no one else.

As it turned out, everyone was in on what was a massive joke, including Gloria Lovell, who had lied to me. The conversion wasn't part of the joke. They *liked* my becoming a Jew. They only wanted to teach me what kind of Jew I really was. The answer was a scrambling Jew. It took me three days and a lot of fast and heavy bullshit to get a series of cheap flights that took me back to London, where they had just left, then on to L.A. Was it mean? Absolutely. Mr. S loved being mean. That was his sense of humor. Yet he gave me a bar mitzvah present of a thousand dollars when he saw me, plus a big hug for being as resourceful as he knew I would be in getting home. Just because he liked torturing me didn't mean he didn't love me. Or so I thought.

8

Generation Gap

B Y 1965, everything about the Hollywood that Frank Sinatra had come of age in was in decline, including Frank Sinatra himself. As if approaching fifty weren't traumatic enough, seeing your city and your business on the eve of destruction made life seem precarious, especially for a control freak like Mr. S. The film industry was in a mess, precipitated by the financial disaster of *Cleopatra*, which ruined a lot more than Eddie Fisher's marriage. Fox, which had produced the Roman scandal, was forced into selling off most of its back lot to create the office park of Century City. It wasn't just *Cleopatra* that was killing the movies, though that was the biggest of all fiascos, the most costly flop. Most films were terrible, and most people were giving up on them and surrendering to television.

Los Angeles itself was going the way of the big screen. The great restaurant/nightclubs like Ciro's and Mocambo and the Trocadero, with their plush banquettes, black-tie crowds, palace-level service, towering and flaming dishes, were all out of style and out of business. These restaurants were like *Cleopatra*, too spectacular for their own good. The stars weren't out at night anymore. The Sunset Strip was a dead zone, in the weird limbo of nothingness between the Eisenhower fifties and the psychedelic sixties, but the sixties, as we would know them, hadn't yet happened in 1965. The Beatles were just emerging from England, and big change was in the air, but Mr. S thought the moptops were a stupid fad like hula hoops and Davy Crockett coonskin caps. They weren't quite as bad as Elvis; at least they're *white*, he joked. He didn't give them long. He wasn't any keener on the Motown sounds of the Supremes or the Temptations, the Brill Building pop of the Drifters, or the surf rock of the Beach Boys, though he was a bit more tolerant of the Four Seasons, mainly out of Jersey Dago chauvinism. The one who drove him completely around the bend was Barbra Streisand, and not because she was Jewish. I thought he might approve of her if only because she wasn't a rocker, but he thought she symbolized how low Broadway had sunk. He didn't like her style of singing. Mr. S thought Barbra was too phony, too forced, too theatrical, rubbing her Brooklyn-ness in your face. He wasn't rubbing Hoboken, at least not when he sang. To Sinatra, modern music was either bubble gum or mediocre. He saw himself as the last bulwark of quality and tradition, the one who cared about something more than the crowd's quick buck. By and large, then, Mr. S was pretty down on America.

In view of these feelings and what a sad place Los Angeles was, Mr. S decided that he'd rather be in Europe, even in his hated Big Italy. So there we went to film his macho World War II picture, *Von Ryan's Express*. Between takes he would listen to Puccini and old Neapolitan folk songs and throw cherry bombs at the elegant but pompous ski crowd of Cortina d'Ampezzo, where we were shooting. He also liked to use extra explosives to blow up the hotel toilets of his tough-guy supporting actors/cronies Brad Dexter and Dick Bakalyan, exactly at the moment they needed them.

Sometime Mr. S's jokes would get so malicious that even *he* couldn't stand them. There was a beautiful Italian production secretary on *Von Ryan* who had recently married a young American film publicist living in Rome. Mr. S had a thing for her, but as a newlywed she was too much in love to cheat on her husband, even with Frank Sinatra. Mr. S simply couldn't fathom this. He said the publicist was "a zero," unworthy of his new bride, and I'd say Mr. S was more jealous of this poor guy than he was of Prince Ranier. Every manifestation of the couple's love for each other just stuck in Sinatra's craw, particularly a lovely white cashmere sweater the husband sent the secretary as a gift. One weekend, when the husband came up to Cortina to visit, Sinatra ran into the couple in the lobby of the Miramonte Majestic Hotel. The secretary proudly introduced her husband to Mr. S, who responded by taking a fountain pen and autographing "Frank Sinatra" in huge letters on the back of the white cashmere sweater. The couple was speechless. Before the secretary broke down crying, Mr. S had left the lobby. The next Monday, when the stores opened, he had me go and buy three identical cashmere sweaters, in red, white, and blue, and deliver them, without any note of explanation or apology, to the secretary's hotel. Mr. S never told me he was sorry, but I know he was. It just wasn't his style to express regrets, outside of his music.

On weekends we didn't spend on Cortina, all Europe was our playground. We went to Spain to see Ava. She was at the tail end of a violent affair with George C. Scott. Until Ava fell in love with Scott while in Rome filming John Huston's epic on the Book of Genesis, *The Bible*, Sinatra had nothing but admiration for Scott. He was a real actor's actor, a Broadway light married to another Broadway light,

Colleen Dewhurst, and now a movie star. Mr. S didn't frequent the theatre, though he loved Scott in *The Hustler* and *Dr. Strangelove*. But once he started with Ava, Sinatra *hated* him. I suppose he felt that way about any man Ava chose over him, like Walter Chiari. He felt defeated, like a loser.

Scott was threatening to Mr. S in other ways than winning Ava and serious acting. He was a genuine tough guy, a former Marine and a brawler who actually beat up paparazzi and nosy journalists, things Mr. S was *accused* of doing but never did. I had met Scott briefly in 1963, when Mr. S had done a one-day cameo (along with Tony Curtis, Kirk Douglas, and Burt Lancaster) in John Huston's murder mystery *The List of Adrian Messenger*, of which Scott was the star. He had a lot of presence. I could feel his seething power just watching him move so determinedly. Scott was also only in his late thirties, younger than Ava, who had crossed forty, and a decade younger than Frank. What Sinatra hated most of all, though, was that Scott used all his brutality *on* Ava. He had beaten her up several times, fracturing her collarbone in Rome and putting her in a neck brace, and destroying a suite at the Savoy in London and leaving her black and blue. Yet Ava kept going back for more, and that drove Mr. S nuts. Eventually, she called the London cops, who arrested Scott, then finally called it quits. Scott went back to Dewhurst, but got so depressed over losing Ava he ended up in a Connecticut sanitarium.

Ava could do that to a guy, even the toughest guys like Scott and Sinatra, to whom she was still doing it almost a decade after their divorce. Although he chased her to Spain, Ava blew Mr. S off romantically. She let him sleep in the garage of her Madrid home but not in her bed. Thwarted by Ava's rejection, Mr. S, in turn, blew up. We flew down to Málaga on the coast to try to relax, but it didn't work out that way. When some Spanish cop came to our hotel and wanted to question Mr. S after a groupie in a Málaga nightclub he had dismissed without an autograph tried to get attention by claiming he had hit her, he flipped out. He called Generalissimo Franco "a Spic faggot." Such talk was not cheap in Spain. Protesting his right to "free speech," Mr. S was thrown in jail overnight, and the *Von Ryan*'s producer, Saul David, had to fly in from Italy to post the heavy bail. "Fascist bastards!" Sinatra yelled as we got on the plane. Luckily Ava was relocating to London, so we wouldn't have to go to Spain again. Until Franco finally died, Sinatra was *persona non grata* in Iberia, while Spain was even more *non grata* in Mr. S's travel book. As with most producers, this was Saul David's first and last film with Sinatra. It was further proof that producing was one career move I could gladly forgo.

This time Mr. S was relieved to be back on American soil. We returned to the Fox lot, where the interiors of *Von Ryan*'s were shot on a sound stage. "One-take Frank" was how Sinatra was known to the Fox executives. At that point his serious acting ambitions were just about over, but nobody expected much from him other than to show up and be the star that he was. Frank did do one double take the day he saw Mia Farrow's underwear-free silhouette. The nineteen-year-old star of the TV hit *Peyton Place* had come over to our sound stage to watch one of her idols at work. The rest was history, love and marriage, then more history.

Mia's looks, her willingness to show all, and the shock of the new that she showed him under her see-through dress, got her through Mr. S's Palm Springs door and into his bed. The rest was accomplished by Mia's cheering squad of Hollywood's Old Guard who were friends of her mother and late father. Pushing Mr. S into the arms of Mia, in what became a campaign To Get Frank Married, were Mr. S's new group of powerful Establishment friends. This cabal was a combination of Old Hollywood Stars, like Roz Russell (*Auntie Mame*) and Claudette Colbert (*It Happened One Night*), and Old Jewish Money, like Bennett Cerf, the star of *What's My Line* and the founder of Random House, and Armand Deutsch, the heir to Sears, Roebuck, and, of course, the Goetzes. Where were the Dagos of yesteryear? The "big" ones had gone the way of Sam Giancana, who had finally been sent to prison for contempt of court (and of Bobby Kennedy). The Jilly boys were in the background, trotted out for after-hours revelry. Basically, Mr. S had ascended to the Swifty Lazar–New York elite "theatah" crowd. It had taken him ten years, plus his expulsion by the mob and by the Kennedys, to land him there, but this was his new life, and Mr. S was convinced by its denizens that Mia had the Right Stuff to be part of it.

Taking time to analyze the eligibility situation, I calculated that Mia scored very high on Mr. S's checklist for what he wanted in a woman:

1. Beautiful.
2. Classy.
3. Pedigreed.
4. Intelligent.
5. Big eyes.
6. Thin.
7. Sleek legs.
8. Irish Catholic.
9. Natural (minimal makeup and perfume).
10. Healthy (doesn't smoke).
11. Immaculate.
12. No kids (now or ever).
13. Blind devotion.

A corollary to the last requirement was that the candidate would give up whatever career she had to make Mr. S her full-time career. Age and maturity were not important criteria for Sinatra, who could be attracted to either young or old, silly or serious.

Where Mia fell most short on the Sinatra Test was on the intelligence part (not that she was stupid, just spacey), the smoking part, and, above all, the kid part. Nor did she act classy, in the Grace Kelly sense. She was a funky hippie. But that could be changed. That was what playing Pygmalion was about, if that's what Mr. S wanted to do. Thus far in his fifty years Frank Sinatra had never found a woman to get the perfect score. Ava was the closest, and she remained his ideal. Then again, maybe he didn't want to find his perfect mate. He often said that his loneliness and longing were what made his singing what it was. If he were content, the music would lose its edge, its soul, its heart and heartbreak. Perhaps it was better that Saturday night be the loneliest night of the week. Once he met Mia, though, he began to think perhaps not.

Where to spend his nights, lonely and otherwise, was becoming an issue. Outside the rarefied world of his first-night, Lazarian crowd, Mr. S was as down on New York, New York, as he was on Los Angeles. He called the Big Apple "the Sewer." Manhattan in the midsixties was at a low ebb, rife with crime, garbage, and flight to Scarsdale. Mr. S had absolutely no nostalgia for the city of the forties that had made him a star. He had less than no interest in taking a walk down Broadway or any other sentimental journey on the sidewalks of the city. Of course, I got a rush out of being in the city, just being out on the town, and he couldn't understand it. "I guess you don't have to worry about being mugged," he said to me. "You're camouflaged." The idea was that blacks didn't prey on each other, and he blamed them, and the Puerto Ricans, for destroying his "wonderful town."

Mr. S gave New York no chance whatsoever of a comeback. His Manhattan was a closed circle of Patsy's and Jilly's, for Dagoism, and La Grenouille and Le Pavillon, the two most expensive French restaurants in the city, where he went with his theatrical friends and society dates like Gloria Vanderbilt. Although he had been intimidated by the equivalent snobby "frog pond" kind of place in Paris, such as Tour d'Argent, the nasty French captains in New York knew how to suck up to Mr. S. They would give him the Jilly treatment that their haughty counterparts would never do on their native soil. Normally, Sinatra would have lit a few cherry bombs to shake up this pretentious bullshit, or do his favorite party trick of pulling the tablecloth from the table, usually leaving the china and silver in place, but sometimes blowing it, and a small fortune in crystal. But now he was buying into the phoniness. I was glad he didn't start making me wear a uniform. I think it wasn't so much that he was aging, but that he had joined an aged elite that behaved in a mannered way. Mr. S wanted to fit in with them, play by their polite rules, go to their rarefied haunts. Yet the Old Sinatra was still there. That's why he insisted on keeping Jilly around, to remind him of where he had come from and the high/low life he had loved to lead. And that's why I was there, for the same reason. To him I was still the old George, his man "Spook." He didn't treat *me* any differently. Mr. S wasn't quite Jekyll and Hyde, but the two sides to him were working out an arrangement of how to peacefully coexist.

Back in L.A., the Goetzes seemed less intimidating to me now than when I was a temp waiter for them. Maybe because Edie's potentate father, Louis B. Mayer, had died, maybe because they were older, maybe because I had gotten around since then, they were much more accessible. They still "Snoogied" each other to death, kissing and hugging and flattering, and their dearest wish was for their boy Frankie to have a marriage as blissful as theirs. I now noticed that Bill Goetz's humor wasn't much more elevated than Jilly's. He, too, loved corny jokes, and for all his art, he'd say things like, I'm going to Madrid to see that naked broad in the Prado, meaning Goya's *Naked Maja*. The Goetzes still gave the best parties in town. Once, during some dinner for visiting royalty that happened to fall during the World Series, they set up twenty televisions, one at each table, inside and out, to make sure no one had baseball as an excuse to miss their glamorous affair. These were the most gourmet TV dinners you could imagine.

While Mr. S was embracing seniority, Dean Martin was getting younger than ever. Drink in hand, he parodied himself on his hit TV series, backed by his famous chorus line of showgirls. He knocked the Beatles off the charts with "Everybody Loves Somebody," which became the number one pop song in America. And he became an American James Bond in his Matt Helm series of spy spoof films. Dean, one hot Dago, chided Mr. S for hanging out with the "Hillcrest Set," shorthand for the old rich Jews of *the* showbiz country club. Frank and Dean always had different temperaments. Now, with the Rat Pack gone with JFK, they remained in their different worlds. One Sunday in Palm Springs, Dean stopped by after a full morning of golf and found Mr. S, Jilly, and Jimmy Van Heusen still asleep with six hookers in various states of undress sprawled around the house. Dean shook his head with the dismay of a serious older brother of a juvenile delinquent. "You'd think they'd be sick of this same old shit by now, wouldn't you, George? Hell, *you* must be sick of it."

"You know I love this job," I said, poured him a drink, and turned on the television so he could watch sports until the boys woke up.

Sammy was pretty much gone as well, doing the "family thing" with May Britt. While Mr. S was hanging out with the "theatah" crowd, Sammy was actually *in* the theatre. He had a huge Broadway smash *Golden Boy,* which ran from 1964 to 1966. And instead of hanging out with Bennett Cerf, as Sinatra did, Sammy actually wrote and published his autobiography, *Yes, I Can,* which was a top bestseller in 1965. Sinatra was pleased for the success of Dean and Sammy, though he seemed somewhat perplexed that they had not only thrived without him but also might be leaving him in the dust

One of the "Old Jews" Dean had teased Frank about who *wasn't* a Jew was the very patrician, very rugged Princeton dropout and agent turned theatrical producer Leland Hayward (*South Pacific, Gypsy*), who was the closest substitute Mr. S had found for Humphrey Bogart. Like Bogie, Hayward was heavy on the booze and loved by the ladies. He had been married to actress Margaret Sullavan (the first wife of his client Henry Fonda), then to Slim Hawks, whom he took from director Howard. Now he was with Pamela Churchill, who had been married to the son of Winston. Hayward was probably the best socially connected man in all show business, and Mr. S hung on his every glamorous success story.

Hayward had his big flops, too, and certainly he would not have won a Tony for child-rearing. One daughter committed suicide, and the son himself was committed by his father to a loony bin for running away from prep school. Mr. S was fond of the boy and even flew to the Menninger Clinic in Topeka to visit him. The boy eventually got out and produced *Easy Rider* (which in Mr. S's current mind-set would have meant that the kid should have stayed in the clinic). Third wife Pamela, who was a famous British adventuress, with affairs with Aly Khan, Gianni Agnelli, and one of the Rothschilds under her belt, had big eyes for Frank Sinatra. Strangely, he had none for her. Finding her dumpy, he called her "the Jersey cow." Pam was forever stroking Mr. S's back, flattering him, flirting. It did her no good. He asked me to seat her away from him at Palm Springs dinner parties. If Pam had been skinny, her ploys might have worked, but her maternal routine didn't play with Mr. S. "I've *got* a mother," he said. I think the problem was one of keeping Mr. S down on the farm, after he'd seen mini-Mia. Once he'd been captivated by her "new look," for Mr. S, Thin was In.

After her "unveiling" on the Fox lot, things between Mia and Frank moved quickly. She was down at Palm Springs and in his bed in short order. I had to stock up on more organic, vegetarian food for her than I did for Greta Garbo, though now it was easier to find. The odd couple did have some history in common. Mr. S told me that Mia's late father, John, an Australian boozer and womanizer, had directed Ava Gardner in *Ride Vaquero* in 1953, at the height of her turmoil with Mr. S, and had had an affair with her. Thus Sinatra had this score to settle, even if it had to be done over John Farrow's dead body. Mr. S had even met Mia once before, when she was about twelve, at the time he was doing his cameo in *Around the World in 80 Days*, for which her father would share the Oscar for Best Screenplay. He claimed to think she was awfully cute back then, and claimed that John Farrow was deeply threatened by those thoughts, given his own transgressions with Frank's wife. There was some chemistry there, but when Mia first showed up at the house with her pigtails and weighing about eighty pounds, what came to my mind were not wedding bells but the teens on *American Bandstand*.

Then the coven of golden oldies got their marriage campaign into high gear. Most of them were friends with Mia's mother, the beautiful Maureen O'Sullivan, who had played Jane in all the Johnny Weissmuller *Tarzan* movies. Ungawa! Mia, it turned out, was one of the most eligible society girls in L.A. She ran with a pack of beauties who had been her classmates at Marymount, the exclusive Catholic girls' school where Nancy and Tina had gone. (That Tina was only two grades behind her dad's new squeeze didn't strike anyone in this crowd as weird. I guess Bogie and Bacall, pillars of this community, had the same spread.) Mia's friends and romantic rivals included Candice Bergen; Tisha Sterling, who was the daughter of actress Ann Sothern; Kris Harmon, the daughter of football great and sportscaster Tom Harmon and sister of future star Mark Harmon; and Sheila Reeves, whose father owned the Los Angeles Rams. Mia was lowest on this list of teen goddesses; she had her own score to settle, to show these little bitches who was Number One. She may have seemed like a meek church mouse, but in fact she was every bit as driven as Sinatra.

At first Mr. S was embarrassed to be seeing this teenager. He wasn't embarrassed by much, but this one was a little beyond the pale. Mia came down to Palm Springs, and they'd never go out. It was a total backstreet deal. The only people who knew about her were Jilly, Van Heusen, Jack Entratter, and Yul Brynner, who was hanging around a lot at the time, sponging off Frank for food, drink, and girls. As I said, Yul was as cheap as Peter Lawford. He may have been the King of Siam, but to us he was Uncle Scrooge, the king of tightwads. Mia seemed more impressed by Yul as a star than she was by Mr. S. Sinatra may have been Mia's idol, but all she was idolizing was an image, a style, a legend. Mia knew zip about Sinatra's songs, his movies, his struggles. I thought the coven's idea that Frank should marry Mia was insane, though of course I held my counsel.

It wasn't that Mia was a Beatles girl or a Stones girl, as opposed to a Frank girl. She was a *nothing* girl, a total space cadet. In a while, she would become a yoga freak, a Maharishi devotee, but in the first bloom of her romance with Sinatra, she was a clueless nineteen-year-old whose main passion was her deaf cat. She was like a kid in a contest with other kids to see who could be the first to get the autograph of a big star. As it was, the real autograph Mia Farrow was after was Frank Sinatra's DNA.

Mr. S himself was like an insecure schoolboy, wanting to know what the guys thought of his girl "She's fantastic, don't you think?" he'd ask, and what could you say? That she was "modern?" "Different?" "Cute?" Yul was the most supportive. He was a closet AC-DC himself, having had a secret affair with Sal Mineo. He pushed the Mia thing, saying she was "divine." Fascinated with colors and fabrics and styles, Yul sounded like a Seventh Avenue fashion designer. Mia was his own little model. As for the tougher critics in the group, Mr. S would have liked us to say what a sex kitten she was, but none of us had a frame of reference for anyone like her. Marilyn Monroe, even dead, was still everyone's ideal.

Julie Christie was the new British look. But Mia was . . . Mia. Twiggy wouldn't hit the scene for two more years. Kate Moss was decades away. Waif was the word, but it wasn't a word Mr. S would have dug. I guess he was way ahead of the curve on Mia.

Eventually, Mr. S, urged on by the coven, particularly Edie Goetz and Roz Russell, went public with his new squeeze. He was most uptight about introducing her to his kids, who were basically her age, and to Big Nancy, who he knew would be appalled. Dean's great joke was that the Scotch he drank was older than Mia, and Ava's great joke about Mia being "a fag with a pussy" was that Frank was a latent homosexual who was finally coming out. She knew better, but she couldn't resist the opportunity to tease Mr. S. No one, absolutely no one, took this romance seriously. Yes, Lauren Bacall was nineteen when Bogart found her, but she was throaty and sexy and seemed twenty-nine. Mia seemed twelve. I was there when he brought Mia to Big Nancy's to meet the family. At first there was a lot of dead air, pregnant silences. It was so weird, seeing the past and future Mrs. Sinatras side by side. It was a true test of Big Nancy's tolerance, and the fact that she didn't try to strangle Mia—or Frank—got her a gold star from me. Big Nancy had basically no comment the whole time, but Little Nancy, who in December had her first huge success with "These Boots Are Made for Walkin'," was over the shock of Tommy Sands leaving her and was feeling secure enough to be gracious. And since Mia and Tina were pretty much contemporaries, they had much more in common than Mia had with Frank. Aside from Frank Jr., who had distanced himself from his father and didn't bother to show, the Sinatra kids were incredibly nice to Mia, and didn't give their dad any shit about her.

Mr. S pressed on, despite an awful beating from the press, with which he had had a dreadful relationship for decades. Reporters hounded him and Mia everywhere they went, including out to sea. In

August 1965, he chartered a big yacht, the *Southern Breeze,* to sail up the rocky coast of New England. Mia's *Peyton Place* producers gave her a hiatus on the show by putting her character on the show in a coma. Soon Mia may have wished she were in one, or at least under the covers. On the yacht were Roz and her husband, Freddie Brisson, an Anglo-Danish Broadway and West End producer, Claudette and her husband, Joel Pressman, an ear, nose, and throat doctor at UCLA, the Armand Deutsches, and the Goetzes. Not exactly a swinging group, the yacht party would turn into *Voyage of the Damned* after a crewman drowned off Martha's Vineyard.

Just before that, Sinatra had taken Mia ashore with the group at Hyannisport to visit old Joe Kennedy, who was still alive but still not talking. I think the Goetzes, who knew Rose, were the prime movers of the excursion, as Mr. S hadn't really spoken to a Kennedy since he asked Bobby for help when Frank Jr. was kidnapped. For all the venom he felt toward Joe, the only reason Mr. S would have had to go see him would have been to pull the plug on Joe's respirator. Maybe he was doing it to show off: "I'm fucking a teenager, and you're a vegetable, Mr. A. Eat your heart out!" All through the cruise, there were daily headlines about the romance. Mother Dolly held forth from Hoboken that the whole affair was a publicity stunt that her magnanimous son was doing to help Mia's career, a fresh air fund for struggling actresses. Mia's mother pronounced that if Sinatra was to marry anyone, it should be *her.* The mama of Mia was only four years older than Mr. S. Although the cruise was supposed to last a month, Mr. S pulled the plug after a week of hell on the high seas.

Mr. S's fiftieth celebration at the Beverly Wilshire in December, 1965, created a new set of diplomatic and logistical problems. This birthday party was being given by the Two Nancys, and at least one Nancy wanted No Mia. Mia threw a fit, Big Nancy threw a fit, Mr. S threw a fit. That the party ever came off at all is a miracle. It was like the Israelis and the Arabs, there was so much fruitless shuttle diplomacy. Big Nancy basically said this was *her* party for *her* husband, and she sincerely would have taken long odds against Frank's actually marrying Mia. She saw her as just another girlfriend, with a limited shelf life. This party was for eternity, for good memories forever. Why should it be spoiled by a passing fancy? At one point, however, Little Nancy prevailed on Big. Let's make Dad happy, was her plea, and Big Nancy, ever the good sport and blessed peacemaker, relented. Little Nancy then invited Mia, but now Mr. S realized Big Nancy was right to begin with. He told Mia to skip this one.

So Mia ended up staying home, as did Frank Jr. The latter's absence really hurt Mr. S. It looked as though Sammy Davis Jr. wasn't going to show, either. Then he jumped out of the birthday cake. That was the only smile Mr. S had all evening. Adding to all the embarrassment, the next time Frank saw Mia, in protest against her exclusion, she had cut off all her hair. "Now I really will look like a fag," Mr. S moaned. But he tried his best to put an Audrey Hepburn spin on the whole little boy look. For all his whining, something about Mia kept turning him on. And on and on. He wanted men, and not just gay men, to find her sexy, but when one did, he went insane with jealousy. When he found out Mia had been dancing, with wild brio, with British singer Anthony Newley (*The Roar of the Greasepaint*) at the Factory, a new disco on Santa Monica Boulevard in Boys Town, Sinatra and Jilly planned an elaborate "ambush" of Newley, who was soon due at the Sands. Newley, who was married to Joan Collins, knew that merely dancing with Sinatra's girl was an act of treason and sedition. He knew that his impure thoughts would come back to haunt him. The guys were going to "lean on the Jew."

Before the rendezvous at the Sands we ran into Newley at Matteo's, the new red sauce, red tablecloth Hoboken-style restaurant in Westwood that was run by Matty Jordan, an ambitious waiter whom Dolly

Sinatra had delivered when she was a midwife. Matteo's had become Mr. S's new favorite hangout. It had toy trains, Mr. S's new passion, running on a ledge around the entire dining room. There was nothing but Sinatra Muzak. It was his kind of place. I was at the bar drinking while Frank, Jilly and some others were having dinner. I was highly surprised to see Newley, who must have been tempting fate by going in there. When the Brit saw Sinatra, he turned a whiter shade of pale. I think he tried to bolt, but Sinatra and Jilly jumped up from their table and beat him to the door. I expected a bloodbath, as did Newley. Jilly grabbed him, and Sinatra put his arm around his shoulder, as a prelude to strangulation. But it was all prelude. Sinatra congratulated him on his newest song, they talked showbiz, and not a word about Mia. Because Sinatra was heading to London to make his next film, Newley offered him the keys to his city, and then some. His groveling was almost comical, were it not so real. The fear was as satisfying to Mr. S, if not to Jilly, as the blood, and the ambush at the Sands never happened.

Jilly's bloodlust was sated in June. Mr. S was at the Polo Lounge of the Beverly Hills Hotel celebrating Dean Martin's forty-ninth birthday. At a nearby banquette was a pillar of the Beverly Hills community, Fred Weisman, who was married to the sister of an even bigger pillar, conglomerateur and art collector Norton Simon. Simon himself was married to Jennifer Jones, another trophy Mr. S had coveted and never got close to. Somehow words, dirty words, got exchanged between the Weisman and Sinatra tables, and because it was a drunken Dago birthday night, "Kike," "Hebe," "Sheenie," and other terms of endearment began flying from Sinatra and friends. That's *amore,* from this crowd. Somehow Weisman didn't feel the love. He got offended, and Jilly, who would stand up for Mr. S's honor even when there was none to stand for, began beating Weisman in the head with one of the phones the Polo Lounge was famous for parvenus wanting to be paged on. Weisman was lying inert in a pool of blood on the deep green carpet. The

Dagos got out of Dodge, pronto, before the cops and the ambulances could arrive. Mr. S was really pissed at Jilly and his mad temper, but he wouldn't ever have ratted him out. He knew that if *he* had been the assailant, Jilly "would take the bullet for me."

We all drove down to Palm Springs that night, to lie low. Two weeks later, when Weisman, who had been in a coma at Cedars-Sinai, finally emerged and decided not to press charges, Mr. S was as relieved as Anthony Newley had been. The fact that Sinatra and Mickey Rudin bought these millionaires off with God knows how many millions more of hush money obviously had a lot to do with it. But wasn't that what all the money was for, to buy your way out of nightmares? To celebrate, and to honor all those superstitions of his, Mr. S decided to "do the right thing" with Mia. He knew that thing was the wrong thing with his family, so he insisted on total secrecy when he went to a trusted, discreet Beverly Hills jeweler and bought Mia a nine-carat diamond engagement ring for ninety thousand dollars. No sooner had he slipped it on her finger than he got *farther* out of Dodge, jetting to London and leaving the future Mrs. S behind to contemplate their glorious future together. Mr. S truly believed he was living on borrowed time and that the good times were starting to run out.

The first few weeks in London on *The Naked Runner* were like a running bachelor party. "Swinging London" was in high gear. There were countless Mia-like waifs in their Biba miniskirts and Mary Quant tights strutting their great stuff on the King's Road. This was heaven on earth for leg men. Mr. S celebrated his dwindling time as a swinging single every second he wasn't filming. His enabler here, as always, was Jimmy Van Heusen, who rounded up gaggles of goddesses to party at the apartment we had rented on Grosvenor Square, across from the American embassy. Sinatra got me a room in the penthouse of the Playboy Club overlooking Hyde Park, another great source for "birds." We also went to visit Ava's new townhouse in

Ennismore Gardens in Knightsbridge. If she had only said she would give their love one last try, Mr. S would have dumped Mia then and there. But Ava was delighted with her low-key life in London. Her heart, she told him, now belonged to her Corgi, Rags. Mr. S even walked Rags for her, to show what he'd do to win her back. It wasn't enough. "I guess I got nowhere to run, do I?" he said sadly on our long walk through the rain back to Mayfair.

By the time we got to London, Mr. S's new record, "Strangers in the Night," was the top single in the world. He was bigger than the Beatles on their own turf. People in England worshipped him. It was amazing going into some trendy restaurant with him, like Trattoria in Soho or Alvaro's in Chelsea. The waters would part. He liked the scene, but he didn't like the food. I'd always have to cook for him back at the flat. Late at night we'd go out to the gambling clubs, Crockford's, the Victoria Sporting Club, and his favorite, the Colony, George Raft's place in Mayfair. It was full of Jersey gangster types and made Mr. S feel right at home. There was nothing to him like feeling at home. We went to some producer's American-style cookout at this stately home out near Oxford. The producer had a really bratty young kid, and Mr. S gave the kid a hot dog. The kid tried to take a bite, but the hot dog was plastic. The kid started to cry. It was a trick Mr. S had bought at some magic store in Piccadilly Circus. He couldn't stop doing practical jokes like that, even to little kids. It seemed kind of cruel, but that was the Sinatra humor. He ate out on the kid's shocked face for days. As for the classic, clubby British aristocratic stuff, nothing turned Mr. S off more. It was funny how he had come to embrace *French* phoniness, at least as it was practiced in snobby Manhattan temples of gastronomy like La Grenouille, but *British* phoniness somehow was different. One night he walked into, and out of, Annabel's in Berkeley Square, the chic-est nightclub in London, because he said the people all reminded him of Peter Lawford and he wanted to throw up.

He was also horrified at the prospect of running into Sam Spiegel, who lived in London like a pasha and was considered the lord of the film business at a time when lots of Hollywood types were living there to take advantage of the highly favorable exchange rate and of the James Bond–Beatles sensibility that had captured the imagination of potential ticket buyers. He often said he would beat the shit out of Spiegel, who had so many enemies that he traveled with bigger and meaner bodyguards than those of Mr. S. The showdown was all talk and no fisticuffs. We did happen to see Spiegel and his entourage of babes a few times at Alvaro's. Spiegel waved, Mr. S imperceptibly nodded recognition, and nothing else happened. The only star we would regularly go out with was Laurence Harvey, who never stopped stroking my inner thigh and trying to stick his tongue in my ear. "What do you expect of a fag Polack Hebe trying to pass as a straight British gent?" Mr. S said. "Let him blow you, George. How do you know he's not good? Just close your eyes and think of England." Contrary to orders, I kept these eyes wide open.

The Naked Runner's plot cast Sinatra as a retired CIA-type assassin whose son is kidnapped to blackmail the killer into going back to work. Talk about two sore subjects for Mr. S, political killings and kidnapping. Was he being masochistic? I think he was making one last effort to get that Best Actor Oscar. He figured, if you suffer enough, confront your worst demons, the Academy will reward you. As a measure of his seriousness, the film had almost no women in it, and no Sinatra trademark wisecracks. Yes, he had some snide comments about his film son's Beatle haircut. Long hair drove him batty, probably because he had so little left of his own, and because our half-hour toupee drill every day was such a tedious ordeal. There was also a big product plug for Jack Daniel's and a scene in a model-train shop, but this was no *Tony Rome* where Sinatra was playing Sinatra. It was more like *The Manchurian Candidate*, where Sinatra was *acting*, playing a man in conflict, a man in pain. On second thought, maybe he wasn't acting after all.

Pain or no pain, Mr. S was taking this film very seriously. He was not only the star but also the producer. (He had produced a number of his own films: *Johnny Concho, Robin and the Seven Hoods, None but the Brave.*) As producer, he had hired a young Canadian director named Sidney J. Furie, whose previous credit had been the Michael Caine espionage thriller, *The Ipcress File,* which had been an international hit. At the beginning of the shoot, Mr. S was very nice to Furie. When Furie's grade school teacher came to visit the set to see how far her star pupil had come, Sinatra took the two out to lunch, and gave the Canadian schoolmarm the thrill of a lifetime. Soon, however, he decided to interrupt the entire production, so he could fly to Las Vegas and marry Mia. He had left her at home because he expected to be terribly busy at the beginning of the shoot. I suppose he came to miss her. We took off in his new Lear jet, which had been a gift from his friend Bill Lear. The Lear replaced the *El Dago,* though Mr. S didn't give the Lear a name. Being Sinatra meant never having to pay for anything, since whoever gave him a gift, whether liquor, a car, or a plane, was assured of being featured in endless free publicity. The whole world wanted to live the way Mr. S lived, warts and all.

I think Mia must have been putting a lot of pressure on him, because the way it happened sure felt like a shotgun wedding. He didn't tell Big Nancy, he didn't tell the kids, he didn't even tell his mother, and he normally told her *everything.* We took the Lear jet back to America, overnighting in New York, where Mr. S had dinner with some old friends, then had a knockout redheaded hooker come over to the apartment. I suppose he was giving himself his own bachelor party, yet there was no joy the morning after. As we flew on to Vegas, Mr. S barely spoke, and I didn't dare make any jokes that came to mind like whistling "Get Me to the Church on Time." He wasn't drinking much, but he was chain-smoking. He looked grim, as if he were on his way to major surgery, or his own execution.

When we arrived in Las Vegas, we went straight to the Sands and did the deed. There was no luncheon, no premarital toasts, no festivities. We just got out in what was 110-degree heat, and drove to the hotel, where Mia was waiting. Mr. S gave her a quick peck on the lips, but it was certainly no *From Here to Eternity* embrace. The ceremony was performed by a judge in Jack Entratter's suite at the Sands. The only guests there were Jack, the Goetzes, Red Skelton, who was performing somewhere in Vegas, and me. Mr. S looked nervous and shell-shocked. Mia looked radiant, as if she had won the Irish Sweepstakes. The girl had gotten her man, at last. Now the even harder part was figuring out how to keep him.

We flew back to L.A., where the Goetzes gave the newlyweds one of their stop-at-nothing dinner parties. Hollywood royalty may have been there, Tracy and Hepburn (in separate cars, as always), Edward G. Robinson, Billy Wilder, George Cukor, but no Sinatras. They found out in the papers, and that was a slap in the face. Mr. S did stop in New Jersey en route back to London to introduce his bride to his parents. Dolly gave them a huge feast, but because of Mia's odd dietary restrictions, she would only eat salad, which was no way to the heart of an Italian mama. All the *scungilli, calamari, mortadella, osso buco,* it all was wasted on the waif. Nor was Dolly impressed by Mia's Broadway friends, such as Liza Minnelli, who was way too la-de-dah for the crowd on the wrong side of the Hudson. It felt like a cataclysm waiting to happen.

Because she understood her son's obsession with beautiful women, Dolly could understand Frank's marrying Mia, something Big Nancy could not. However, Dolly, who was as much a social and achievement snob, New Jersey-style, as Mr. S was, thought Mia was beneath Frank's station. He deserved a major movie star. In Dolly's view, Marilyn Monroe would have been the right girl for her famous son. So what that Marilyn couldn't cook? Neither could Mia, and at least Marilyn liked to eat. Dolly took me aside and said, with a combination of annoyance and defeat, "She's a little nothing. Is that the best he can do?" Dolly didn't believe Mia would amount to anything. This time she was wrong in underestimating her.

Big Nancy was too polite to complain to me about Mia. Her approach, as before, was a disrespectful silence. She didn't berate Frank for what Big Nancy's maid told me her boss saw as a sneaky, cowardly "Pearl Harbor" approach to the marriage. Big Nancy had this view of herself as Mr. S's only legitimate wife. All the rest was a Hollywood show. That he now had taken this child bride, behind Nancy's back to boot, was the cruelest insult he could have dealt her. The girls, while supporting their mother, both thought Mia was totally cool, and would try to hang out with her as much as they could, without rubbing it in Big Nancy's face.

Mr. S simply couldn't deal with the whole thing. He escaped to London, taking Mia with us to the Grosvenor Square flat. And there the troubles began. Mia knew far more people in England than Frank, including half the rock stars on the radio, and she wanted to see all of them. Mr. S wanted to see all of them dead, so that was a big conflict. Now Mr. S refused to go out at all, for fear of Mia's running into her young hipster friends. So she became his Prisoner of Zenda. Mia would stand at the window staring out across the square at the ugly modern American embassy with its huge and scary American eagle sculpture perched on top of it as in some monster movie. She reminded me of a teen who had been grounded by her folks. There was so much action in London, she complained to me, and her husband was "an old fuddy-duddy." She never said that to *him*. Mr. S never mentioned anything to me, that wasn't his style, to bellyache about his new bride. But he didn't seem happy. Neither Frank nor Mia acted like a blissful newlywed. Mr. S may have wanted to walk across Hyde Park and cry on Ava's nearby shoulder, but she told me, on my own occasional visits to Ennismore Gardens to walk her Corgis with her, that she wouldn't have it. He made his bed, let him sleep in it, she said. And so he did. There were few displays of affection outside the closed door of the bedroom, where Frank and Mia did spend most of their time together. Once shooting resumed on *Naked Runner*, the picture seemed to fall apart. Mr. S was both testy and unfocused. He was sleepwalking through his part, and the times when he would wake up, he would go into a rage. I felt sorry for the director, who was half in tears all the time.

Every weekend we would take the jet and go visit some rich old fart, like Jack Warner, who had a villa on the French Riviera. The idea was to keep Mia away from young and therefore bad influences. Eventually, Mr. S got the brilliant idea to shoot the rest of the movie in Palm Springs, which was kind of a stretch substituting for the green and gray of East Germany that the story required. "It's my picture and I'll shoot where I want to," was Mr. S's dictatorial attitude. When Brad Dexter, who was titular producer of the opus, tried to speak up for the "integrity" of the film, Mr. S basically cut him off and never spoke to him again, sending his hatchet man Mickey Rudin to do the dirty work. An even bigger hatchet was taken to the film by the critics, who saw it for the incoherent jumble it ended up being. So much for Mr. S's Oscar plans. At this point in his life, he was in such a deep depression that he seemed ready, willing, and able to self-destruct.

One thing Frank Sinatra missed terribly was the excitement of being a political kingmaker that he had tasted in the JFK election, before being stabbed in the back by the kings and princes he had made. With Lyndon Johnson in office, Yankee Dagos couldn't have been less welcome in Washington, D.C. Mr. S was a fighter who had been barred from the ring. He knew he was the champ; all he wanted was the chance to prove it. He got that chance in 1966 in the California gubernatorial campaign. The Democratic candidate was incumbent Pat Brown, who asked for Sinatra's help against his Hollywood challenger Ronald Reagan, in his first bid for public office. Mr. S was apoplectic that a bozo, or *Bonzo*, like Reagan would have the audacity to run for any office higher than dogcatcher. If anyone in Hollywood should be governor, it was Mr. S. Besides, at the time, Sinatra was still a liberal. He saw Reagan as a right-wing John Bircher, a Pacific Palisades Klansman. He also made fun of Nancy Reagan as both a failed actress and a failed Sinatra groupie (he claimed she had come on to him as a starlet in the forties, and he had said no), plus she had fire- hydrant legs. This election was a piece of cake. Just look at the entertainment lineup of Mr. S's Democratic superstars versus the Republican lineup: Roy Rogers, John Wayne, Pat Boone. It didn't seem close. It wasn't. Reagan won handily. Once again, Mr. S ate humble pie.

The only place where Sinatra could get the respect he deserved was at his desert fiefdom, the Sands. But even in Vegas, the times were beginning to change. Sinatra's first engagement as a new husband saw him sinking to a new low in tasteless humor. With Mia in the audience in front of the stage, Mr. S began a routine about his wife that was more appropriate for Henny Youngman ("Take my wife . . ."). He introduced Mia saying, "Finally I found a broad I can cheat on." He didn't stop at Mia. He joked that Sammy wasn't there because he was at his own opening, of a gas station in Watts that sold three varieties of petrol: regular, ethyl, and burn, baby, burn. As noted before, comedy wasn't Mr. S's forte, though that didn't stop him from trying. He came up with these routines himself. Because he was Frank Sinatra, the audiences would laugh, if only as a knee-jerk reaction, and often with their jaws dropping in bewilderment.

Mr. S could give, but he couldn't take. When his onetime buddy Shecky Greene made his famous joke; "Frank Sinatra saved my life. His goons were beating me up and he said, 'Enough,'" Mr. S did not laugh and excised Shecky from his buddy list. Jackie Mason might as well have been a dead man walking with his jokes about Sinatra's toupees and dentures and Mia's braces. Both Shecky and Jackie were badly beaten up by anonymous assailants. Although Mr. S had long broken with Sam Giancana and his genuine Mafia connections, he still knew a lot of tough guys who liked to *pretend* they were made men and did thuggish "favors" for Mr. S, favors he didn't want done. The press had a field day playing Guess Who. Mr. S felt he was being crucified.

Nothing was safe for Mr. S, not even the Sands. The hotel, and much of Vegas, was about to be bought up by Sinatra's old rival for the affections of Ava Gardner, Howard Hughes. The mob was having so much trouble of their own, they welcomed the opportunity to unload their casinos. Hughes was the sucker they had dreamed about. By now Sam Giancana was out of prison and had left the country, living in walled splendor in Cuernavaca, Mexico, and devoting his energies to criminal opportunities in Latin America, Colombian cocaine, Panamanian shipping, things of that sort. Mr. S sometimes reminisced about the old days in Chicago, Cal-Neva, early Vegas. He missed Mr. Sam like a lost uncle, or godfather, as it were. Johnny Rosselli was still around, actually helping broker the sting of Hughes. Now that Mr. S had gone the way of the Goetzes, he and Rosselli never crossed paths. Besides, after Cal-Neva and the split with Giancana, Rosselli was probably under mob pressure to give Sinatra the silent treatment.

An even worse treatment for Mr. S was the humiliation of having his credit cut off at the Sands, the House that Frank Built, but now it was Hughes's house. The Apollo astronauts, heroes of Mr. S's, had come to see his show. It was a total mutual-admiration society. The astronauts were completely snowed, particularly when Mr. S sang "Fly Me to the Moon" for them. Sinatra wanted to further show off by staking the moonmen to bets at the tables. But all bets were off. Again I stood back as Mr. S went wild. He hijacked one of the golf carts that the bellhops used, put Mia in shotgun, and proceeded to play bumper cars with everything in the lobby before crashing the cart into the all-glass entrance. He didn't intend to drive through the glass, for that would have put him and Mia at a risk even he, in his worst rage, wouldn't have taken. But the cart, like Sinatra, went out of control and hit the window, shattering it but not going through it, as the press reported for more dramatic effect. Somehow, neither Frank nor Mia was hurt in the demolition derby. He then tried to do a burn, baby, burn number to some couches and drapes in the lobby, which, luckily, didn't catch. When Mr. S failed to light his, or anyone else's fire, he took Mia and left. During the tantrum, no one, no guard, no clerk, dared to interfere with him. They still treated him as if he owned the place and had the right to destroy it if he wanted to.

If Jack Entratter, who was still managing the Sands but was somehow away from the place that night, had been around, this scene would have never happened. Yet without Entratter there to bend them, the new Hughes rules were strictly enforced. Mr. S was no longer God. It's hard not to be God anymore. The next day, Mr. S had a confrontation with Carl Cohen, Entratter's Number Two, a why-hast-thou-forsaken-me kind of man to man. And instead of kissing Mr. S's ring, as in the not-so-old days, Cohen, a mean Jewish brawler, knocked Mr. S's two front teeth out, provoked by Sinatra's having called him a "kike bastard motherfucker" (shades of Dolly's diction). Mr. S got new caps and, suffice it to say, never played the Sands again nor spoke to his lifelong friend Entratter, whom he accused of having intentionally disappeared from the showdown out of fear of his new boss Hughes. Sinatra signed with Caesar's Palace the next year, but this man did expect to be a prophet in his own country. When he wasn't, it was cruel and unusual punishment.

For Frank Sinatra 1967 was a very bad year. His biggest career accomplishment was the throwaway song "Somethin' Stupid," the only father-daughter love song ever to hit number one on the pop charts. It was a little incestuous, but, as Mr. S said, "Number one is number one. Take it any way you can get it." His other big achievement was being named chairman of the Italian-American Anti-Defamation League, "The Dago NAACP," as he termed it. Now that he was an elder statesman, he would have to can the racist humor. That was a major sacrifice. His being honored by the league made Mr. S feel old. The death of Spencer Tracy made him feel older. Being a pallbearer tagged all his Sicilian superstitious bases. He worried about being "in line."

But nothing bothered him more than what was happening in San Francisco, and Mr. S wasn't even there. In fact, he rarely went to the City by the Bay. It was cold and it was damp and it belonged to Tony Bennett anyway. At least it *used* to belong to Tony until it was taken over by Janis Joplin and Grace Slick and Jerry Garcia and the hippies in Haight Ashbury whose cancer of psychedelia, as Mr. S saw it, was spreading like a stoned contagion across America and the world. Everybody caught it, even the goddamned Beatles, on whom Mr. S would have taken long odds in Vegas that they would have been long gone by now. But here they were with even longer hair and this spaced out *Sergeant Pepper* album and this other freak from UCLA Jim Morrison and "Light My Fire," and Mr. S knew exactly what they were all selling. Drugs, drugs, drugs, his most despised commodity. He could sell all the Jack Daniel's in the world with *his* music, one more for the road, baby, but drugs, no way. He wished that Sgt. Barry Sadler ("Ballad of the Green Berets") would come and blow Sergeant

Pepper into oblivion. These hippies were body-snatching America's youth, brainwashing them, poisoning their minds. And worst of all, the most prized body these spaced invaders had snatched was that of his new wife.

Mia Farrow was a poster child for hippiedom. She loved going to San Francisco, she loved wearing flowers in her hair, she had every Beatle record, and would soon inspire some of them herself. There was no Eastern religion she wouldn't embrace, no astrologer she wouldn't consult, and no famous rock star, or cult figure, she wouldn't want to get to know. I never knew her to have cheated, physically if not spiritually, with Mr. S, but the times were loose and anything was possible. She was young and experimental and open to everything, and my job was to babysit her through her coming of age, the Age of Aquarius.

I turned forty in 1967. I didn't like turning forty any more than Mr. S liked turning fifty. We may not have been part of the "youth culture," but we both believed we were forever young. Unlike Mr. S, I was excited by the changes in the world outside. I did my share of drugs as well in my off hours. I let my hair grow, bought some bell bottoms and big collars, a chain or two, even got a Harley-Davidson. Mr. S scrutinized every slight change the way a seismologist checks fault lines for the slippage that signals disaster. "What's with the sideburns, George?" he'd ask. "What's with the long collar?" "Are those *flowers* on your tie?" I rolled with the times, but held the line. I never "freaked out," never went to a love-in, never joined a sit-in, or burned a bank.

Mr. S made a big point about the difference between *freedom* and *license*. "Don't go thinking that by growing your hair or getting high that you're gonna save the world, save your people, even save your ass," he warned me. He didn't go so far as to claim the whole hippie movement was a Communist plot, but he came close, blaming it on those insulated, permissive rich folks he called "Scarsdale liberals," whose bleeding hearts were about to be broken when they saw the country in bedlam. He suspected a radical, anarchistic element behind the big party America's youth was having. Mr. S didn't mind a welfare state, but he insisted on a state of *some* kind, and not the state of confusion where he thought we were heading.

Even though he had never served, he was a huge supporter of the military as a bulwark of our freedom. He was appalled at the way kids were attacking our soldiers over Vietnam when all the guys were doing was their duty. Once he saw I had an antiwar petition someone had given me to sign, and he gave me a long lecture on how, as a veteran, I would be committing a sacrilege by signing it. He warned that the JFK assassination could have been "just the beginning." In the next year, 1968, when both Martin Luther King Jr. and Bobby Kennedy were killed, I realized Mr. S may have been more than an aging reactionary. He *loved* America, and he would give his all to protect it. War or peace, Mr. S also really cared about me. He was worried I'd go wrong. If it weren't for him, I might have indeed gone too far. He was a stabilizing influence. For Mia, however, he was the Bad Daddy.

The unwritten social contract between Frank and Mia had two key points, no career, and no kids. In 1967 Mia was already flagrantly violating one and, from my perspective, calculating how to violate the other. Just to humor her, Mr. S "allowed" Mia to make one film a year. He assumed she would get it out of her system. Was he wrong on that one! She spent months in London and Berlin making her own spy thriller, *A Dandy in Aspic,* about an assassin hired to kill himself. Mr. S was so down on Swinging London he never went over to visit Mia on the set. He wasn't seeing anyone else in L.A., other than the occasional call girl, so I'd say he was being faithful. Mia was, too, but not according to the press, which Sinatra hated, and often with good reason for its sensation-seeking inaccuracy. The papers had a field day with *Dandy,* manufacturing big stories about Mia's torrid affair with her costar Laurence Harvey. The paparazzi caught them dancing together, in embraces that looked naughty and suspicious. That dancing. Mia should have been a go-go girl, she loved dancing so much. (I came to wish she hadn't.) The world press's blow-up of this "scandal" confirmed Mr. S's dim view of celebrity journalism as just another branch of creative writing. We both knew that the only member of our family that Larry wanted to have an affair with was *me*. So we let that slide. To appease her husband and thank him for his "permission" to let her act, she brought him home a gift of a black London Austin cab. He hated it. He was a Dual-Ghia guy, a swinging convertible racer. Austin cabs were drab, slow clunkers, for old ladies and square bankers in bowlers. Is *that* how Mia saw him? A James Bond Aston-Martin maybe, the one with the ejector seat, but an *Austin*? All the gift did was create more tension.

A far bigger problem was Mia's next project, *Rosemary's Baby.* Mr. S got the heebie-jeebies over that one. He saw the plot line about a waif who gets impregnated with the child of the devil as way too close to his home, a reflection of Mia's scarcely veiled wishful thinking. The girl envisioned herself, as she often told me, as a master-race breeding machine. How could a great man like Frank Sinatra *not* give her a child that would be more than a mere child. It would be a national treasure. It would be Rosemary's Baby. She talked to me about it all the time, saying what a crazy, selfish attitude he had and how she was going to turn his mind inside out. She made me drive her to go browsing at all the maternity boutiques for baby clothes. We'd go to furniture stores where she would imagine how she would decorate the child's room. If Mr. S ever heard some song on the radio like "Baby Love" he'd just cringe. Mia liked to sing the words to the hit song "If I Were a Carpenter," ". . . and you were a lady, would you marry me anyway, would you have my baby?" I think Mr. S may have tried to avoid sleeping with her at times for fear that she would get pregnant. She loved the challenge, always thinking of original ways to seduce him. Some "little boy," as the press tried to make her out. She was a total femme fatale. The only one who knew how seductive she was was Mr. S, the ultimate connoisseur of women. Mia was the equal of the Chairman of the Board.

Mia was a creative genius at starting fights that got Mr. S crazy. She'd push all his hot buttons, long hair, drugs, mysticism, rock, Vietnam, making him feel like the Ancient Mariner for being so out of it to disagree with her. "How can you *say* that?" was her favorite expression, delivered in a tone of insulting intolerance, the idea being that Mr. S was either an idiot or an animal. But Mia would find a way to bring these arguments or "discussions" around to a romantic resolution. I think what she most enjoyed was getting someone widely considered one of the planet's coolest ladies' men so hot and bothered over her. From where I sat, it was the most passionate relationship Mr. S ever had, including the aftermath beddings of his big rows with Ava.

Sometimes Mia could be sweet as sugar, as helpless as a lost choirgirl. And at other times she could outhooker the hookers, trying on some thousand-dollar dress, leaving it half open or unzipped, saying, "Don't I look *ridiculous* in this?" So ridiculous that Mr. S would rip it off and have his way with her. Unless she would play hard to get, like saying, not *now*, I have to meditate, which would make Mr. S even hornier for her. Mia's favorite outfits were the tie-dyed hippie dresses, which the classically old-fashioned Mr. S was embarrassed for her to wear in public with him. Yet she'd find see-through ones, or wear the rags in such a way as to turn Mr. S on, despite his aversion to the style. Once she got him into bed, she must have declared herself the winner, regardless of what Mr. S thought. I guess in Mia's case, love conquered all. Still, for all his passion for her, the baby threat concerned him.

Mia had Mr. S in such sexual thrall that love might have conquered all, except for one of Mia's fatal dancing spells. This one was with the last man on the planet that Mr. S wanted to touch his wife, and it wasn't someone like H. Rap Brown or Bob Dylan or Allen Ginsberg. It was worse than all of Mr. S's folk-villains combined. It was the Antichrist himself, Robert F. Kennedy! How Mia could have made such a false step was beyond everyone. Frank Sinatra was the one guy in Hollywood who was backing Hubert Humphrey. Yet given that she knew so little of what her husband was all about, outside of the boudoir, she may well not have even known about his backstory with the Kennedys and how they had nearly destroyed him. That was history, and Mia wasn't interested in history. She lived in the now, or somewhere in space. Wherever she was, her mind was in the wrong place when she hit the floor over and over with Bobby Kennedy at a Democratic fundraiser at the Factory, the same place Mia had done her thing, the wrong thing, with Anthony Newley. Mr. S was in New York, preparing for his new movie, *The Detective*, where he had a big role written in for Mia. Although *Rosemary* was the ultimate New York film, aside from exteriors at the Dakota, most of it was shot at Paramount, hence Mia was here and Frank was there.

Frank was way out there, when he heard the news. He didn't even call Mia to discuss it. What could she say? Some sins were simply unpardonable. She had already refused to abandon *Rosemary*, which had gone way over schedule, and start work on *Detective*. Mr. S was forced to look for a replacement actress. Might as well replace Mia everywhere. This was strike three, four, five . . . And she, as the umpire would say, was outta there! What was going on in his world, Mr. S wondered. He had just learned his "son," Sammy, was going to shoot a movie in London with Peter Lawford. It was called *Salt and Pepper,* and it was supposed to be a hip comedy. Hip my ass, Mr. S sneered. Sammy and Peter, Mia and Bobby, Jesus Fucking God. Acting as judge, jury, and high executioner, Mr. S sent Mickey Rudin to deliver divorce papers on the *Rosemary* set.

But as another baseballer said, it ain't over til it's over. Mr. S and

Ava had open divorce papers for years and years, and even a decade after the divorce was official, Mr. S was seriously in love with her. His greatest fantasy was that she would marry him once again. Dreams don't die. Mr. S's flirtations on *The Detective* with Lee Remick and Mia's substitute, Jackie Bissett, were more retaliatory than romantic. He had no one, nothing. Besides, the 1967 Christmas holidays were approaching. The coven, Mia's coven of Social Oldies, including Ruth Gordon herself of *Rosemary* (it *was* too close for comfort), were coming down to Palm Springs for the Christmas holidays. Mr. S was too embarrassed to spoil his own party. He had turned the compound into a resort, with a new New England-style cottage called the Christmas Tree House, which would be strung up with lights year round, plus another bungalow, a new screening room, and other amenities, including one whole cottage for his vast model train collection, which at the moment was giving him more pleasure than sex.

Mr. S had been crazy about toy trains since he was a boy, and his parents never had enough money to buy him more than a small set of Lionels. Mr. S would tell me how he'd go to the biggest toy store in Hoboken to look at the huge train display in the window, and dream. Now this was one dream he could make come true, even if the others were fading. Being married again had given Mr. S more time on his hands, which he devoted to building up his model train empire. There were Japanese Bullet Trains, French TEEs, Spanish Talgos, American Superchiefs. Mr. S would sit alone there all night, drinking Jack and playing Casey Jones. The two shadow careers he had were engineer and concierge. He had me so crazy buying the best sheets and towels and robes and toothbrushes and laundry bags that the Ritz had nothing on us. I started calling him HoJo, for Howard Johnson of the Orange Roofs and 21 Flavors. Frank Sinatra was Hollywood's Innkeeper.

What was an inn with no guests? So he begged Mia to come back and be his hostess, although she was devoid of all social graces and had no idea who to seat next to whom, pissing off lots of people. After two weeks and the coven had dispersed; however, so had Mia. Mr. S couldn't take the baby rap. He went off to Miami to sing at the Fontainebleau and to shoot *Lady in Cement,* which we all said was where he wanted to put Mia, gangland style. Mia went to India to visit the then current guru. She later told me one of his followers tried to seduce her while she was in a trance. So much for prophets. Once Mia left, Mr. S did show occasional signs of life. One night when we were at a Palm Springs restaurant, Ruby's Dunes, at a dinner with Liz Taylor and Richard Burton, the hairdresser Jay Sebring showed up at another table with a stunning, blond, six foot tall, sixteen-year-old "assistant." Like a homing pigeon, Mr. S dumped Liz and Dick, who were bitching at each other so much they hardly noticed, and joined Sebring's table.

Within fifteen minutes he was literally *under* it, ostensibly look-ing for his pen, but in reality going down on the Amazonian supermodel-to-be. I could see her giggling and loving it. This was "strangers in the night" at its ultimate. But nothing further tran-spired and Mr. S lapsed back into his Mia funk.

Mia eventually came back to L.A. and stayed at the mansion in Bel Air that Mr. S had redone for her. But they rarely intersected, in any way. When Mr. S's multiple stresses combined to give him pneumo-nia on the *Cement* shoot, Mia did fly down to Florida, but the vibe was more that she had come to bury him than to cheer him up. She gave up after a few days and went back to California. Nobody could seem to cheer up Mr. S, even Ava, who got so pissed off that he really wasn't dying, that when he got back to his old tricks of jealous recriminations about Ava's recent romance with the batterer George C. Scott and excavations of ancient history about Spanish bullfight-ers and Italian gigolos, Ava also packed up and left. She had barely lasted twenty-four hours. For the first time since we had been together, this man didn't want to depend on anyone. And I guess the person he most depended upon was *me*. No matter how he lashed out at everyone who came down to his Florida bedside, Mia, Ava, even Dolly and Marty, he never once raised his voice or said one nasty word to me.

I was very worried about his health. I assumed he was indestructible, and here he was, at the mercy of the place he hated above all others, a hospital. His skin was sallow, greenish. He was too weak to insist on wearing a hairpiece. He seemed to have given up. He looked frail and old and helpless, as well as furious at himself, and the heavens, for letting him get this way. Mr. S managed to recover, but he didn't recover his sense of humor. The minute he was strong enough to get out of bed, the tantrums resumed. Hookers were hired and fired. Rooms were trashed. Dishes were hurled against the walls of restaurants. Paintings were cut up. Even the assassination of Bobby Kennedy by Sirhan Sirhan brought him no sense of satisfaction or retribution. "It wasn't even one of *us*," he mumbled, staring into his increasingly frequent tumblers of Jack, as if he still belonged to the Outfit that had long cut him from its rolls that he was never really on. Through it all, however, he remained incredibly nice to me.

Any hopes for a happy ending with Mia evaporated when *Rosemary's Baby* became the number one hit in America, blowing *The Detective* off the screen and establishing Mia as a bona fide movie star. Hers was one career that was not going to end, not even for the Chairman of the Board, as Dean had recently christened him. Mia was already looking down the road. I remember when we went together to see *Casino Royale,* the star-studded James Bond spoof, the *Austin Powers* of its day, how she raved on and on about Peter Sellers, what a genius he was, that she had met him in London and how much he liked her and he was the next Charlie Chaplin and how "heavenly cool" he was. Woody Allen was in the same film, and to my mind much funnier than Sellers. Mia hardly noticed him. When I said how great I thought he was, she shrugged her shoulders sweetly and vaguely. "Stand-up," she dismissed him. I saw then that Mr. S was history, one that would not repeat itself.

What I didn't know was that I would soon be history as well. In the truly weird party that was Frank and Mia, the belle of the ball was saving the last dance for me. If I hadn't tried to kill time in the Candy Store that jinxed night in the summer of '68, I probably would still be working for Frank Sinatra. After all, until then, I hadn't made one false move. When all the others had been drawn and quartered, I was the last man standing. He was making big plans with me for parties he was going to throw for the upcoming presidential campaign. The Dems were coming to Chicago, Sinatraville to most, and Mr. S was planning to be there, rolling out the red carpet. He had declared for Humphrey, and HHH had made him his point man in showbiz, which was what politics was becoming. It seemed as if happy days, JFK days, were going to be here again. And I was going to be right there with him. We had talked about it. He was going to do another inaugural. Ol' Blue Eyes was going to be back—in power.

Right at that time, that very night, Mr. S was entrusting me with his most precious cargo, Ava Gardner. Maybe, once Mia was gone, Ava would relent on her perpetual refusal to take Mr. S back. I had fantasies of being part of one happy family, for once in my life. But it was not to be. I took that fatal turn into the Candy Store, and I took that fatal spin on the dance floor with Mia, and his enemy the press made Mr. S lose face and despise me more than he despised them. The idea that Frank Sinatra's black valet was having a thing with his young movie star wife was the stuff tabloid dreams were made of. That kind of gossip sold millions of copies. THE BUTLER DID IT! The butler *didn't* do it, but it didn't matter. The butler was gone.

9

Aftermath

I HAD pretty awful withdrawal symptoms for about a year after getting the axe from Mr. S. I actually tried to call him a few times, but he refused to speak to me. I tried to console myself that I was in the same boat with many of his other dearest friends, Hank Sanicola, Jack Entratter, Peter Lawford, Lauren Bacall, Mia Farrow, but to me that boat felt like a sinking ship. After fifteen years, I had a very distinct identity as Sinatra's valet, and I was immensely proud of it. Now I was nobody. I had some money saved. I was very well paid, and months after being fired, Mickey Rudin sent me a big check. But who wanted this kind of "fuck you" money? It came with another of Rudin's threatening letters telling me, in gangstery legalese, never to darken Sinatra's door again. Nigger Go Home. Yet my home was Sinatra's home. I felt more betrayed by him than he had felt betrayed by his beloved

Kennedys. I tried my best to stop feeling sorry for myself, and I finally found that the only way to do it was to start feeling sorry for *him*.

The Mr. S who fired me simply wasn't the Mr. S who had hired me. Not even close. The Mr. S of 1953 was a boyish thirty-seven-year-old romantic dreamer who was about to perform the miracle of reconstructing the dreams that a heartless entertainment industry had shattered. Having been a teen idol and then having the idolization stop on the cusp of what was in the 1950s middle age had understandably made Sinatra hideously insecure. It also made him an incredibly nice and humble guy. He made me feel that he was lucky to have me, and as his luck got better and better, he made me feel like his lucky charm. The Mr. S of 1968, on the other hand, was on the downhill slope from the pinnacle of that heartless entertainment industry. From being a discarded teen idol, he had become a world idol, but now at fifty-two he was on the border of old age. No one despised old age, not even the "don't trust anyone over thirty" sixties hippies, more than Mr. S, who, by that token, was coming to despise himself. He had sung and won, but he had also loved and lost. That crucial defeat in the game of life had made him one sore loser, a frustrated angry man. His days of hope were over. He wasn't looking for lucky charms anymore. He was looking for scapegoats.

As part of my healing process, I began taking a perverse pleasure as Mr. S's world continued to crumble around him almost the minute he locked me out of it. He and his Sicilian superstitions. If he believed in any of those witches' tales, he should have regarded me as his good luck charm, for just about every great thing that happened to him occurred when I was there. I am sure that when the shit started to rain down on him that August, he had to be saying "Where the fuck is that goddamn Spook?" But his pride was such was that he would never be able to admit he was wrong. Having crossed the Rubicon of hatred, he couldn't double back to the land of love.

No sooner was I gone than the *Wall Street Journal* broadsided Mr. S with a big exposé about his Mafia connections. It was ridiculous, because all those connections, like Mr. Sam, had long ago disconnected from Sinatra. When I read it, it appeared to be an anti-Humphrey hatchet job, because the Democratic convention was about to start, and Mr. S was HHH's main man, only man, in Hollywood. Now Humphrey and his team distanced themselves from Sinatra just as the Kennedys had turned away from him. Sinatra was political poison. He had Mafia "cooties." Mr. S may have wanted to relive his Kennedy glory days, when he could boast that he was the man who put *his* man in the White House, but the magic had vanished. To lose to *Nixon* was pretty ignominious. So was the public's reception of *Lady in Cement* when it opened, and promptly closed, that fall. And so was Mr. S's big return to Vegas, to his new home of Caesar's Palace. There may have been no Carl Cohen to knock his teeth out, but Vegas itself had become so uncool, so tacky, so *Nixon*, that Frank Sinatra's association with it was less a triumph than an admission of defeat. Once the mob had sold Vegas to Howard Hughes, the thrill was gone. The fun was the danger, the vice, the crime. It was becoming Disneyland with slot machines, and this was just the beginning.

Mr. S seemed desperate, grasping, wanting to be accepted by young audiences, and all he could get were the blue-haired package tourists on the Strip. Imagine trying to do songs like "Little Green Apples," or trying to team up for an album with the guy from the Four Seasons. "Let's Hang On," could have been Mr. S's new theme song. When I saw a picture of him in a Nehru jacket and beads, I thought it was a trick shot, but it wasn't. And when I saw that his newest "best friend" was Vice President Spiro T. Agnew, I knew that something had gone way wrong. With his attacks on the "nattering nabobs of negativism," Agnew was America's favorite buffoon. His politics made Sam Giancana look like Franklin Roosevelt by comparison. Maybe Mr. S was looking for a Giancana substitute in Agnew. If he looked at the Greek vice president as a Jack Kennedy substitute, then he was in more trouble than I thought. Yet there Spiro was, sleeping in JFK's bed in Palm Springs. How the mighty had fallen. Sinatra finally got a hit again with "My Way," but he sang it like an obituary for himself. I was feeling bad for Mr. S, and that felt good to me.

My gloating turned to tears in early 1969, when Marty Sinatra died of heart failure. If the biggest tragedy of Frank Sinatra's life was his failure to win the heart of Ava Gardner, his failure to win the mind of his father couldn't have been far behind. All the glitter, all the fame, nothing was enough to convince Marty Sinatra that his son wouldn't have been better off going to Stevens Tech and getting a *real* job. To Marty neither the Sands, nor the Cal-Neva, nor Warner Brothers itself counted as a real firehouse. The old boxer went down in the last round, and Mr. S had never been able to make peace with him. This was a big death in the family, and I still couldn't help but think of it as *my* family. I wanted at least to call or write Dolly with my condolences, but in light of all of Mickey Rudin's threats, I didn't want him to try to get me arrested as a stalker. I had to keep my own grief to myself.

I was surprised when I heard very reliable rumors that after Bill Goetz died in 1969, Mr. S had made a play for his widow Edie. It reminded me of what happened with Betty Bacall when Bogart died. Mr. S didn't let grass grow, and, even though she was about fifty years older than Mia, and sixteen years older than Frank, Edie Goetz had been Mr. S's dream girl since he had laid eyes on her in the 1940s. If he couldn't have the princess of Monaco, he would have the princess of Hollywood. Apparently, Edie was horrified at the idea. Princesses like her didn't marry commoners, and certainly not Jersey Italian commoners. She thought he was joking. Mr. S didn't joke about romance. She wanted to remain "just friends." Those words were a profound insult to Mr. S. He never spoke to Edie again, either. His way.

For me, the final nail in the coffin of the Frank Sinatra I knew was his romance with Barbara Marx. We had known Barbara for years. She was a pretty Vegas showgirl, a classic California beachy, bleachy blond without an idea in her head. I'm wrong. There was one big idea, to marry a rich man. To achieve her goal, she was always trying to put herself in harm's way. She was often at the Sands, the Racquet Club in Palm Springs, Romanoff's in Beverly Hills. She finally found Mr. Right, or Mr. Better than Nothing, in Zeppo Marx. Zeppo was the fifth Marx Brother, which was sort of like being the fifth Beatle. If you can't remember what he was funny for, don't feel bad. He wasn't supposed to be funny. He was an agent. Zeppo lived close to us near the Tamarisk Country Club fairways. Zeppo was in his sixties and sick all the time, and often at night when he had gone to sleep, Barbara would sneak out and visit Mr. S. I asked him what he saw in her. "Grace Kelly with my eyes closed," he answered. I never thought he took her at all seriously.

After Marty Sinatra died and Edie Goetz turned him down, Mr. S began seeing Barbara Marx a lot more. She divorced old Zeppo and became Sinatra's official main squeeze in 1972. The minute that happened, I abandoned all hopes of getting that magical call at four A.M.: "Hey, Spook, you wanna play some cards?" One person who broke all Mr. S's rules and sought me out was Dolly Sinatra, when she moved to Palm Springs after Marty's death. It was like a miracle from the blue when she called me, a long-lost friend returned. No one could have hated California more than this Jersey girl. Mr. S had bought her the house next door to his compound on Wonder Palms Drive from the Beverly Hills furrier Abe Lipsey. It was a luxurious home, but that didn't matter to a homesick Dolly.

The only thing Dolly hated more than California was Barbara. To Dolly she was the personification of all that Dolly detested about the Golden State. We'd go for rides to old coffee shops where Mr. S wouldn't see or hear about us. Dolly didn't care. She wanted to shame him into taking me back, but I put my foot down. It wasn't going to happen with Barbara there. "He's better off with you than her," Dolly said in her typically outspoken style. I tried to play devil's advocate, saying that Barbara was what Frank needed at this stage of the game, the autumn of his years, a Barbie Doll type. She already had a son and was out of the kid game, and unlike Ava, unlike Mia, she wasn't going to foul things up with the demands of a career.

I'm sure Mr. S knew about his mother's violently negative attitude toward the woman who became his wife in 1976. Barbara's best friend was fellow showgirl Bea Korshak. The local buzz was that Bea's husband, Sid, Mr. S's last tie to the Chicago mob, ordered the Chairman to do the right thing by Barbara. Frank and Barbara did double date all the time with the Korshaks, and Mr. S did enjoy the feeling of old times with the powerful *consigliere*. However, a more likely impetus for Frank to make it legal with Barbara was the unlikely marriage of his dearest bachelor buddy Jimmy Van Heusen. That Chester the serial playboy and sex addict had succumbed to monogamy in his late fifties may have been the key event that propelled an isolated Mr. S to the altar with Barbara. Dolly felt betrayed by her son, and by what she saw as his "weakness." She refused to fly on the same plane with her new daughter-in-law. In January 1977, the separate plane that Dolly had demanded to go to a Caesar's Palace concert crashed into the mountains on takeoff from Palm Springs. I know Mr. S blamed himself for the rest of his days. He didn't blame Barbara, only himself. He was more than aware that his mother didn't want him to marry Barbara and he did it anyway. No woman ever loved him like

Dolly and he knew it. That pain would never go away. The rest of his life would be anesthesia.

I can't really blame Barbara Marx for not wanting me around. Dolly told me how any time my name came up, Barbara would badmouth me and Frank wouldn't say a word. Barbara wanted a clean slate and a fresh start. Amen. At that point, so did I. I had gotten a few other valet positions, for Steve McQueen, George Hamilton, Bill Cosby. But my heart wasn't in it. I could only serve one master. All the rest were anti-climactic. Instead I used my nest egg to travel, go back to New York, Europe, see the world through my own eyes instead of the Old Blue Ones. I lived as large as I could, and sometimes my paths would cross with some of my old Sinatra friends. For instance, I was at the Hotel Negresco in Nice when I ran into Prince Rainier and Princess Grace, who were there for some benefit. They spotted me first, and called me over. At first they seemed hurt that Mr. S was on the Riviera without letting them know. They had no idea that he and I weren't together anymore. I was too embarrassed to say how he had fired me, so I mumbled something about something. They insisted I come to the palace for a meal, but I made up another excuse. I didn't want to be dining out on Mr. S. The idea was to do Europe *my way,* though I was sorely tempted.

I let my hair grow, wore clothes Mr. S would have created a bonfire of, rode my motorcycle. I was in my early forties, but since I had missed my twenties and thirties, I was making up for it. Eventually I came back to L.A. I went on *The Dating Game* three times. On one of them I won a trip to France. I also sang on *The Gong Show,* and was a contestant on *You Bet Your Life,* when Buddy Hackett was subbing for Groucho. One of my ground rules was that I didn't want to discuss having worked for Mr. S. Of course, the first thing Buddy did was start asking all about Sinatra. I got mad and walked off. So much for my brilliant television career.

In 1978, for the first time since the Mia incident, I ran into Frank Sinatra at Don the Beachcomber in Palm Springs. He wasn't with Barbara or anyone I knew, just a bunch of new guys. We crossed paths at the bar, face to face. I took one look at him and broke down into tears. I couldn't stop crying. Mr. S put his arm around me. "Forget about it, kid," he said. "It isn't so bad." I guess I *couldn't* forget about it, because the tears didn't stop. Mr. S gave me one last squeeze and was gone. He looked older, heavier, harder. I was sad he wasn't as sentimental about us as I was. In that split second, my life flashed before me, and my first thought, my first hope, was that Mr. S would invite me back to work. That, I suppose, answers the question, if I had it to do all over again, would I? I would then, and I probably would now. But Mr. S didn't give me the chance.

Eventually I decided to do something I was good at, which was carpentry. If I were a carpenter and you were a lady . . . Oddly enough, by doing my carpentry I met a real lady, Terri Taylor, a very lovely girl from Tennessee whose father was the minister at the Westwood Presbyterian Church near UCLA. Like my second wife, Sally, she was white and fair and beautiful. Opposites attract. We had two beautiful daughters, Rachel and Jennifer, who are now getting to college age. We had a wonderful marriage for a decade, until we drifted apart and got an amicable divorce. Of my three sons by Sally, Guy, who became a film projectionist with dreams of becoming a director, died of an unexpected heart attack at thirty-seven in 1993. Gregory, the oldest, has become an accomplished artist, with shows around the country, while his baby brother Sean is still with his mother in Hawaii, earning a good living as a deep sea fisherman.

I wish I could say as good things about the three kids of my first wife, Dorothy, my Louisiana childhood sweetheart, who went back home and remarried several times. She never let me see my kids, so I could say it wasn't my fault, but I won't. Once they grew up, in the years after I left Mr. S, the kids' lives all went to hell. Our daughter became a dope dealer, had six husbands and six kids and was murdered. Our second son became a transsexual and killed himself when his gay male lover wouldn't marry him. And our first son is nearing the end of a long prison term for armed robbery. He has a son, my grandson, who is also in prison. I hadn't seen any of these kids since they were babies, so the pain I feel is fairly abstract. I wish now I could have had my hand in raising them. Maybe I could have helped.

Just this last year, I got a letter from my first born and namesake George. He's now fifty-four, which seems amazing. He had tracked me down and wrote me from prison. Now we have a correspondence going. I'm going to see him soon. And maybe then I'll see my grandson. It's a beginning, and it's never too late to begin. I'm not sure how my own Sicilian superstitions come into play here, but there's enough tragedy for Shakespeare. My mother, on the other hand, had a full, rich life and died at ninety in 2001. Throughout all my years with Frank Sinatra, she expressed no interest whatsoever in either meeting him or attending one of his concerts, though he frequently asked me to invite her. He never impressed her as a singer. She was old New Orleans, and she preferred old New Orleans jazz and blues, and that was her way.

I still live in Palm Springs, which is absolutely nothing like the exclusive Hollywood hideaway it was when Swifty Lazar tried to house me in the stables of the Racquet Club. Native American casino gambling is on the way, and I'm sure the place will become the new Las Vegas. Almost the whole Sinatra crowd is gone. Jack Entratter died young, Jilly Rizzo died in a freak auto accident, Jimmy Van Heusen passed on, too, in 1990, still happily married, believe it or not.

I never saw Mr. S again face to face. He rarely left the compound in Palm Springs, and in L.A. the only place he liked to go was Matteo's, with its ever-chugging electric trains, the sole survivor of the Rat Pack scene. For some reason, I stayed away. I had my life. I didn't want to get tempted by the siren call of the past, no matter how faint it had grown.

In 1998, when Mr. S died at eighty-two, I couldn't believe he was gone. One of the highest livers of the twentieth century had failed at making it into the next, a goal he often talked about. Because he had lived so hard, played so hard, tried to love so hard, many of those who had shared his life felt that he had indeed been on borrowed time. However, because I knew how much he dreaded the idea of dying, and, despite his prayers for an Oscar and for his son's return, how little faith he placed in the hereafter, I personally thought he'd summon up the power to go "all the way," or at least to one hundred. He was a century kind of guy. At his later concerts, I saw how he toasted the audience with the Italian phrase *"Cent'anni."* He'd say, "May you live a hundred years, and may the last voice you hear be mine."

I tried to go to Mr. S's funeral, but Barbara cut me from the list. I wept for him on my own, across the street from the old Romanoff's on the Rocks, and thought about the great times that we had. What did I learn from the man? That life was but a dream, that it could change on a dime, that you should nail your lines on the first take and move on to new ones. Every few months I'll go for a walk and lay a desert flower on Mr. S's simple gravestone. FRANCIS ALBERT SINATRA. 1915–1998. "THE BEST IS YET TO COME." Let's all hope so.

Acknowledgments

We would like to extend special thanks to the following people who have helped us with this book with valuable recollections and insights: Josephine Abercrombie, Sheila Allen, Sidney Beckerman, Baby Bryan, Jeanne Carmen, Olivia de Havilland, Rob Fentress, Sidney J. Furie, Nadia LaCoste, Betty Lussier, Deborah Markland, Stuart Phelps, Rick Ross, Penn Sicre, Chris Silvester, Ed Walters, and Sandy Whitelaw. Special thanks to Henry Bushkin and Walter Seifert, who introduced us and made this book a reality; to our tireless agent, Peter Miller; and to our inspired editor, Mauro DiPreta, whose passion for Frank Sinatra helped ignite our own.

—George Jacobs and William Stadiem
Los Angeles, December, 2002

About the Authors

GEORGE JACOBS has refused countless offers to tell his story. Until now. A master chef and carpenter, he lives not far from the old Sinatra compound in Palm Springs, California, where he continues to be one of the toasts of that star-filled town.

WILLIAM STADIEM was a Harvard JD-MBA and Wall Street lawyer before embarking for Hollywood, where he has written the screenplays for such films as Franco Zeffirelli's *Young Toscanini*, starring Elizabeth Taylor. He wrote the bestselling *Marilyn Monroe Confidential*, and *Lullaby and Good Night* with Vincent Bugliosi. Formerly the Hollywood columnist for *Interview* magazine as well as a food critic for *Los Angeles* magazine, Stadiem lives in Santa Monica, California.

To receive notice of author events and new books by George Jacobs and William Stadiem, sign up at www.authortracker.com.

Printed in the USA
CPSIA information can be obtained
at www.ICGtesting.com
LVHW031750070824
787457LV00011B/227

9 780060 596743